The Original Amos 'n' Andy

The Original Amos 'n' Andy

Freeman Gosden, Charles Correll and the 1928–1943 Radio Serial

ELIZABETH MCLEOD

McFarland & Company, Inc., Publishers
Jefferson, North Carolina, and London

The present work is a reprint of the illustrated case bound edition of The Original Amos 'n' Andy: Freeman Gosden, Charles Correll and the 1928–1943 Radio Serial, *first published in 2005 by McFarland.*

LIBRARY OF CONGRESS CATALOGUING-IN-PUBLICATION DATA

McLeod, Elizabeth, 1963–
The original Amos 'n' Andy : Freeman Gosden, Charles Correll and the 1928–1943 radio serial / Elizabeth McLeod.
p. cm.
Includes bibliographical references and index.

ISBN 978-0-7864-4584-4
softcover : 50# alkaline paper ∞

1. Amos 'n' Andy (Radio program)   2. Gosden, Freeman F., 1899–1982. Correll, Charles J., 1890–1972.   I. Title.
PN1991.77.A6M36   2009
791.44′72—dc22   2005009060

British Library cataloguing data are available

©2005 Elizabeth McLeod. All rights reserved

No part of this book may be reproduced or transmitted in any form or by any means, electronic or mechanical, including photocopying or recording, or by any information storage and retrieval system, without permission in writing from the publisher.

On the cover: old radio ©2009 PhotoSpin; two 1932 publicity portraits (photograph restoration by Osborne Design and Development, Newton, New Hampshire)

Manufactured in the United States of America

*McFarland & Company, Inc., Publishers
Box 611, Jefferson, North Carolina 28640
www.mcfarlandpub.com*

for D. C. E.
who always said I should write a book

and

for A. L. O.
who helped me understand that I could

ACKNOWLEDGMENTS

Research for *The Original Amos 'n' Andy* began in the mid–1970s, and in the years since many individuals and institutions have provided research assistance and access to necessary source materials. The cooperation and encouragement of Freeman F. Gosden, Jr., Jane Gosden, and Richard Correll were especially valuable.

Among those making essential source materials available were the staff of the Manuscript Division at the Library of Congress, J. David Goldin, Bryan Cornell at the Library of Congress Recorded Sound Reference Center, Harlan Zinck at the First Generation Radio Archives, Ed Carr, Michael Kieffer, Michael Biel, Tom Hood, Anthony Tollin, Frank Kelly, Frank Absher, Michael Hayde, Danny Willis, and Derek Tague.

Special thanks to Amanda Osborne for her meticulous work on restoring the fragile bits and pieces of *Amos 'n' Andy* memorabilia that illustrate this work, and—most important—for her friendship.

CONTENTS

Acknowledgments vi
Preface 1
A Note on the Script Excerpts 5

1. Origins 7
2. Correll and Gosden—Perfect Harmony 17
3. Airtime 23
4. Here They Are … 29
5. A Coast-to-Coast Hookup 47
6. Meet the Cast 69
7. Speaking the Language 87
8. Tales to Tell 95
9. Black and White? 115
10. Dissonant Voices 127
11. The Later Years 139
12. Making the Point 153

Appendix: By the Numbers 163
Cast and Credits 179
Chapter Notes 187
Bibliography 201
Index 209

"They wanted to hear 'Amos 'n' Andy.' Perhaps it is closer to the truth to say they wanted to be with *these two people, to pass fifteen minutes of their lives with two men whom they never saw and whom they knew in the same way that they knew their own friends...."*

—Gilbert Seldes, *The Public Arts*

PREFACE

"One time someone very aptly called 'Amos 'n' Andy' the Great American Disease. You couldn't go into any town in any part of the country at any time of the year without hearing 'Amos 'n' Andy' coming out of homes and stores and everything else."

—Bill Hay, 1973

THIS IS THE STORY OF two performers who are among the most influential figures in the history of American broadcasting.

They created and performed the first original serial to be devised for the broadcast radio medium—and the first dramatized broadcast radio series to feature continuing characters. Storytelling techniques they pioneered and conventions they established endure to the present day.

In distributing their creation, they invented the concept of recorded broadcast syndication—an idea that has grown into a multibillion dollar industry.

The program they created and performed commanded the attention of more than 40 million Americans, six nights a week, at the peak of its success—nearly one-third of the nation's total population at that time.

And today, more than three quarters of a century after their premiere, few performers make historians and social critics more uncomfortable: because these two white men spent most of their professional lives portraying African American characters.

The men are Freeman F. Gosden and Charles J. Correll. For over 30 years, they were *Amos 'n' Andy*.

The modern-day view of their creation was summed up as early as 1972 by William Manchester, who dismissed the program as "a nightly racial slur" and argued that the show used its Depression-era popularity to illustrate the casual racism that pervaded that time.[1] Since then, a popular view of *Amos 'n' Andy* has grown in which the very title has become a synonym for the excesses of crude and vicious racial stereotyping, an embarrassment to observers looking back from our more progressive age—or, especially among academics, a talking point in the eternal debate over the politics of racial identity.

Because of this reputation, few cultural historians have actually made the effort to read and study the thousands of pages of the program's original 1930s scripts. Consequently the image of *Amos 'n' Andy* usually presented to the modern media student is a negative and grossly distorted one—with the central role Correll and Gosden played in the development of American broadcasting often minimized, glossed over, or ignored.[2] And as the cycle continues, a body of scholarship is created that has more to do with latter-day cultural-studies theory than with any real connection to the substance of the actual program. To condemn *Amos 'n' Andy* as a mere artifact of America's racist past may offer modern commentators a comfortable platform from which to assert their own enlightenment, but it does nothing to explain why Correll and Gosden attained a unique status among entertainers of their era—not just as popular comedians but as beloved inspirational figures about whom a *New York Times* critic once observed, "Their power for good is said to be amazing to the nth degree."[3]

Before one can credibly attempt to interpret the program's social history, one must first clearly understand its performance history. To form an assessment of *Amos 'n' Andy* based on the 426 episodes aired in a half-hour situation comedy format between 1943 and 1955 or on the 78 episodes of the television series filmed between 1951 and 1953 is to reach a judgment based on only a fraction of the program's total run, thereby ignoring the 4,091 episodes of the series that aired in a nightly 15-minute serial format between March 1928 and February 1943. These serial episodes differ sharply from the later versions of the program in both format and in overall tone—and it was this original version of the program, now almost totally forgotten, that most clearly spelled out the vision of its creators. And it was this original series that captured the attention of a nation only beginning to come to grips with the media revolution wrought by radio broadcasting in the 1920s.

Modern observers likewise are hampered in coming to terms with the program by the lack of substantive insight into the ideas behind the series from its creators themselves. Freeman Gosden, the program's creative mastermind, granted almost no serious interviews over the final two decades of his life, and those published in earlier years were generally of a press-agent nature. Several late-in-life interviews with Charles Correll exist, but these are generally of a casual, nostalgic nature and rarely address the content of the program in any depth. Neither performer is known to have kept a personal journal nor to have engaged in extensive personal correspondence that would have offered insight into the ideas behind the program. With Correll and Gosden no longer able to speak for themselves, their scripts stand alone as a primary source—and one must bypass volumes of secondhand academic analyses and go back to these original works if one hopes to fully understand what they were trying to say to their audience.

The history that follows is not presented as a work of sociopolitical criticism, since examination of the series from that perspective is available in the works of many other authors. Nor does this work discuss in any detail the production and content of the *Amos 'n' Andy Show* television series, a project with which Correll and Gosden came to have little day-to-day creative involvement. Rather, the intent and purpose of this work is to provide accurate documentation of the development and content of the original *Amos 'n' Andy* radio serial and, by doing so, to explore both the intent of its creators and the basis of the program's unique appeal to its original audience. This study is based not on secondary sources or on latter-day academic deconstruction but, rather, on close and complete readings of more than 2,700 consecutive *Amos 'n' Andy* scripts in the author's possession, covering the entire first decade of the program's run, as well as an extensive personal collection of primary sources dating from the 1920s and 1930s.

Speculative interpretation of what the program said about the nation's view of race only tells a fraction of the *Amos 'n' Andy* story. Smug condemnation tells none of it. Before one can truly understand the grip that *Amos 'n' Andy* exerted on its audience in the years of its greatest success, one must first understand what the program actually was.

A NOTE ON THE SCRIPT EXCERPTS

QUOTATIONS FROM ORIGINAL *Amos 'n' Andy* scripts presented in this work are formatted exactly as they appear in the original typed pages. Freeman Gosden and Charles Correll prepared their material phonetically, in order to ensure that all lines were delivered with precisely the correct pronunciations for each specific character portrayed. Given that Correll and Gosden consistently used variations in dialect as signifiers of social class, this level of precision was a necessary element in their writing.

Certain conventions were used by Correll and Gosden in the typing of the scripts, which should be kept in mind while reading them. Scripts were intended to be read by the performers exactly as written. Pauses in the delivery of lines were indicated in the scripts by the presence of dashes between sentences: the more dashes, the longer the indicated pause. Performance directions, indicating changes in mood or vocal shading, were inserted parenthetically into the text, and have been retained where present in the excerpts. Correll and Gosden were meticulous in sticking to the prepared script, and ad-libbing generally occurred only when necessary to cover a cough or a misread line.

Excerpts are presented here without internal editing wherever possible, in order to preserve the flow and flavor of the original material. However, in a few cases, it has been necessary to internally abridge lengthy quotes from the scripts in order to improve readability; in such cases, omissions are indicated by the presence of an ellipsis (…). In no case has the omission of material been allowed to alter the essential meaning of any excerpt.

1. ORIGINS

"I never wanted to do anything but act in those shows."
—Freeman Gosden

It is often assumed that Freeman Gosden and Charles Correll built their career on the timeworn foundation of blackface minstrelsy—that Amos Jones and Andy Brown are simply the twentieth-century descendents of the nineteenth-century minstrel end-man figures generalized by modern historians as "Jim Crow" and "Zip Coon." It is true that the end men of minstrelsy were the inspiration for the very concept of the two-man comedy team, whether in blackface or not, and their influence has endured in American popular entertainment for more than a century and a half, and the basic characterizations of the luckless patsy and the scheming rogue were minstrel staples, deeply rooted in traditions of American folk humor, which have in fact outlived blackface to continue little changed to the present day.[1] But to draw a straight and exclusive line from minstrel shows to *Amos 'n' Andy* not only grossly oversimplifies the actual content of the radio program, it also overlooks other factors that influenced Correll and Gosden and their work, ranging from popular comic strips to the day-to-day experiences of their own lives.

While Correll and Gosden had both appeared in amateur minstrel shows before entering radio—at a time when such homegrown productions could be found in virtually every community in the United States—neither man could claim a long-standing personal background in professional minstrelsy. They spent approximately five years working in the field as professionals, and much of that time was spent in production and administrative capacities rather than onstage. Nor were Correll and Gosden vaudevillians—their exposure to the aggressive, fast-moving humor of the pre–World War I era was as spectators, not as performers, and the brash show-business traditions that nurtured the careers of such performers as Eddie Cantor, George Burns, Jack Benny, and Fred Allen were utterly foreign to their experience. Instead, Correll and Gosden entered show business by an entirely different route, on the lowest possible rung of the professional ladder: as touring home-talent coaches who achieved sudden and extraordinary success through a combination of luck, timing, and instinctive ability. And, as will be demonstrated in the pages to follow, their work diverged from the simple-minded stereotypes of minstrelsy far more than it coincided with them.

Freeman Fisher Gosden was born in Richmond, Virginia, on May 5, 1899, the youngest of five children born to Walter W. Gosden, Sr., and Emma L. Smith. Although Gosdens had been present in Virginia since the colonial era, and although publicity articles in the 1930s frequently stressed the family's deep Virginia heritage, census records reveal that Freeman's branch of the family in fact traced its immediate roots to Ward Six in Baltimore, Maryland—a neighborhood populated not by Southern aristocrats but by middle-class merchants, tradesmen, and petty professionals. Walter Gosden was born there in 1845, as the fourth of five children of John T. Gosden—a music teacher, born in England in 1806—and his Maryland-born wife Sarah Ann. The family was not wealthy: in the year of Walter's birth, court records reveal that a mortgage foreclosure cost his parents their investment in two hotels.[2]

Little is known of Walter Gosden's childhood until the age of 16, when he joined the cause of the Confederacy at the start of the Civil War by enlisting in the Army of Northern Virginia. Before reaching the age of 20, he served with the 43rd Battalion of the Virginia Cavalry—better known as "Mosby's Rangers"—an elite partisan unit of near-mythic reputation led by Colonel John Singleton Mosby, well known for their daring guerrilla raids behind Union lines. Gosden served with distinction as a Ranger and was under Mosby's command when the "Grey Ghost" chose to disband his unit in April 1865 rather than submit to a formal surrender. In the Rangers' final skirmish, a confrontation with units of the 8th Illinois Cavalry near Fairfax, Virginia, on April 10, 1865—a day after the formal surrender of the Confederate forces at Appomattox—Private Gosden distinguished himself under fire by risking his own life to pull a wounded comrade from the battlefield and carrying him to safety while simultaneously returning fire on his pursuers.[3]

Walter Gosden carried the effects of his wartime service for the rest of his life, walking with a limp resulting from a bullet wound. Growing up in an era that heavily romanticized the Civil War, young Freeman Gosden took great pride in his father's military record and frequently boasted of his father's exploits.

> Some days when Dad would go by on his way home, I would tell the other kids how brave he had been. I used to tell them about the Civil War, and how he was wounded in battle. Then, one day, my older brother overheard the conversation and asked me to come into the house. He wanted to have a talk with me in his room. He told me that on several occasions he had heard me tell of my father's bravery, of his being shot in battle. My brother said, "I'm going to tell you the true story. Our father asked Colonel Mosby if he could have a few days off to go to Richmond. He had heard so much about Libbie Prison that he wanted to go and take a look at it. He was granted leave. While he was looking at Libbie Prison from the outside, one of the [Yankee] prisoners escaped. A guard shot at the runaway soldier, but the bullet hit Papa in the behind. And that is how our father was wounded."[4]

After the war, Walter Gosden settled in Richmond and, in contrast to his adventurous teenage years, he became a bookkeeper and spent more than a quarter of a century toiling over the ledgers of the Planters National Bank, where he was eventually joined by his oldest son, Walter, Jr. Though the Tennessee-born Emma Smith's father had been a doctor, wealth continued to elude the family. Walter and Emma and their children lived in a series of rented houses along the boundaries of Jackson Ward, Richmond's thriving African American district. Most of Freeman's childhood was spent in a duplex house at 711 East Marshall Street, along the lower slope of Richmond's Navy Hill. Close to the city's theatrical district and just a few blocks from the center of Jackson Ward, the neighborhood marked a point of intersection for Richmond's white and black communities in the early years of the twentieth century, and its mix of cultural influences would determine the future course of Freeman Gosden's life.

Considered the commercial and cultural capital of the black Southeast during the years of Freeman's childhood, Jackson Ward was a neighborhood alive with black-owned businesses, schools, churches, and social organizations. The first African American public school in the United States was opened at Jackson Ward's Ebenezer Baptist Church in 1858, followed by the establishment of the Virginia Union College for Negroes in 1867 and Hartshorn Memorial College in 1887. In 1883, the Richmond *Planet* began publication, giving Jackson Ward residents an able and articulate voice, particularly under the outspoken editorial pen of John Mitchell, Jr., who was described by the *New York World* as "a man who would walk into the jaws of death to serve his race." In 1890, Mitchell became Richmond's first black city council member, and he aggressively protested the increasing influence of segregation laws in the early 1900s, leading a 1904 boycott of the city's Jim Crow streetcar system, which drove the streetcar company into bankruptcy. After the ratification of a restrictive and overtly anti-black state constitution and the gerrymandering of Jackson Ward shattered his political power, Mitchell turned from politics and focused his efforts on the development of African American economic solidarity by vigorously promoting black support for black-owned businesses. Others in Jackson Ward followed Mitchell's lead: in 1904, Jackson Ward resident Maggie L. Walker—whose home stood just eight blocks from the Gosden residence—established the St. Luke's Penny Savings Bank, emphasizing business loans for black entrepreneurs. These achievements symbolized the initiative and determination of Richmond's black residents in coming to grips with the constraints placed on them in an officially segregated world. Even as segregation laws were formalized, codified, and strengthened during the early 1900s, Jackson Ward residents refused to be beaten down. Their community, built on a foundation of entrepreneurship and a philosophy of economic self-sufficiency, offered young Freeman Gosden a daily window into a complex urban black culture, which most white Americans of the early twentieth century never knew existed.[5]

Freeman Gosden was a quiet, sensitive child: he was thin and rather shy, with an unruly bush of kinky, sandy-colored hair that earned him the nickname "Curley"; his most unusual physical feature was a mismatched set of eyebrows, one white and one brown. Attending the Ruffner School in Richmond, five blocks from his home, Freeman was considered a good student, but his gentle, studious demeanor led to taunts of "mama's boy" and "teacher's pet" and to frequent confrontations with schoolyard bullies. Shyness and self-consciousness continued to haunt Freeman as adolescence approached. At 12, he won third prize in a patriotic essay contest, but when he was called to the stage in the school auditorium to accept his award, he panicked and fled from the auditorium.[6]

After completing his grammar school education, Freeman spent a year living with his sister and brother-in-law outside Atlanta, Georgia, where he attended a military school for boys. Returning to Richmond after that year, he enrolled at John Marshall High School, but, due to his family's worsening financial situation, he was forced to drop out at 16 and obtain a job. Working at first as an errand boy for the Tarrant Drug Company in Jackson Ward, the youth eventually secured a full-time job as a shipping clerk with the Craddock-Terry Shoe Corporation.

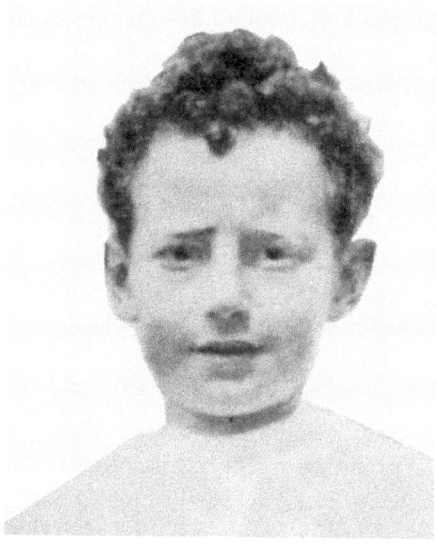

"Curley" Gosden at the age of eight, 1907. The nickname is self-explanatory.

The family's financial worries only added to the air of uncertainty that lingered over Freeman's childhood and adolescence, a period during which the Gosden family was shaken by a procession of deep personal tragedies. In 1902 the family's second son, William—despondent over the failure of his marriage—took his own life 19. Nine years later, Walter Gosden died after a long illness at the age of 66. Finally, in September 1917, Emma Gosden and her only daughter Minnie lost their lives in an automobile accident caused by a reckless driver. Of Freeman's siblings, only his brothers Walter, Jr., and Harry survived into the 1920s—and Walter would not survive into the 1930s.[7]

Freeman Gosden found refuge from the uncertainties of his youth in the fascinating world of small-time vaudeville. At Richmond's Bijou Family Theatre, just a block away from his home, the boy sat transfixed Through acts of every kind: song-and-dance teams, comedians, and novelty performers. Despite his shyness he dreamed of a stage career of his own. "I never wanted to do anything but act in those shows," he recalled years later. The stagestruck youngster made his first appearance on a stage at the age of ten, competing in a diving contest promoted by vaudeville swimming star Annette Kellerman. Although stage fright compromised his performance, Freeman was awarded an honorary prize of a few dollars as the youngest boy in the competition. Another early stage venture found the boy volunteering to assist famed magician Howard Thurston, and he pretended to fumble the eggs he was asked to hold—his first attempt at stage comedy.[8] Soon, attending shows wasn't enough—Freeman developed an interest in putting on shows of his own, and in this he was aided by his closest childhood friend, a black youth named Garrett Brown.

An orphan taken in by the Gosdens in early childhood, Garrett Brown lived ten

1. Origins 11

The Bijou Family Theatre in downtown Richmond, where Freeman Gosden's childhood dreams of a show-business career first took root.

years with the family and earned his keep by running errands and doing odd jobs. He and Freeman were roughly the same age and shared similar personality traits: both were intelligent, quick-witted, and skilled observers of the people around them. While Freeman attended his classes at the Ruffner School, Garrett—who had been tagged in early childhood with the nickname "Snowball"—attended a nearby school for African American children. The Gosdens were strict, devoutly religious parents, and they required both boys to apply themselves energetically to their schoolwork, applying physical discipline as required to emphasize the point. "Sometimes we learned our lessons standing up," mused Brown in 1930. While the Gosdens regularly attended the Second Presbyterian Church in Richmond, they allowed Garrett to attend an African American church of his own choosing—but required that he do so regularly.[9]

But it wasn't all schoolwork and discipline for Freeman and Garrett. Both boys enjoyed sandlot baseball and other casual neighborhood sports, and Freeman carried into adulthood fond memories of begging adult smokers for the picture cards of professional baseball players that then came with popular brands of cigarettes. Although Garrett Brown recalled that Freeman was not noted for his athletic skills, Freeman nonetheless joined the local YMCA, where he developed an interest in swimming and handball and also picked up a reputation as a gifted dancer. Garrett, meanwhile, sharpened his skills as a semiprofessional boxer, taking on all comers in informal, winner-take-all bouts staged in various Richmond basements. Although Emma Gosden strongly disapproved of Garrett's pugilistic activities, Freeman was invariably in

The only known photograph of Garrett Brown, ca. 1930. Freeman Gosden's close childhood friendship with Brown proved an indelible influence, helping to shape the characterizations Gosden later brought to life in *Amos 'n' Andy*.

attendance for these matches—where onlookers contributed to often substantial cash purses—and more often than not, Garrett emerged the winner. "We always had money," Brown recalled. Both boys were also excellent mimics and enjoyed imitating the various dialects heard on the Richmond streets. They took special pleasure in putting on impromptu shows for the entertainment of Freeman's ailing father. Often these performances took the form of minstrel shows: with Garrett as end man and Freeman as interlocutor, the boys exchanged wisecracking comedy lines and swapped dialect jokes.[10]

Garrett Brown left the Gosden home after a decade, moving to Roseton, New York, with a companion to seek his fortune, but he and Freeman exchanged letters for many years thereafter. In the absence of his closest friend, Freeman turned increasingly to theatrical activities to pass his free time, and he went on to gain a reputation as a budding entertainer, appearing occasionally in amateur-night shows in Richmond theaters as an eccentric dancer. As a craze surrounding film comic Charles Chaplin swept the nation in 1915–16, Gosden donned a derby hat and used a whangee cane to compete in a local Chaplin look-alike contest, impressing the audience with his imitation of the comedian's distinctive waddle. Around this time, Gosden met Lewis "Slim" O'Neil, a fellow Richmonder around his own age who further encouraged his interest in show business. Together, O'Neil and Gosden studied "buck dancing," an eccentric dance style drawn from a combination of African American and Celtic techniques, in which fast, flat-footed steps contrasted with the near-immobility of the upper body. Gosden and O'Neil practiced until they had mastered the technique and worked out a routine. They made their professional stage debut on April 27, 1917, in a benefit minstrel show in Fredericksburg, Virginia, organized by the United Daughters of the Confederacy. Despite his youth, Freeman had developed as a well-rounded entertainer, but his progress was interrupted by a bad case of war fever. On April 6, 1917—even as Freeman and "Slim" were rehearsing for their debut—the United States entered World War I. Five days after that initial performance in Fredericksburg, and three days before his eighteenth birthday, Freeman Gosden exchanged minstrel regalia for a sailor's uniform, enlisting, along with Lewis O'Neil, in the U.S. Navy.[11]

Although originally assigned to the USS *Montgomery*, Gosden ended up spending the war stateside after his vulnerability to seasickness led his superiors to classify him as Unsuitable For Sea Duty. Instead, Seaman Gosden was sent to a Navy communications school at Harvard University—where he was trained as a wireless operator, beginning a lifelong interest in the newest communication technology. His trip to Harvard marked his first visit to the North, and as Lewis O'Neil had also been assigned to the school, they were able to continue their off-duty entertainments for fellow sailors, with Freeman taking up the ukulele during his tour of duty in Boston. When his training was completed, Gosden was transferred to the Navy base at Virginia Beach, where he waited out the war by monitoring radio traffic.[12]

Following his discharge in early 1919, Freeman took a job as a traveling salesman for the American Tobacco Company but found the work uninteresting, giving it up for a sales job with a Petersburg, Virginia, automobile dealer. He also continued to pursue his interest in show business by sharpening his skills as an all-around entertainer and working with O'Neil and several friends in an amateur song-dance-and-comedy troupe that appeared in local benefit shows all around the Richmond area. It was his appearance in one such show that brought Gosden to the attention of a Chicago-based theatrical entrepreneur by the name of Joe Bren.[13]

Bren was a songwriter and former vaudevillian who had found a new and profitable niche for himself: managing a company that produced benefit shows for fraternal and civic groups all over the East, South, and Midwest. The Joe Bren Producing Company provided scripts, music, and a qualified director while local citizens competed to fill the parts. Gosden's appearance in a Bren production sponsored by the Richmond Benevolent and Protective Order of Elks in mid–1919 caught the eye of the director, who sent a report back to the home office praising the 20-year-old's facility with black dialect. After a brief correspondence with Gosden, Bren offered the young man a job as a traveling director.[14] So it was that in the late summer of 1919, Gosden was paired with another Bren representative in producing "The Jollies of 1919" for the B.P.O.E. of Durham, North Carolina. His partner in this endeavor was a stocky, smiling, 29-year-old pianist named Charlie Correll.[15]

Charles James Correll was born in Peoria, Illinois, on February 2, 1890, the oldest of three children born to Joseph Boland Correll and Anna Fiss. Living in a brick-porched one-story house at 711 Hancock Street, the family was working class.

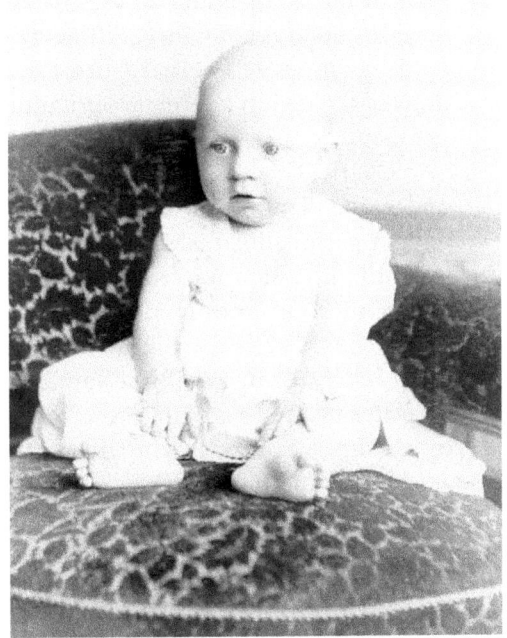

A picture of Victorian innocence, albeit slightly stunned by the flash, Charles James Correll poses for the camera in 1891, at 18 months. *(Correll Family Collection)*

Charles's father was a brick mason with the Peoria construction firm of Ebaugh & McFarland, and his grandfather was an Irish immigrant who had married a Georgia woman prior to the Civil War and had relocated to Illinois after spending time in a Tennessee refugee camp following the war.[16] Joseph Correll was a friendly, ebullient man, and young Charlie inherited much of his father's personality. "You couldn't feel melancholy under the same roof with Charles. He wouldn't stand for it," remembered his uncle, Joseph Fiss, in 1930. Joseph Correll agreed. "Full of pep from morning to night," he described his son. "Trying hard at everything and always on the go. Charlie comes home and when the front door opens we know that all the peace and quiet around the house has departed. He would toss his cap on a stand, and his books on a chair, and go straight for the piano."[17]

Around 1895, the Corrells moved to a home at 1318 North Adams Street in another working-class Peoria neighborhood. Paved with rough creosote blocks, and not far from the American Pottery Company's ceramic works and a Central Railway Company streetcar barn, North Adams Street was the backdrop for the next 12 years of Charles Correll's life. The local firehouse formed the hub of community activity, and young Charlie would spend many hours watching the firemen and listening to their stories. "On North Adams Street, we lived next to Fire House No. 5," Correll recalled in 1949, "and of course in those days we watched them train the horses. The firehouse had the only telephone in the block, and the house was the gathering place for all the men in the block at night and most of the kids in the daytime. The memories of the firemen and all the wonderful things they did for all the people of the neighborhood is something I'll never forget."[18] Correll also carried into adulthood fond memories of Peoria's Corn Carnivals, which were colorful, exciting celebrations of the region's primary agricultural crop featuring games, parades, and entertainment.

Charlie Correll delivered his first lines at the age of seven, appearing in a second-grade play put on by the Greely Grammar School. As he grew up, the boy's bouncy personality made a stage career seem inevitable. Throughout his school years, up until his graduation from Peoria High School in 1907, Charlie Correll was a regular participant in dramatic productions, and he became the leader of the Peoria High School Orchestra. Like young Freeman Gosden, Correll spent much of his boyhood fascinated by smalltime vaudeville shows, and as a teenager he earned a job as an usher in Peoria's Main Street Theatre, where he was occasionally reprimanded by his supervisor for leaving his post to mingle backstage with the actors. Encouraged by his mother, who was an accomplished amateur singer and guitarist, Charlie began at 13 to take piano lessons, studying under a classically trained instructor by the name of Joseph Hornbacher. The lessons continued for ten months before Charlie's jaunty approach to music clashed with the more conservative tastes of his teacher, and the instruction came to a halt. At the same time, he delivered newspapers and worked odd hours in the mailroom at the Peoria *Journal*, where he acquired a reputation as something of a comedian and practical joker among his coworkers. "The boy is a born actor," commented pressroom superintendent Charles Malm, who was a frequent victim of Correll's pranks.[19]

After completing high school, Correll spent a year working as a stenographer for the Peoria architectural firm of Hewitt & Emerson (he had learned shorthand as part of his school's "commercial" course) and then devoted several years to learning his father's trade, eventually leaving his father's employ for a job with the office of Illinois state architect James Cole in Springfield, where Correll served as an assistant to the superintendent of construction on the Illinois Supreme Court Building. After completing this assignment, Correll returned to Peoria to become a stonemason with the construction firm of V. Jobst & Sons, where among other assignments he helped to build Peoria's new Orpheum Theatre. All along, Joseph Correll sensed that his son's heart wasn't in his work. "Charles was interested in plays and dancing," he told *Radio Digest* in 1930, "and I let him work out the problem for himself."[20]

Twelve-year-old Charlie Correll tries to stifle a grin as he attempts to assume a pose of adult dignity next to his father, Joseph B. Correll, in 1902. *(Correll Family Collection)*

As his father suspected, Charles Correll was not destined to spend his life holding a trowel. "I liked music and everything better than bricklaying," Correll confessed, and while working in the construction business, he maintained a continuing interest in the stage. Beginning in 1911, Correll put his piano skills to work as a film accompanist, performing nightly at Peoria's Columbia Theatre, a job that continued until he left Peoria in 1914 to move to the nearby city of Rock Island. He had begun appearing in local amateur minstrel productions during his high school years, receiving his first training in blackface characterizations and eccentric

After his graduation from high school, Charles Correll spent a summer assisting his father and uncle on a construction job at the Southern Illinois Penitentiary. Even in such grave surroundings, Correll found his prankish streak difficult to suppress. *(Correll Family Collection)*

dancing from Peoria fire chief Benjamin Butler, who was himself a former small-time minstrel and had frequently entertained Correll during his days as hanger-on at Fire House No. 5. Throughout the 1910s, Correll jumped at any opportunity for stage work. His appearances in amateur and semiprofessional productions around

Peoria and the nearby Quad Cities areas eventually led to a job as accompanist for the Metropolitan Quartet, a Rock Island–based singing group much in demand for local minstrel and variety shows. Correll's involvement with the Metropolitans led ultimately to his first professional work as a singer. Fellow Metropolitan Jack Pardidon recalled that Correll was asked one night to take the place of one of the baritones, who failed to appear for a scheduled engagement. "You know, that boy had a natural voice," Pardidon told a reporter in 1930. "Real good stuff. Of course, it needed a little trimming around the edges, but the voice was there, and that's more than you can say for a lot of boys that make a living singing."[21]

Theatrical activities continued to fill Correll's evenings even after he took a wartime job as a munitions worker at the Rock Island Arsenal in 1917. He was performing in a benefit show organized by the Joe Bren Producing Company in Davenport, Iowa, in 1918 when he came to the attention of a Bren representative, who recognized both Correll's talent and his friendly way with people and offered him a job. With the end of World War I, Charlie Correll left his job at the arsenal, put down his stonemason's tools, and hit the road coaching talent for Joe Bren. This road eventually led Correll to Durham, North Carolina—and a lifelong partnership.

2. CORRELL AND GOSDEN—PERFECT HARMONY

"They seemed to have mike sense naturally, and they went out very well."
—Joe Bren

WHEN THEY FIRST MET in that Durham rehearsal hall, "Gos" and Charlie hit it off from their first night together. "From the minute I introduced myself to Charlie," Gosden recalled in 1933, "I liked him. At that time I knew nothing about staging amateur theatricals, having worked only in a few in Richmond. It so happened that we were scheduled to be together for a week. Charlie, realizing that I had not had sufficient time to get the entire routine together, stayed up with me practically all night, went to the train with me, and gave me every possible help until he said goodbye." Correll, for his part, was immediately drawn to the eager young Virginian. "The day we met," he recalled, "was the beginning of the most congenial and happiest association I have known."[1]

As their friendship developed during the early 1920s, it became evident that Correll and Gosden made an especially well-matched team—even though on the surface the men were quite different. Gosden was tall and thin, Correll was short and stocky. Gosden was sometimes uncomfortable with people he didn't know well, while Correll was outgoing and friendly on and off the stage. And where Gosden was an intense, driven man who displayed an uncompromising attitude of perfectionism in everything he set out to accomplish, Correll was almost always calm and relaxed and trusted fully in his partner's judgment. Gosden soon became the dominant, innovative member of the team, while Correll provided a steady, stabilizing influence. "One who knows the pair once commented that Correll (Andy) is the balance wheel of the combination," wrote the *New York Times* in 1933. "His is the jovial personal-

Charles Correll and Freeman Gosden, "The Life of the Party," ham it up for the publicist's camera, ca.1925.

ity that moves on an even keel throughout the year. Gosden is the dynamo that drives hard as long as there is an ounce of energy left. Correll, he said, is the rudder, Gosden the motor of the ship."[2]

Thanks to their complementary personalities and the sly sense of humor they both shared, the two quickly became close collaborators and even closer friends—a friendship that endured for the rest of their lives. "I asked why on Christmas Day every year the Gosden family would always go over to the Correll family's home," recalls Freeman F. Gosden, Jr. "I asked, 'Why can't they come to our house?' The answer was 'Charlie is my partner and I always want him to know that outside family, he is the most important person in my life.'"[3] Correll also felt an intense personal bond with Gosden, and for the rest of his life he credited his partner for his own success. "I don't know of any team that didn't at sometime or other decide to go their own ways," observed Correll more than five decades after he and Gosden began their partnership. "We never even gave that a thought—and still don't. I know very well if it wasn't for him, I'd be in Peoria someplace laying bricks."[4]

The Joe Bren Producing Company's productions were usually sponsored by fraternal orders—Masons, Shriners, and Elks were the firm's steadiest clients, and Correll and Gosden themselves became active Shriners during their years with Bren. The sponsoring organization split box office receipts 50–50 with the Bren Company. The shows followed a master script prepared by the Bren office, often titled "Jollies of 19—," with the same script used throughout an entire season. The Bren shows would open with a singing minstrel chorus, followed by comic interplay between the "end men" and the Interlocutor, or master of ceremonies. This first act would be followed by a straightforward series of musical specialties, and the show would conclude with a broadly played comedy sketch in which the entire company participated. The Bren companies were usually quite large, the idea being to involve as many leading local citizens as possible, and in most cases only the end men—the comedy stars of the show—appeared in blackface makeup. The climactic sketches in the Bren shows were often built around slapstick parody of "high culture" such as grand opera or Shakespearean drama—skits in which the humor flowed as much from the deflation of these often self-important genres as it did from the malapropisms and stage dialect of the parodists.[5]

Correll and Gosden were not primarily performers during their days with Bren—but they did step in when needed, sometimes as minstrel end men, and sometimes harmonizing on comic songs with Correll at the piano and Gosden on the ukulele, tiple, or banjo. Gosden occasionally danced in Bren shows and also gained a reputation as a skilled comic monologuist.[6] Their experiences on the road also taught them how to read an audience, how to relate to a broad range of personalities from all walks of life, and also how to think on their feet. "One time the boys and I were together playing a show in Aberdeen, South Dakota," recalled Joe Bren in 1930. "Just after the show went on, a tornado with all the accompanying stage effects burst into town with angry persistence. The lights went out, the storm raged and the audience was panic stricken, but Correll and Gosden took matters into their own hands and saved lives as well as the show. For one hour they cracked jokes, sang songs, and entertained generally to a crowded gathering of terrified people in a pitch black house. When the storm had blown itself out, the show went on. Correll and Gosden slipped back into their parts and five minutes later no one would have known that anything unusual had happened."[7]

In 1924, both men were recalled to the company's home office in Chicago, where Gosden was assigned by Bren to organize and oversee a circus division and Correll took on administrative duties in the amateur show department. For both men, 1924 marked the end of their active participation in minstrelsy. Instead, they turned their attention to a new form of entertainment—taking a room together and working up an act on their own with the idea of breaking into local radio. Their inspirations were vaudevillians like Gus Van and Joe Schenck, recording artists like Billy Jones and Ernie Hare, and radio performers like Ford Rush and Glenn Rowell—all acts that emphasized crisp two-part harmonies combined with a slick line of comic patter between selections. Correll and Gosden developed an act quite similar to those of other harmony duos of the day, and although their style was far from unique, they presented their selections with a genuine sense of fun.[8]

Correll and Gosden had dabbled in radio as far back as 1921 and had occasionally participated in broadcasts between 1922 and 1924 during promotions for local Bren productions, including several appearances over Chicago station WLS as members of a Bren minstrel company. In early April 1925, they presented their harmony act for the first time over the Calumet Baking Powder Company's station in Chicago, WQJ, an engagement made as a promotion for a Bren show then playing in Joliet. Bren himself arranged the broadcast. "They only knew one song well enough to put on the air," he recalled, "so they sang that. It was a medley starting with some sort of a verse about everybody happy or something to that effect and then swung into a number of popular songs of the day. Correll played the piano and Gosden strummed the banjo. They seemed to have mike sense naturally, and they went out very well."[9]

The performers themselves sensed that the act had gone over and were in high spirits when they returned to the Bren office. Bren Company office manager Louise Summa, a close friend of Correll and Gosden, who would go on to spend more than 30 years as their personal secretary, recalled their enthusiasm. "I'll never forget the day they got back from Joliet," she told an interviewer in 1935. "Gozzie was sitting on my desk telling me how scared he and Charlie had been. Gozzie was going through his mail as he talked to me and pulled out a gaudy calendar with a picture of a ship, an advertisement of some insurance company. He held up the calendar and said, 'Well, Louise old kid, here's our ship come in at last.' There was something prophetic in that---both Gozzie and I felt it as we looked at each other."[10]

That same week, Bren arranged for Correll and Gosden to audition for Robert Boniel, the manager of station WEBH, owned by Chicago's Edgewater Beach Hotel. Performing the same selections they had used in the WQJ broadcast, the team impressed Boniel, and they were offered a regular engagement, appearing Wednesdays and Fridays through the spring and summer of 1925 under the billing "Correll and Gosden, the Life of the Party." The WEBH programs packaged the team with an assortment of other conventional mid–1920s radio acts—the Oriole Orchestra, the Three Musketeers, Fowler and Tamara's South American Troubadours, soprano Rita McFawn, and tenor Robert York—and there was little to set Correll and Gosden apart from any other act on the schedule.[11]

A trademark was needed and the performers hit on it accidentally. Louise Summa recalled the precise moment when Correll and Gosden gave their act a distinctive twist. "One night they sang 'The Kinky Kids Parade,' a hit song of the time [by Gus Kahn and Walter Donaldson], and interpolated a line of patter done in Negro dialect. Correll was the blustering, bullying major. Gosden, the persecuted private…. The routine was very successful and they were called upon again and again to repeat it. With each repetition it grew more elaborate. Gosden kept introducing more and more characters, all of whom he impersonated."[12]

"The Kinky Kids Parade" was a typical comic-sentimental pop tune of the mid–1920s, its jaunty 6/8 melody evoking the image of a group of black children staging their own backyard parade, but Correll and Gosden's interpolations set their version apart from that of other radio performers and recording artists. During the summer of 1925, the Correll and Gosden version of "Kinky Kids" emerged as their signature selection, capturing the imagination of Chicago-area radio listeners not just for the use of dialect but also for the use of that dialect as a foundation for multiple voice characterizations. The two performers had, quite casually, hit on a vital radio technique: through careful manipulation of the voice and by taking advantage of the directional properties of the microphone, two actors could create the impression of an entire group of people, using distinctive vocal traits to sketch out details of personality, and counting on the listener's imagination to fill in the rest. Black dialect was just one feature of Correll and Gosden's act—more often, the dialogue interpolations in their songs revolved around the doings of "Gos" and "Charlie," nondialect variations on their own personalities, augmented by falsetto female voices done by Gosden—but the strong response created by "The Kinky Kids Parade" ensured that black characterizations would take on increasing prominence in their performances. But even more important would be their growing realization that two men plus a microphone could equal an entire roomful of characters.

As their act evolved, the performers had to balance their WEBH assignment with their continuing work for Bren. "We didn't get any money—we didn't get nothing," recalled Correll. "There *was* no money in those days. We got nothing except a blue plate dinner at 1 o'clock in the morning."[13] But money wasn't the objective. Instead, the pair hoped their radio work would lead to stage work—and indeed, in the late summer of 1925, they were able to sell a collection of some of their best material to popular Chicago bandleader/entertainer Paul Ash, including, of course, their trademark dialect-interpolated version of "The Kinky Kids Parade."

The resulting "tabloid revue," entitled "Red Hot," gave Correll and Gosden their first taste of big-time success. They took a week's leave of absence from the Bren Company in September 1925 to appear with Ash on the stage of Chicago's McVicker Theatre, performing five shows daily as a prologue to a feature picture and earning a total of $250 for their week's work. Correll and Gosden were billed as providers of "Harmony Syncopation" and also presented a featured comedy sketch parodying a mind-reading act. Critics were impressed—and the performers were convinced more than ever that their act had a future.[14]

3. AIRTIME

"We didn't want any part of it until we knew if it was going to go or not—we didn't want to be a part of any flops."

—Charles Correll

THE SUCCESS OF "RED HOT" propelled Correll and Gosden to greater heights of popularity on radio, and it was followed by an equally successful sequel, "Paul Ash in Hollywood," in which the performers honed their skills as topical parodists, sending up the "sheiks and shebas of Filmland." Correll and Gosden toured briefly on the strength of this latter production, making radio appearances in St. Louis, Missouri; and in Columbus, Ohio. Finally, on returning to Chicago in October 1925, the partners were offered a staff position at WGN, the powerful *Chicago Tribune* station. This job enabled them to quit their positions at the Bren Company, and for the first time they devoted their full attention to broadcasting.[1]

At first, Correll and Gosden were general utility men at WGN. They performed their harmony act nightly over both WGN and its shared-time affiliate WLIB, sometimes making multiple appearances between 7 PM and midnight. Their announcer for these programs was one of the most popular and most distinctive radio personalities of the era—a burr-voiced 39-year-old Scotsman named Bill Hay, who had arrived in Chicago earlier that year by way of Nebraska. As Correll and Gosden became established at WGN, they soon realized that the popularity of "The Kinky Kids Parade" had carried over from WEBH—much to the increasing annoyance of the performers. "The mails were loaded with requests for that number," recalled Hay, "and although the boys themselves became terribly weary of it the radio fans besieged them to repeat and repeat it."[2]

On the strength of their increasing popularity with Chicago listeners, Correll and Gosden were signed by the Victor Talking Machine Company in November 1925, and on December 20th they made their first recordings. "The Kinky Kids Parade" was a natural choice for their first side, complemented by "Blinky Moon Bay," a generic pop ballad by Haven Gillespie and George A. Little. But for whatever rea-

Song publishers took advantage of Correll and Gosden's increasing popularity with Chicago radio audiences in 1925–26 by using their picture to sell sheet music. As this example suggests, the team specialized in upbeat novelty numbers.

son, both sides were rejected and were never issued. Subsequent sessions proved more satisfactory for Victor executives, and between March 1926 and December 1927, Correll and Gosden recorded a total of 21 songs, 16 of which were released.[3] The records sold moderately well, and the act continued to build a following on radio. But as the fall of 1925 wore on, the management of WGN began to look for something different—and found the answer within the pages of the *Chicago Tribune* itself.

During the 1920s, the newspaper comic strip was in its golden age; beginning with Sidney Smith's *The Gumps* in 1919, a craze for continuity strips swept the nation. *The Gumps* was syndicated by the *Chicago Tribune*—and *Tribune* promotion manager Benjamin T. McCanna was convinced that what worked in print could work equally well on radio. McCanna's idea was revolutionary: radio drama was still in its infancy, and no one had ever tried what he was suggesting: an open-ended, continuing dramatization, to be aired in nightly installments. Knowing Correll and Gosden's skill with dialogue, McCanna and WGN station manager Henry Selinger approached them in the fall of 1925 with the idea of adapting the strip for the air.[4]

The Gumps was the first American comic strip to use daily continuity in order to tell a dramatic story—and the themes treated in this strip and even its storytelling style would profoundly influence the work of Correll and Gosden. Andy Gump, the chinless patriarch of the Gump family, was a grasping, scheming character, always striving to climb beyond his lower-middle-class station. His speech was bombastic and self-important, and his self-confidence seemed boundless, even when faced with the failure of his latest venture—and this tendency often made him an easy target for bunco artists. Not unlike the serialized fiction of the nineteenth century, the story lines in *The Gumps* unfolded gradually—and carried on for weeks at a time, with readers hanging on every panel, anxious, say, to learn whether Andy Gump's fabulously wealthy but hopelessly idealistic Uncle Bim would be enticed into an ill-advised marriage with the scheming Widow Zander.[5] But unlike prior forms of literary serial fiction, in *The Gumps*, each individual story line was in itself a segment in a larger, unending story—the overall daily lives of the Gump family. This story line continued onward through the years with no final resolution—with the events of each succeeding episode building up an elaborate backstory for the characters, creating for readers an effective real-time simulation of day-to-day reality.

Correll and Gosden were reluctant to accept the proposal. They had made a name for themselves with their harmony act and were reluctant to place that reputation on the line by associating their names and voices with a potential flop. They also found themselves intimidated by the material—much of the action in the Gump home revolved around the interplay between Andy Gump, his no-nonsense wife, Min, and their mercurial son, Chester, and these middle-class married life themes seemed beyond their ability to portray, since Gosden's falsetto female voices could hardly be taken seriously as part of a realistic story. "If it had been a couple of years later, we might have tried it," Gosden recalled in 1939. "But I didn't marry Miss Leta Schreiber until June of 1927, and Charlie was single too. We knew nothing of married life."[6]

The performers pondered the assignment and immediately found additional flaws in the idea suggested by Selinger and McCanna. "The original idea was to have four or five actors," recalled Correll. "But Gos and I talked it over and decided such a cast would be unwieldy for a nightly feature. There would be too little time for rehearsal and we did not think things would move smoothly enough." Instead, Correll and Gosden suggested that they play all the parts themselves—eliminating any potential for problems with a large cast. The focus would be on two central characters, with additional characters to be added by voice doubling—a technique for which Gosden had already demonstrated remarkable skill.[7]

Correll and Gosden turned next to the subject matter and agreed that they would prefer to build a series around characters of their own rather than the established characters of *The Gumps*. Drawing on the success they had had in recent months with interpolated black dialect sequences during their musical performances, the performers at first suggested simply a more formalized version of those comic interludes—expanding the characterizations they had casually inserted into their version of "Kinky Kids Parade" into a series of their own, an approach that suggests that they hadn't quite understood what McCanna was trying to achieve with his "radio comic strip" idea. "We said, 'Maybe we could come up with a couple of characters doing jokes,'" Correll recalled in 1972. "We had a whole stack of jokes we used to do in these home talent shows … some of these old gags, you'll still hear 'em once in a while." And as Gosden elaborated to a newspaper reporter in 1981, "we chose black characters because blackface comics could tell funnier stories than whiteface comics."[8]

In this comment, Gosden made reference to a principle that was widely understood by performers of the early twentieth century—the liberating anonymity of blackface. Blackface had long been used by stage comedians as a generic "comic mask," as a technique for adopting an anonymous comic identity—the legendary African American stage comedian Bert Williams once noted of his first experience in burnt cork, "It was not until I was able to see myself as another person that my sense of humor developed."[9] Radio took away the visual cue of literal blackface. But the use of black *dialect*, coupled by alteration of vocal pitch, could sufficiently disguise the voices of the performers to the point where they would no longer *be* Correll and Gosden, harmony singers: instead, they could portray characters totally separated from themselves. And if the series failed, Correll and Gosden themselves could walk away unscathed. As Correll recalled more than 40 years later, "We didn't want any part of it until we knew if it was going to go or not—we didn't want to be a part of any flops."[10]

Once Correll and Gosden began the process of expanding their offhand dialect characterizations into actual personalities, they realized that the use of black dialect opened the door to interesting dramatic possibilities that would be more in line with McCanna's original idea. Since World War I, Chicago's black population had increased dramatically, as black men moved North in significant numbers, lured by the promise of industrial jobs. The "Great Migration" had been the topic of much discussion, and a vibrant black community had coalesced on Chicago's South Side—a community that, for Gosden, must have seemed reminiscent of the Jackson Ward of his youth.

Correll and Gosden quickly abandoned the idea of a joke-oriented series in favor of the story of two young black men from the rural South seeking their fortunes in the big city, a story that could easily be constructed around very basic human themes. "We decided that instead of doing those old jokes," Correll recalled, "we'd just take two colored characters from down South, bring 'em to Chicago and give 'em a job." And given that the lead characters would be portrayed as single men always struggling to get by, these themes seemed far more accessible to the performers—given their own paycheck-to-paycheck lives—than the petit bourgeois world portrayed in *The Gumps*. Correll's "bullying major" character from "The Kinky Kids Parade" offered the basic foundation for the gruff, deep-voiced Henry Johnson; Gosden's "persecuted private" formed the first hazy outline of Sam Smith. These basic vocal characterizations, using the contrast between Henry's imperious bass and Sam's gravelly tenor to create a vivid aural impression of the characters' size, were coupled with a simple continuing story line about the daily challenge of earning a living in an unfamiliar city. The result was the first "radio comic strip"—*Sam 'n' Henry*.[11]

On the surface it might seem that this idea had taken Correll and Gosden a long way from *The Gumps*. But by the time *Sam 'n' Henry* premiered on January 12, 1926, the performers had managed to work much of what had made that comic strip popular into their own creation. Like *The Gumps*, *Sam 'n' Henry*'s plots would most often revolve around money. Like Andy Gump and his naïve but wealthy uncle, Sam Smith and Henry Johnson often became involved with petty chiselers and confidence men. And most striking of all, the lead characters combined key personality traits echoing those of Andy Gump and Uncle Bim. Like Andy Gump, Henry was often an arrogant blowhard who didn't know as much as he thought he did but who never let that fact interfere with his constant pontifications. And like Uncle Bim, Sam's trusting nature left him an easy mark for every bunco artist that came along. Even the pacing of *The Gumps*—slow, meandering story lines punctuated by sudden bursts of action and an undertone of suspense—would be absorbed by Correll and Gosden into their own storytelling style. Just as in *The Gumps*, each day in the life of Sam and Henry was a small fragment of a much bigger picture—a gradual, linear flow adding texture and detail to the overall story of their new lives in the North.

Correll and Gosden drew from other comic strips as well. The dominant theme of the continuity comic strips that, following on the coattails of *The Gumps*, became a major fad in the early 1920s was "the little man against the world"—from the sleazy racetrack schemer Mutt and his naïve and trusting companion Jeff to the derby-wearing, cigar-chomping, work-dodging poolroom lowlife Moon Mullins; from the hapless dreamer Barney Google, ever beaten down by the cold, hard world around him, to the nickel-and-dime machinations of the lazy, shiftless Castor Oyl and his hapless dupe Ham Gravy. This theme resonated strongly throughout the work of Correll and Gosden. Likewise the mixture of old-fashioned sentimentality and working-class philosophy that would characterize Correll and Gosden's radio scripts echoed the tone of any number of contemporary comic strips, most notably the *Tribune*'s own *Little Orphan Annie*.[12]

It becomes obvious, then, that most of the basic plot devices that would later be found in *Sam 'n' Henry* could be found throughout the first half of the decade in the comic pages of almost any newspaper, and while the basic figures of Sam and Henry may seem at first glance to owe their identities to the conventions of blackface, it is evident on closer examination that the real roots of Correll and Gosden's characterizations extend less to the minstrel stage than to the striving, contentious figures of the 1920s American comic strip. But radio, telling its story in an intimate, individualized manner throughout the medium of sound alone, would give these characters an edge of humanity and a sense of realism beyond that of any of their contemporaries in print.

4. HERE THEY ARE ...

"We have all been close to tears at times when real trials and tribulations beset either of our beloved friends."
—Fan letter, 1929

CORRELL AND GOSDEN SUBMITTED their proposal for *Sam 'n' Henry* to Henry Selinger and Ben McCanna in November 1925, but their innovative format and characterizations failed to make much of an impression. "I guess our outline didn't sound so good," Correll recalled. "The management of the station said it wouldn't do so we almost forgot about it." The performers continued with their regular harmony-team programs and gave little additional thought to the rejected series.[1]

Then, in early January 1926, Correll and Gosden received an abrupt summons from WGN management and were told to prepare their program for its first broadcast—to be aired the following night. Although the performers had assembled a rough outline for their original proposal, they had no finished script. Locking themselves into an office, Correll and Gosden worked through the night to assemble their first episode. "Boy what a night that was," recalled Gosden. "It was January 11, 1926. It was an all-night session, and then on the night of January 12 we broadcast *Sam 'n' Henry* for the first time. Boy, were we scared."[2]

The first episode of *Sam 'n' Henry* mixed a few familiar elements with techniques never before heard on the radio. The recognizable dialects provided easy identification of Sam Smith and Henry Johnson as rural Southern blacks. But listeners expecting typical blackface comedy would have been baffled by that evening's broadcast—for that initial script contained not a single real joke, not a single comic situation. Sam and Henry engaged in none of the usual snappy repartee associated with minstrel end men. Instead, they simply talked—not as flamboyant entertainers but as two ordinary people. And in the course of their conversation, their dialogue slowly and deliberately told a story.

For ten minutes on that January evening, the audience followed the conversation as Sam and Henry made their way by buckboard to the Birmingham, Alabama, railroad depot. Through dialogue alone, Correll and Gosden helped their listeners visualize the mule-drawn wagon creaking slowly along the dusty road, as Sam and Henry discussed their plans for a new life in the North and met their friends at the depot who had assembled to see them off on their journey. Like many real-life participants in the Great Migration, Sam and Henry had been recruited for jobs in Chicago by an agent from a Northern company, and they had accepted the offer sight unseen.

>Mr. Johnson---What are you boys doing going to Chicago?
>
>Sam---We goin' up dere to wuk fo' a contractor, Mr. Johnson.
>
>Henry---W'y don't you show de man de lettah we got --- show de man de lettah.
>
>Sam---Heah's de lettah I got Mr. Johnson --- I'll read you part of it.
>
>Henry---Read de man de whole lettah - don't read him no part of it -- read de man de whole lettah.
>
>Sam---Here it is, Mr. Johnson - it says Mr. Sam Smith - Dear Mr. Smith - Our Southern rep'sentative, Mr. Mathews, handed us yo' name statin' dat you would be willin' to come to Chicago and wuk fo' our comp'ny durin' de restruction of sev'al buildin's now bein' 'rected in Chicago. Please re'pot to our Mr. McCarthy, who is now in charge of employment on de new skyscraper under restruction in de loop and he will assign yo to yo' wuk. 'Pon yo' 'rival in Chicago, phone our office, State 7264, and we will tell you whar you kin fin' Mr. McCarthy at that time. 'Range to leave Bummin'ham as soon as possible. Yo's ve'y truly -- de Chicago Construction Co.
>
>Mr. Johnson---Well that's fine, boys --- good luck to you.
>
>Henry---We ain't gonna have no luck --- I can see dat --- 'cause Sam ain't lucky and I'se wid him and I guess all dat bad luck's gonna come to us too [*Sam 'n' Henry*, Episode 1, 1/12/26].

Although the basic idea behind *Sam 'n' Henry* was a breakthrough in broadcasting technique—the first dramatized feature presenting continuing characters in a continuing story line ever to be heard on American radio—Correll and Gosden did not master that technique without considerable trial-and-error experimentation. Neither performer had ever entertained literary aspirations, and the only real writing experience they had had was in creating broad comedy material for the Bren Company's stage shows. With Correll and Gosden having had no experience in the creation of even semirealistic characters, it was inevitable that the earliest episodes of *Sam 'n' Henry* would lean heavily on overt stereotypes. Sam Smith was invariably naïve and whiny, while Henry Johnson was not just dour but *mean* as well. Both characters smoked and were fond of bootleg gin, and within the first month of their arrival in Chicago, they were arrested for shooting craps.

But as the series went on, the characters began to take on substance. Sam and

4. Here They Are ...

Henry soon ran into hard times when they were laid off from their construction jobs and found themselves struggling to find work in an unfamiliar city. The first weeks of the new series chronicled their efforts to find employment, carrying them to an assortment of South Side businesses. They worked briefly as shipping clerks for the mail-order firm of Montgomery Ward, and then in a Chicago meatpacking plant, and they finally ended up going into business for themselves by opening a cartage company using a rickety wagon and an elderly horse named "Gram'pa."

As the series unfolded, Correll and Gosden allowed their characters to explore their new world. Sam and Henry marveled at the splendor of Chicago's skyscrapers and elevated trains and made friends among their neighbors on the South Side. During their employment at Montgomery Ward, a coworker enticed the newcomers to enroll in the mysterious and forbidding Mother Lodge of the Jewels of the Crown of Chicago, presided over by a manipulative man known only as The Most Precious Diamond—a deep-voiced charlatan whose imperious manner provided an impressive mask for a henpecked husband desperate for an escape from his troubled household.

Other elements of the story line worked to underline the subtle character traits with which Correll and Gosden were gradually learning to endow their characters. Despite the warnings of both Henry and the Diamond of the dangers posed by marriage, Sam pined for his girlfriend Liza back in Birmingham and waited anxiously for her regular letters, suffering desperately about Liza's rumored dalliance with a smooth-talking Pullman porter back home. Henry, meanwhile, bluffed and boasted his way through life; he was an arrogant, egocentric poseur who disdained his friend's sentimental nature and took a perverse pleasure in sabotaging Sam's long-distance romance. From one day to the next, Correll and Gosden were learning how to write, how to act, and—most of all—how to create vivid and believable human characterizations.[3]

>Sam---Henry, whut in de worl' is de matteh? I'se goin' to Bummin'ham.
>
>Henry---Shut up now.
>
>Sam---Henry, you gonna 'cause me to lose 'Liza heah now --- whut did we say in dat valentine dat made her so mad?
>
>Henry---We ain't said nothin' --- 'Liza's jes' tired o' you --- she done foun' herse'f another man down in Bummin'ham, dat's all.
>
>Sam --- No, dat ain't it Henry --- dat ain't it --- 'Liza ain't dat kin'a girl -- I know her --- I done knowed her fo' fo' yeahs now.
>
>Henry---Now ca'm down --- ca'm down.
>
>Sam---Ain't no ca'min' down now Henry --- I don't wanna lose 'Liza --- I wanna marry dat girl.
>
>Henry---I'se gonna hit you oveh de head wid a stick in a minute now.
>
>Sam---Henry, I'se in love wid dat girl -- I loves her --- you ain't neveh been in love --- you don't know how it feels --- I lay in bed an' I think 'bout her --- I cain't go to sleep 'cause I thinkin' 'bout her.

Henry---Yeh --- an' yo' cain't wake up in de mornin' fo' de same reason [*Sam 'n' Henry*, Episode 32, 2/17/26].

Radio drama was in its infancy in 1926, and there were few models for Correll and Gosden to study. Their experiences with the Bren Company had never prepared them for the work they were doing—and consequently, *Sam 'n' Henry* was developed on a sink-or-swim basis. Although no recordings exist of any of the actual broadcasts from this period, phonograph records made by the team for the Victor Talking Machine Company in 1926 and 1927 preserve several examples of *Sam 'n' Henry* skits. These recordings reveal that both men were still learning how to use the microphone. Correll and Gosden deliver the dialogue in a stilted and stagy manner, with Gosden shouting out his lines and Correll, by contrast, mumbling out his responses with a peculiar under-the-breath delivery.[4]

For more than two months after the premiere of *Sam 'n' Henry*, the performers were uncertain about the program's potential. Still convinced that its failure would detract from their marketability as a harmony team, Correll and Gosden insisted on maintaining complete anonymity and kept their identities secret even from coworkers at the radio station. They went so far as to broadcast their nightly episodes in total isolation from a private room in the Drake Hotel, rather than from the regular WGN studio on the tenth floor of that building. But attempts to preserve their anonymity proved futile. "For a while we endeavored to keep their identities secret," recalled Bill Hay, "but a great many people recognized their voices from the Kinky Kids song which they had put over so tremendously." The true identities of Sam and Henry were soon an open secret.[5]

Despite its occasional coarseness, *Sam 'n' Henry* offered listeners something no other radio program in 1926 could offer: a sense of a casual nightly visit with familiar friends. Listeners came to know Sam and Henry not simply as voices in the evening air but as distinctive personalities in their own right and as personifications of universal human qualities. "You know, we rather like Sam. He is so unashamedly ignorant and anxious to learn that he deserves a better teacher than Henry," wrote a critic in the *American Appraisal News* during the show's first year. "But it was his fortune, as it is the fortune of so many of us, to be attracted to the ponderous bulk of Henry, who is but an impressive wind

The release of this phonograph record by the Victor Talking Machine Company in March 1926 marked the first public acknowledgment that the increasingly popular Sam and Henry were, in real life, the harmony team of Correll and Gosden.

bag, having neither pith nor substance, and to mistake his oracular mouthings for the real minted coin of wisdom."[6]

As interest in the series grew, Correll and Gosden poured themselves into the program—writing all the scripts, playing all the characters, and, when their identities were officially revealed in late March 1926, squeezing in a grueling schedule of personal appearances to promote the program. Across the Midwest, listeners continued to respond to their characterizations, as the serial grew to become a regional favorite.

> What's the matter with WGN?
> All day we look forward to 10 PM.
> All day we murmur, 'What shall we do?
> If *Sam 'n' Henry* don't come through![7]

By the end of 1926, *Sam 'n' Henry* had built a strong following throughout the Midwest—and Correll and Gosden realized that what worked in Chicago could just as easily work all over the country. The performers had begun making recordings of short *Sam 'n' Henry* sketches for Victor just four months after the series began, and these had sold well. The success of these discs suggested to the performers that live broadcasting over a single station need not be their only option. The result was an idea that would threaten to revolutionize the way in which radio programming was produced and distributed.

Correll and Gosden were not the first broadcasting figures to suggest the idea of pre-recorded radio features, nor were they working in a vacuum when they developed their own strategy for implementing this plan. The concept of radio syndication was being actively discussed by a number of individuals with an active role in Chicago-area broadcasting during 1927, most notably Maurice Wetzel, a former announcer with Westinghouse's Chicago outlet KYW who had moved from radio into an executive position with the phonograph division of the Brunswick-Balke-Collender Company. During 1927, Wetzel experimented in his home with technology for recording live radio broadcasts off the air, with an eye toward making them available for future rebroadcasts, and this idea led logically to the notion of creating pre-recorded original features, which could be distributed to individual radio stations on discs without the need for broadcast network lines. Using the facilities of Brunswick's Chicago studio, Wetzel prepared a sample program demonstrating his idea, but he failed to successfully market the venture.[8]

The world of Chicago radio was a close-knit one, and while there exists no documentation to prove that Correll and Gosden knew of Wetzel's experiments firsthand, it is entirely possible that they learned of his idea through their mutual friend E.C. Rayner, who published an extensive article about Wetzel's experiments in *Radio Digest*. It's possible that Wetzel's work, therefore, indirectly influenced their own development of the idea. But where Wetzel had focused on the technique of producing a recorded radio program without developing a practical system for distribution, Correll and Gosden were able to develop a workable plan for marketing a recorded version for *Sam 'n' Henry* directly to participating radio stations, using the syndication department of the newspaper that employed them as their model.

Correll and Gosden proposed this plan for the syndication of *Sam 'n' Henry* to WGN's management, and it became a source of significant dissension between the performers and management for much of their tenure at the station. But station executives were absolute in their rejection of the idea. WGN was the leading radio station in the Midwest, with a vast reach blanketing much of the middle of the United States. To allow other radio stations to air *Sam 'n' Henry* could, in effect, place the station in a situation where it would be competing with itself—an unacceptable possibility for the Tribune Company executives. *Sam 'n' Henry,* by contract, was an exclusive WGN feature, and the *Chicago Tribune* was determined to keep it that way.

Correll and Gosden chafed at the dismissal of their idea, which could have brought them considerably more exposure and, in turn, more money from personal appearances. Already, such personal appearances had ballooned into an unexpected financial bonanza for the performers. During 1927, Correll and Gosden had parlayed the popularity of *Sam 'n' Henry* into a series of stage appearances along the Balaban & Katz theater chain in and around Chicago, for which they were paid $2,000 per week—a sum that far surpassed the $100 per week each they earned from WGN. The performers took note as well of the possibilities offered by licensed merchandising of their characters, as the *Tribune* was profiting from the regional sale of a hardcover collection of scripts from the first two months of the program, a *Sam 'n' Henry* candy bar, and a metal toy express wagon, complete with Gram'pa the horse and rubber figures of Sam and Henry themselves on the driver's seat.[9]

Even without the additional exposure of recorded syndication, Correll and Gosden were already attracting national notice. In September 1926, accompanied by E.C. Rayner, the performers traveled to New York as the only Chicago radio act to be invited to perform at the prestigious Radio Industries Banquet, held in conjunction with the annual Radio World's Fair—a gala trade show that attracted the attention of the leading figures in the broadcasting industry. The trip offered the performers dramatic evidence of radio's explosive growth, and, in providing them with the venue for their network radio debut, it emphasized their act's potential as a national attraction.

On the night of September 15, 1926, Freeman Gosden and Charles Correll shared the microphone at New York's Astor Hotel with an array of nationally known performers, in a broadcast heard over 33 stations associated with the Red Network (still two months away from transforming itself into the National Broadcasting Company). Correll and Gosden performed a *Sam 'n' Henry* sketch, along with a sampling of their comic harmony act, sharing headline billing with humorist Will Rogers—a personal hero of Gosden's—along with Metropolitan Opera stars Mary Lewis and Reinhold Werrenrath, and United States Vice President Charles G. Dawes.[10]

The following year, Correll and Gosden made the trip to New York again and the 1927 banquet engagement gave them even greater national exposure, with the broadcast heard over the combined Red, Blue, and Pacific networks of the National Broadcasting Company, as well as the newly established Columbia Broadcasting System and a group of independent New York stations—a vast hookup combining 100 of the nation's leading stations. In just two years' time, Correll and Gosden had clearly grown too popular to be confined to a single outlet—even an outlet as powerful as WGN. But they were under contract with the Tribune Company through the end of 1927, so there was little they could do but wait.

The contract ended following the 586th *Sam 'n' Henry* broadcast, on the night of December 18, 1927, and Correll and Gosden swung into immediate action, negotiating a deal with WGN's arch-rival, the *Chicago Daily News* station WMAQ. Correll and Gosden were bargaining from strength, and they knew it; they insisted that their WGN announcer Bill Hay be included in the deal, as part of a financial package totaling $25,000 for the first year. Most important, the performers applied the hard lessons they had learned from their unpleasant break with WGN and insisted that they exclusively retain all copyrights on the scripts and the trademark on the series title. Although the $25,000 contract required that the annual budget for the station be doubled, WMAQ program director Judith Waller convinced *Chicago Daily News* publisher Walter Strong to agree to give Correll and Gosden whatever they wanted by arguing that future revenues from the syndication of the program would mean additional profits for the station.[11]

With Strong's blessing, the contracts were signed, and immediate arrangements were made with Marsh Laboratories of Chicago to manufacture recordings of each episode. The recording studio's founder, Orlando Marsh, a portly, cigar-chomping electrical engineer, had independently developed his own process for electrical recording in the early 1920s, and his Autograph label held the distinction of releasing the first electrical recordings to be commercially sold in the United States. Marsh was also an associate of Maurice Wetzel, whom he had assisted in developing recorded radio program experiments during 1927, so he readily understood the concept that Correll and Gosden proposed. Marsh's recordings were not especially well made, producing audio that tended to be hollow and noisy, but his studio was the most experienced in Chicago in dealing with the new challenges of microphone recording, making Marsh Laboratories an ideal choice for Correll and Gosden's purposes.

Under the plan devised by Correll and Gosden, each episode would be recorded in two parts, each side fitting neatly onto one face of a 12-inch 78 rpm record. The recordings would be made in batches, several weeks in advance of the scheduled broadcast date, and subscribing stations would be required to play each specific episode once and once only, on the same night that episode aired live from WMAQ. If possible, the recordings were to be aired at the same time as the WMAQ airings, to further simulate a live network broadcast. Each station would receive two copies of each disc, in order to encourage the use of double turntables, a technique that allowed each episode to air as a continuous unit, without the need for a pause to turn over the recording. But in a concession to those stations with only a single turntable, Correll and Gosden added "stalling" dialogue to the end of the first half of each episode—penciling in an irrelevant line or two at the midpoint of each script in which a character would make some offhand remark that would cover for the brief silence as the station operator flipped over the record and re-cued the needle.[12] Following the broadcast of each episode, the discs were to be returned immediately to the *Chicago Daily News*, where they were destroyed to ensure against unauthorized reuse.

Interested stations were sent ten episodes on a free trial basis, with the privilege of becoming a paid subscriber to the service if the series caught on. Cue sheets were sent with each shipment of discs, making it possible for each station to personalize the broadcasts by using a local announcer to read the introductory remarks for each episode. Stations under newspaper ownership or management were the most likely prospects for such a service, given their prior experience with print syndication, and for such operations an additional incentive was available: the *Chicago Daily News* also offered a daily *Amos 'n' Andy* newspaper comic strip tying in with the continuity of the radio feature, with staff artist Charley Mueller illustrating dialogue supplied by Correll and Gosden themselves.[13]

With their business manager Alexander Robb overseeing the administrative details of the operation and the *Chicago Daily News* Syndicate handling the distribution, Correll and Gosden had created their own de facto network. They called it a "chainless chain"; realizing the value of the concept, they attempted to secure a patent. They were unable to do so, however, and even before the end of 1928 other entrepreneurs were capitalizing on the success of the chainless chain by promoting syndication ventures of their own. By 1930, dozens of firms were involved in the production, promotion, and distribution of recorded radio programs, providing the foundation for the present-day broadcast syndication industry.[14]

Meanwhile, the Tribune Company was determined to prove that Sam and Henry were radio's top attractions and not Correll and Gosden. Following the departure of the program's originators, *Sam 'n' Henry* vanished from WGN's schedule for a two-

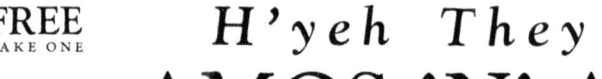

During the spring of 1928, the *Chicago Daily News* introduced *Amos 'n' Andy* to Chicago listeners with this free pamphlet reprinting the first week of *Amos 'n' Andy* comic strips and encouraging readers to follow the story on the air as well as in print.

4. Here They Are ...

Drawn in the broadly caricatured manner of the time by *Daily News* staff artist Charley Mueller, the *Amos 'n' Andy* comic strip ran just over a year, closely following the story line written for radio by Correll and Gosden It filled in scenes only alluded to in the radio broadcasts. Despite Mueller's reliance on the era's standard visual stereotypes, the strip often captured the sense of poignant melodrama that lay at the heart of Correll and Gosden's radio work.

week vacation. And then the program returned in mid–January, with station management hoping that listeners would fail to notice that Sam and Henry were no longer quite themselves. The station had replaced Correll and Gosden with two other performers on the WGN staff, a novelty team named Henry Moeller and Hal Gilles.

The choice of these two performers was not accidental. Moeller and Gilles and Correll and Gosden were colleagues at the Bren Company, where Gosden had taught Moeller and Gilles African American dialect, just as he had taught it to Correll. Moeller and Gilles then toured as a team, producing Bren minstrel shows for service clubs and lodges around the Midwest, just as Correll and Gosden had done. When Gosden was promoted to the position of manager of the Joe Bren Circus in 1924, he hired Hal Gilles as his advance man and worked closely with him until leaving the Bren Company. Under the circumstances, Moeller and Gilles were eminently logical choices to continue *Sam 'n' Henry* and it doubtless galled Gosden to no end to see the Tribune Company using his one-time protégé as a pawn in a corporate power play.[15]

Unfazed by the idea of competing directly against their old characters, Correll and Gosden continued to plan for their new series, working furiously through the early months of 1928, with the goal of premiering the new program in March 1928, over WMAQ and 24 "chainless chain" affiliates. Following a brief personal appearance tour that carried them as far south as Shreveport, Louisiana, Correll and Gosden focused their entire effort on their new venture.

From the beginning it was clear that the WMAQ series would take the same basic approach that had made *Sam 'n' Henry* so popular—a combination of character-driven comedy and melodrama. But a vital difference between the two programs was that the new characters would have a softer edge than the often-crude Sam and Henry. There was no more gin drinking, no more crapshooting, and the "unluckiness" and gullibility that had characterized Sam was replaced by a combination of earnestness, common sense, and a sincere desire for self-improvement. In addition, Correll and Gosden had by this time become well versed in microphone technique. Their new series would prove to be a better crafted production than its predecessor, with the past two years having given the pair a thorough understanding of how to bring their characters to life.

The most difficult aspect of planning for the new program, however, was settling on the title. Convinced that "Sam" and "Henry" were the best possible names for their characters, and with a two-year emotional investment in those names, Correll and Gosden struggled with the question for nearly a month. Halfheartedly, the partners attached Correll's first and middle names—Charles and James—to the characters, and the first two scripts of the new series were called "Jim and Charley." Unsatisfied with these names, Correll and Gosden next turned to their families for inspiration: Correll's brother Thomas was in the construction business back in Peoria, and Gosden's brother Harry worked for a newspaper in Asheville, North Carolina, Thus, "Jim and Charley" became "Tom and Harry" in episodes three and four. But Gosden still wasn't happy. To his painstaking ear for detail, the names just didn't work, didn't give precisely the right impressions of the characters. As the team worked on the script for the fifth episode, Gosden began riffling through the glossary of common names at the back of a desktop dictionary and noticed "Amos." Immediately, he knew this was the name he wanted: it summed up in four simple letters the essence of his character. And then it didn't take long to name Amos's friend—"Andy" sounded just right for a big, deep-voiced, "round and juicy" sort of character. Grabbing the first four scripts, the performers scratched out "Jim" and "Charley" and "Tom" and "Harry," knowing that they finally had their title.[16]

On the night of February 25, 1928, *Amos 'n' Andy* were introduced in a brief pre-recorded promotional announcement—the first such recorded announcement in the history of American broadcasting. That announcement ran six nights a week at 7:11 PM for the next three weeks[17]—until Monday, March 19, when WMAQ listeners heard Bill Hay open the first episode of the new series with a simple, low-key introduction.

> Amos and Andy, two lifelong buddies, from Dixie, have spent most of their life on a farm just outside of Atlanta, Ga. Amos is a hard working little fellow who tries to do everything he can to help others and to make himself progress, while his friend Andy is not especially fond of hard work, and often has Amos to assist him in his own duties. As the curtain goes up, we find the boys returning to the farmhouse with a bucket of milk—both are enthusiastic about going to Chicago where they have heard good high salaried jobs are available: -- Here they are: --

Correll and Gosden in character as Amos and Andy, February 1929. Over 100,000 copies of this photo were sent out in response to listener fan mail by the end of 1929. This photo session marked the performers' final use of stylized blackface makeup.

> Amos---I was sittin' here dreamin' 'bout Chicago an' 'stead o' putting de milk in de bucket, I put half of it on de ground.
>
> Andy---Dat's what yo' git fo' not tendin' to yo' bizness. If I'd been milkin' dat cow, son, I wouldn't-a wasted a drop o' milk [Episode 1, 3/19/28].[18]

The first lines spoken by the new characters defined them. Amos was portrayed as a naïve but earnest young man, plagued by self-doubts, while Andy was older, more worldly, and absolutely convinced that he had the answers to everything. The first week's worth of episodes found Amos and Andy preparing for their trip to Chicago, with Andy filling Amos's head with images of the fortunes just waiting to be made in the North. Even when a friend warns the pair about the difficulties of finding good jobs, the cold weather, the high price of food and lodging, and all the other pitfalls that awaited, the two remained determined to push forward.[19] Finally, with $24 in their pockets and four ham and cheese sandwiches to see them through the trip, Amos and Andy said goodbye to their friends and their old life and boarded a train for Chicago.

> Andy---Listen heah son, when we gits in Chicago, de minute we step off de train, dey is liable to come right up to us an' grab us.
>
> Amos---Grab us fo' whut? Put us in jail or sumpin'?
>
> Andy---No, no --- grab us an' ast us if we want a job.
>
> Amos---You heard whut John told us though back dere at de depot, ain't yo'?
>
> Andy---Whut yo' mean ---- about dem two boys goin' to Chicago?
>
> Amos---Yeh --- he say dem boys went up dere an' starved to death.
>
> Andy---De trouble wid dem boys is -- both of 'em was like you. Dey didn't have no sense --- but wid a man like me along dat knows how to handle big bizness men, we ain't goin' have no trouble [Episode 5, 3/24/28].

But despite Andy's bravado, Chicago proved as cold and cruel for the newcomers as Amos had feared. The two were greeted at the depot not by an employment agent, but by a desperate panhandler—who got a quarter out of Amos by revealing that he'd been jobless for more than six months.

That first night in Chicago set the stage for the next two weeks. Amos and Andy managed to find a cheap rooming house on the South Side, operated by the sympathetic Fred Washington, but employment proved more elusive. As Andy continued to declare his managerial aspirations, Amos hit the pavement and looked for work as the duo's funds steadily diminished. Their fortunes turned, however, when they met a young man named Sylvester—a soft-spoken but intelligent teenager who worked as a garage mechanic and was directly based, according to Gosden, on his childhood friend Garrett Brown.

Sylvester helped Amos and Andy find their first jobs in Chicago as day laborers on a new gymnasium project, and when Andy hit upon the idea of buying a decrepit old topless touring car for $75 in order to go into the taxicab business, it was Sylvester who managed to get the vehicle running, leading to the successful introduction of "The Fresh Air Taxicab Company Of America, Incorpulated." And most important, it was through Sylvester that Amos and Andy would meet a prosperous businessman by the name of Taylor—and Taylor's bright, attractive daughter Ruby.[18]

The introduction of the Taylors in *Amos 'n' Andy*'s second month marked the series' most significant departure from the precedents established in *Sam 'n' Henry*. While the earlier series had focused exclusively on uneducated working-class characters, *Amos 'n' Andy* not only acknowledged the existence of an educated, prosperous black middle class, but the new series also made members of that class integral players in the continuing story.

> Amos---Dis heah Ruby Taylor's a sweet gal a'right Andy -- ain't no two ways about dat.
>
> Andy---If her old man is goin' give you a job, she ain't bad. But if you is jus' goin' sit around an' talk love talk to de gal all de time, den you betteh let her alone.
>
> Amos---Yo' see, her papa's got a lot o' money.
>
> Andy---Whut do her old man do?
>
> Amos---He doos a lot o' things. He's a contractor --- he builds buildin's --- den he got a store dat he sells clothes in --- den I b'lieve he's got a garage or sumpin'.
>
> Andy---Well, out o' dem three places, you ought to be able to git a job. An' if Ruby is pullin' fo' yo', she kin make her old man give yo' big money.
>
> Amos---De only thing about it --- I hate to go to her father an' git a job jus' 'cause I know Ruby.
>
> Andy---Dere you go again now.
>
> Amos---Whut yo' mean, dere I go?
>
> Andy---Whut diff'ence do it make to you how you git de job jus' so you git one?
>
> Amos---Well, de thing I'd like to do is git a job widout Ruby he'pin' me if I could. I kind-a feel funny goin' to her father jus' 'cause she sent me up dere [Episode 13, 4/5/28].

Far more so than Sam's long-distance relationship with Liza, Amos's relationship with Ruby Taylor quickly became—and remained—the emotional heart of the series. The romance blossomed gradually through the spring and summer of 1928. While Amos had come North determined to remain faithful to his childhood sweetheart Mamie Henderson back in Georgia, there was no denying the attraction that had developed between Ruby and himself. Then, when Mamie suddenly broke off her engagement to Amos to marry one Ivan S. Peters, a traveling man from New York, Amos slowly rebounded from his grief to realize that quite without intending to do so, he had already fallen in love with Ruby.

Andy---Did yo' talk any love talk?

Amos---Yeh -- we talked love talk -- but I ain't goin' tell yo' 'bout dat 'cause dat's kind-a pussonel.

Andy---Come on now --- you know I is yo' buddy. Tell me whut you was talkin' 'bout.

Amos---Well, I was tellin' her all about my life --- whut I done down in Atlanta an' she started tellin' me some o' de things dat she used to do an' den all of a sudden, she spoke up an' say dat she never met anybody dat she liked like she do me.

Andy---Dat's a lot o' mush -- dat's all dat is.

Amos---She is plenty sweet Andy --- I is crazy 'bout her.

Andy---Listen, I'm goin' to bed --- is you goin' undress or not?

Amos---I'se too happy to go to bed now --- I ain't goin' to bed now -- I couldn't go to sleep noway. I wanna sit up heah an' think [Episode 119, 8/11/28].

Powered by simple yet absorbing story lines, *Amos 'n' Andy* steadily built a national following, with the syndicated recordings airing on stations from Boston to San Francisco by the end of 1928. While the program was broadcast on a sustaining basis over WMAQ, some of the "chainless chain" affiliates arranged for local sponsorship. In the West, the program was heard over San Francisco station KFRC, under the sponsorship of the Shell Company of California, and Shell promoted the program through giveaways at its chain of gasoline stations, helping to make it a major success with California audiences.[21] In 1929, California would mark the crowning point of Correll and Gosden's tour of the Pantages vaudeville circuit, attracting turnaway audiences and proving beyond a doubt that a single well-produced radio program could appeal to listeners all over the country.[22]

In the spring of 1929, motorists throughout Northern California affiliated themselves with the Fresh Air Taxicab Company with this windshield sticker, distributed by the Shell Company of California, sponsors of the program aired at KFRC, San Francisco. Regional promotion of the program by local sponsors helped boost its popularity during the "chainless chain" era.

Fan mail began pouring in for the performers, and the letters capture the sense of personal identification many listeners felt for the characters. In this Correll and Gosden marked their most important accomplishment: the creation of characters and situations to which listeners could develop an attachment on the most basic emotional level. As the series developed, the characters evolved, and the audience grew, it became evident that in the hands of skilled performers, radio could be far more than simply a vehicle for vaudeville-style comic turns or musical acts; well-chosen words could bring an entire world to life in the minds of the audience. Old-fashioned blackface comedy was nothing unusual for radio listeners in the latter half of the 1920s—performers such as the Two Black Crows, the WENR Weener Minstrels, the KOA Minstrels, the WLW Burnt Corkers, and the Gold Dust Twins were already widely known. The ancient jokes and the familiar characterizations of minstrelsy were a common attraction in 1920s radio broadcasts. Had Correll and Gosden merely perpetuated this tradition, their impact on the audience would have been minimal, and the performers themselves clearly understood this. "We don't wisecrack," Gosden stressed to an interviewer from *Psychology* magazine. "If we had nothing but wisecracks to rely on, we'd lose most of our friends. In the first place, we couldn't get enough wisecracks to go around for three hundred and thirteen nights a year. Not good ones, anyway. We have to diversify the emotional appeal. A laugh here, a little pathos there, and some good advice everywhere. The biggest response from our audience comes from the pathetic and instructive side."[23]

Listeners had tuned in other early radio acts to laugh at familiar jokes or be entertained by familiar tunes, but during 1928 and 1929, even more so than during the two-year run of *Sam 'n' Henry*, it became evident that millions of listeners were tuning in on Correll and Gosden's nightly broadcasts because they were drawn to the compelling stories. Listeners truly *cared* about Amos and Andy.

> We have been inspired by the high aims and rigid honesty of Amos, and we have all been close to tears at times when real trials and tribulations beset either of our beloved friends.[24]

Even before the end of *Amos 'n' Andy*'s first year, the program's wide appeal was noted by advertising executive William Benton, the assistant general manager of the Lord and Thomas agency's Chicago office. In late 1928, Benton suggested to agency president Albert Lasker that the program might be a good fit for one of the agency's clients. The Pepsodent Company, a Chicago-based manufacturer of toothpaste, was looking to reverse a declining sales trend, and Benton and Lasker—who was himself a significant Pepsodent stockholder—suggested to advertising manager Harlow P. Roberts that the firm sponsor *Amos 'n' Andy* on a national network.[25]

Pepsodent had been approached before about using radio and had shown little interest, but the Lord and Thomas proposal struck a spark. "When we were first approached on the idea of using radio, musical programs were the vogue," recalled Roberts in 1932. "There was little else on the air. And frankly, we couldn't get enthused. If Pepsodent was to use radio at all—and we weren't so sure we wanted to—we wanted something different. Well, we waited for a long time, we listened to many auditions ... but we didn't warm up to radio. This went on for about three years.... then, right under our noses in Chicago we found a program we thought might be the thing for us."[26]

Lasker and Roberts together brought the package to Niles Trammell, Chicago manager of the National Broadcasting Company. "We went to the chain with it," Roberts remembered, "and now it was their turn to be discouraging. They sold time, exclusively they told us, in units of hours and half hours. They had never broadcast any quarter-hour programs, and weren't sure they wanted to start doing so. It might make a bad precedent. Also there was no other advertiser putting on a program six times a week. Once a week was the customary procedure.... It was nearly nine months after we broached the subject before NBC lined things up to put Pepsodent on the air."[27]

After weighing the proposal for several months, in June 1929, Trammell finally turned to NBC-Chicago announcer A.W. "Sen" Kaney, a former colleague of Correll and Gosden from the WGN days, and asked him to get in touch with the duo. Kaney located them in Kansas City, where they were nearing the end of their lengthy Pantages vaudeville tour. After exchanging pleasantries, Kaney got to the point: "As soon as you get back to Chicago, Niles Trammell wants to talk to you!"[28]

The Lord and Thomas proposal to NBC was not the first time the program had been pitched to a network. At that time, WMAQ was an affiliate of the Columbia Broadcasting System, and in early 1929, even as Lord and Thomas and Pepsodent were considering Benton's suggestion, WMAQ program director Judith Waller traveled to New York to suggest that CBS pick up *Amos 'n' Andy*. Columbia executives dismissed her offer, unable to see its potential.[29]

The performers were interested in the network proposition for both financial and practical reasons. Although the "chainless chain" had been very successful (by mid–1929 *Amos 'n' Andy* was being heard nationwide, on more stations than carried any NBC program) quality control was becoming a problem. Correll and Gosden had occasion to listen in on stations carrying the recorded programs—and were often appalled at what they heard. "When they got them out on the road, you couldn't control them," noted Correll. "You'd send them to a station and they were playing them at 78 [rpm] and 85 and everything else. We heard them a couple of times and they were all garbled up." The necessity of having to work weeks ahead in the scripting of the program in order to make the advance recordings was also beginning to wear on the performers.[30]

At the same time, the success of *Amos 'n' Andy*'s as a syndicated feature was being monitored with increasing concern by NBC's sales department. "We were on at 10 o'clock," Correll recalled, "and the network that we had of our own had 10 o'clock sewed up all over the United States. NBC sent out a fellow to take a survey on this thing, and see 'what is this 'Amos 'n' Andy' thing that has tied up a lot of stations at 10 o'clock at night?' And they sent a fellow out, and he found out it was us, so they said 'well, we better get them on NBC if they can hold an audience that well.'" After initial discussions with Trammell and Roberts in Chicago, Correll and Gosden traveled to New York in mid–July 1929 to discuss the Pepsodent/NBC proposal with additional representatives of both the toothpaste firm and the network. The performers approached the appointment with a mixture of determination and amazement at how far they had come in so short a time. "Now there's one for the books," mused Correll. "Sending a couple of punk actors like us down to talk to a big sponsor for a program on the networks."[31]

There were still misgivings: while the Pepsodent Company was interested in sponsoring Correll and Gosden, company officials began to feel that the simple two-man dialogue format of the program was a bit too humble. Instead, it was suggested, why not present Correll and Gosden as end men in an elaborate minstrel show, complete with orchestra and chorus? Correll and Gosden vigorously opposed this idea, arguing that it went against everything they'd accomplished in the more than three years they'd been on the air. They well realized that they owed their success to their innovative serial-drama technique.[32]

The performers' arguments finally prevailed. On July 27th, it was announced that Correll and Gosden had signed a one-year contract guaranteeing them $50,000 each, and plans were made to bring the show to the coast-to-coast NBC Blue network.[33] The program would come to the chain just as it had been heard over WMAQ and the "chainless chain." As he had since the first episode of *Sam 'n' Henry*, Bill Hay would announce *Amos 'n' Andy* for the network. The only new addition to the format would be a theme song: after much discussion, WMAQ musical director Joseph Gallicchio selected a plaintive, yearning melody from Joseph C. Briel's nearly forgotten score for the 1915 film *Birth of a Nation*. Gallicchio's small string orchestra played this song at the open and close of every episode—and this made "The Perfect Song" one of America's most familiar melodies.[34]

Correll and Gosden spent several days in mid–July familiarizing themselves with the geography of Harlem, and the final weeks of the syndicated *Amos 'n' Andy* revolved around the lead characters' relocation from Chicago to New York. In the final "chainless chain" episode, broadcast on August 18, 1929, Amos and Andy sat in a rooming house in Pennsylvania, pondering their future in a scene that mirrors, perhaps, the uncertainty of Correll and Gosden themselves as they stood at a career crossroads.

> Andy---Just think Amos --- if it hadn't been fo' me, you wouldn't-a seed all dis country. I brought you up heah from Georgia. De only mountains you would eveh see would be Stone Mountain down near Atlanta.
>
> Amos---Yeh, but I done seed some pretty mountains in de last day.
>
> Andy---Dem boys dat lives down in Georgia --- dey ain't NEVEH seed nuthin' like dis, is dey?
>
> Amos---No, but dey ain't takin' de chance dat we is takin' neitheh.
>
> Andy---Whut yo' mean, ain't takin' de chance.
>
> Amos---I mean dat dey know where dey goin' sleep an' dey know where dey goin' eat an' dey know dey got a job. Heah we is goin' to New York ---- we don't know whut we goin' do.
>
> Andy---Dat IS right too. Yo' know, I been thinkin' 'bout dis heah thing. We was crazy to come heah.
>
> Amos---We was gittin' 'long alright in Chicago.

Andy---We had friends dere. Dat Kingfish is de cause of all dis. He done talked us into all dis.

Amos---Yeh, de Kingfish talked us into it alright ---- but it ain't no use to git cold feet now.

Andy---Oh no --- ain't no use to git cold feet. We gotta keep a stiff uppeh lip AN' loweh lip.

Amos---We just gotta do de best we kin when we git dere, dat's all [Episode 438, 8/18/29].

The following evening, in the WMAQ studios at the LaSalle Hotel, at the stroke of 10 PM Chicago time, Bill Hay leaned into a microphone marked "NBC" and spoke nine simple words. "Monday night, August 19th. Amos 'n' Andy, in person." And with those nine words, the lives of Freeman Gosden and Charles Correll would change forever.

5. A COAST-TO-COAST HOOKUP

"They have made their characters real people; each characteristic makes listeners exclaim, 'Why, I know somebody exactly like that!'"
—Harlow P. Roberts

AMOS 'N' ANDY MADE THE transition from syndication to network in a barrage of publicity, as NBC and Pepsodent heralded their new acquisitions with breathless press releases, advertisements, and magazine articles—and these announcements suggest that at this stage in their relationship neither the network nor the sponsor truly understood the program or the performers. Advance publicity for the network series emphasized the comedy aspects of the series while downplaying the dramatic, and hailed Correll and Gosden as figures of unprecedented national acclaim.

> Freeman Gosden and Charles Correll are the full names of Amos 'n' Andy, whose droll Afro-American witticisms have captivated the nation. Their tremendous popularity is pointed to by broadcasting officials as complete evidence of the hold of radio on the American public.... A recent tour of personal appearances not only resulted in packed houses everywhere, but made them the central figures at civic receptions that rivaled in enthusiasm and numbers those tendered to heroes of war and peace.[1]

Correll and Gosden began their network series on August 19th by continuing the story line from the chainless chain episodes without interruption. Rather than reintroducing the characters from the beginning, the opening episode found Amos and Andy having finally completed their drive from Chicago to New York, only to end up stranded on the Battery, out of gas and with a punctured tire—and bickering angrily over what to do next.

> Amos---De thing we ought to do is git some gasoline in de taxicab. How much money is you got?

An advertisement for *Amos 'n' Andy* flashes over Times Square from Pepsodent's gigantic animated billboard in the spring of 1930—a sure sign that Correll and Gosden had reached the pinnacle of national esteem. (*Correll Family Collection*)

> Andy---I'se almost broke. I ain't goin' put no money in gasoline. Dat's just like burnin' money up.
>
> Amos---Well yo' don't speck me to buy ALL de gasoline, do yo'?
>
> Andy---I'se bringin' you to New York, ain't I? Tryin' to make sumpin' out of yo'. If I'se doin' dat, look like to me dat you kin buy a little gasoline now an' den [Episode 439, 8/19/29].

Correll and Gosden made little effort in that opening episode to elaborate on the backstory of their characters, instead focusing on establishing the personality traits of Amos and Andy for new listeners. And, in keeping with their usual policy, the script contained no jokes, wisecracks, or snappy repartee. The result was less a blackface act than a subtle character sketch introducing Amos and Andy to their new surroundings. But the less-than-subtle publicity buildup given the program in New York—where the chainless chain episodes had not been heard—led to a scathing review from one of the city's leading radio columnists. Unfamiliar with the serial format, and expecting to hear conventional blackface comedy instead of character-driven dialogue, *New York Sun* critic Kay Trenholm welcomed Amos and Andy to New York with withering derision.

> It may be that the actors themselves were too hasty in assuming that their audience here would naturally fall in line with the public sentiment of Chicago and not wait to be won over, much less dare an opinion of its own. We were personally bewildered by their apparent casual treatment of the event which brought them here at all and were left uncertain as to just what their broadcast was all about. Their lines are not good and there is no pretense whatever to carry out the illusion of comedy. It is straight dialogue between two common-place "darkies" and is without even the saving asset of a well thought-out situation. Perhaps after knowing "Amos 'n' Andy" for four or five years one might take a friendly interest in their "doings, " but on first acquaintance they hardly attract a second glance.[2]

Correll and Gosden were deeply stung by Trenholm's review and responded directly to it by opening the program's second network episode with a detailed recapitulation of the story line to date, giving New York listeners a clearer idea of who Amos and Andy were, where they had come from, and what they had experienced over the past year and a half. But like the opening broadcast, the second episode continued to avoid the usual setup-and-punchline formula of blackface comedy. New York listeners gradually came to realize what the rest of the nation already knew: with *Amos 'n' Andy*, story line and characterization were the essential elements.

Although Trenholm's comments were soon proven wrong by an enthusiastic response from ordinary New York listeners as the story line unfolded, Trenholm's caustic review stuck in Freeman Gosden's mind—and he still seethed about it more than 20 years later, when he told columnist Ben Gross, "I still remember that only you and a few others among professional critics saw anything in our first broadcast. Most of them did not realize that we were after the creation of character, not gags."[3]

At first, the program was heard at 11 PM Eastern time—allowing the series to keep the 10 PM timeslot it had held in Chicago for most of its "chainless chain"-era run. "The time didn't suit us," commented Pepsodent advertising manager Harlow Roberts. "Ten PM in the middle west was fair enough, but eleven o'clock in the east seemed pretty late. So NBC maneuvered and finally was able to clear a period for us at 7 PM."[4]

The change was to take effect with the November 18 broadcast. As soon as the change was announced, chaos erupted. "The result of that move was a revolution—which may be strong language," marveled Roberts, "but I can think of no other word to describe the situation—in the Middle West. Complaints poured in by the thousands—there were letters from individuals and petitions signed by all the employees of business houses—one from a railroad had 2,500 names attached."[5]

> On behalf of the 115 employees of the Secretary of State's office, and several hundred other employees of the state of Colorado, I ask you to reconsider the time of broadcasting Amos and Andy, which under the new schedule brings it to the Rocky Mountain region at 5 PM. This does not allow them to enjoy this program, and one hour later

would be greatly appreciated by all who have followed this most interesting entertainment program.⁶

Correll and Gosden agreed to a best-of-both-worlds solution. Beginning on November 25, they would broadcast twice nightly, with the early broadcast going out at 6 PM Central for Eastern stations, and stations from Chicago westward taking the second broadcast at 10:30 PM Central time (later adjusted to 10 PM). *Amos 'n' Andy* would continue to broadcast on this twice-nightly schedule until February 1943, and the dual-broadcast format would be adopted by many other sponsors to ensure a maximum national audience for their features.⁷

The outcry over the time change offered just a hint of what was to come. By the start of the New Year, *Amos 'n' Andy* had become a fad. By March 1930, it had become a nationwide mania.

Beginning in the Washington, DC, area and spreading rapidly through February and March of 1930, advertisements like this one from a theater in Dover, Maryland, reassured movie patrons that they needn't worry about missing *Amos 'n' Andy*'s nightly episode.

It is related that some time ago, the proprietor of a Washington cinema theatre observed his audiences were unusually sparse around the hour of 7 PM. He was told that Washington housewives, husbands, and children, instead of flocking to his theatre after dinner, were staying home by their radios to hear the daily ten minute broadcast of a blackface team called Amos 'n' Andy. To the proprietor it seemed incredible that such a brief radio feature could substantially affect his profits. But he wired his theatre for radio, broadcast *Amos 'n' Andy* regularly from the stage, and with amazement watched his empty seats fill up. Other nationwide theatres soon found it profitable to follow suit.... Observers have recently been forced to the conclusion that *Amos 'n' Andy* are essential to the early evening entertainment of a large proportion of the U.S. public.⁸

Amos 'n' Andy have gone beyond all control. The radio has never had a more amusing feature, nor one that has created so much havoc. For Amos 'n' Andy, like Sidney Smith with his Andy Gump, have finally mastered the trick of creating suspense. With half a dozen plots running through their sketches, they hold the dramatic tension in a way to arouse the admiration of Professor Baker. For a week, the King Fish's Great Home Bank tottered on the brink of ruin and thousands of families all over America never ate a dinner in peace. The night that the Great Home Bank toppled over, with Madam Queen's fifty dol-

5. A Coast-to-Coast Hookup 51

lars involved in the ruin, was the blackest since that night in October after the stock market dive.[9]

The sketch they broadcast nightly is the latest wrinkle in entertainment—a comic serial on the air. Yet not too comic—it has a rare human touch. The ups and downs of Amos 'n' Andy are in the reality the ebb and flow of most lives. Every day you and I meet such characters in real life.[10]

Their nightly 15 minutes is almost indescribable to an English reader, hardly to be understood to an English listener. There is so little in it to describe. It is not a joker's act, nor a mere jumble of wisecrack jokes. The listener laughs, he laughs with a fellow feeling, not as at a smart saying. Here, in fact, is a serial story, a continued drama in two simple lives.[11]

I believe that the success of *Amos 'n' Andy* in arousing that interest is due to the fact that their creators are such good psychologists. They have made their characters real people; each characteristic makes listeners exclaim, "Why, I know somebody exactly like that![12]

With the craze came an explosion of interest in the program, its creators, and its characters—and Correll and Gosden quite unexpectedly found themselves caught up in the swirl of Celebrity. The anonymous small-timers of five years before were suddenly the talk of a nation. Where five years before they had gladly worked for a warmed-over hotel blue-plate dinner, by the summer of 1930, they were bringing in from all sources a combined weekly income of $11,000. And where five years before they would have been excited to find a passing reference to their names in a local Chicago radio column, now they were being sought out for interviews by the most prestigious national magazines. In just five years Correll and Gosden had shot from the bottom of the show business world to its very peak. "We're not kidding ourselves for a moment about the true facts," mused Gosden in an interview with *Psychology* magazine. "We just put on a show. We were hicks when we put it on—I don't mean small-town rubes, but we didn't know anything about 'big propolitions.' Because our show happens to go over with a smash doesn't make us any the less what we were a few months ago."[13] Interviewing Correll and Gosden in the spring of 1930, the hard-boiled New York journalist O.O. McIntyre was surprised to find the performers both candid and modest about their sudden and explosive popularity. "In all my years of interviewing successes, accidental and deserved, I never saw more conspicuous examples of complete bewilderment," McIntyre wrote. "They act as if they were holding something that would at any moment explode in their hands."[14]

Certain that the bubble could burst at any moment, the performers were quick to seize opportunities for capitalizing on their success. Continuing a policy they had begun during the chainless chain era, Correll and Gosden licensed their characters to carefully chosen manufacturers; an array of *Amos 'n' Andy* merchandise was soon on the market. The toy firm of Louis Marx and Sons produced a detailed tinplate wind-up model of the Fresh Air Taxicab, complete with figures of Amos, Andy, and Amos's dog. That was followed by wind-up walking figures of Amos and Andy. The Williamson Candy Company of Chicago produced a popular *Amos 'n' Andy* candy bar: a vanilla-flavored honeycomb wafer enrobed in chocolate. Other licensed manufacturers flooded the dime stores with card games, novelties, and stationery prod-

The Lord and Thomas art department created these cartoonish standup counter display figures to tie in with an *Amos 'n' Andy*–themed advertising blitz for Pepsodent in the spring of 1930. Life-size versions of these figures stood in hundreds of drugstore windows from coast to coast at the peak of the campaign. As usual, Amos does all the work.

ucts. The demand for *Amos 'n' Andy* merchandise attracted fly-by-night manufacturers as well—and legitimate items soon jostled for counter space with cheap knockoff products—featuring "Amos and Sandy," "Amis and Ande," and sometimes, for the boldest of the rogue manufacturers, crudely rendered images of Amos and Andy themselves.[15]

With the craze at full pitch, Correll and Gosden were quickly signed by RKO-Radio Pictures, a recently established RCA subsidiary, for a full-length motion picture. The performers traveled to Hollywood in the summer of 1930, and the resulting production, *Check and Double Check,* premiered on October 24, 1930, as the opening attraction for the new RKO Mayfair Theatre in New York. Correll and Gosden themselves were present for the premiere, which was preceded by an onstage introduction by NBC president M.C. Ayelsworth, and Will H. Hays, president of the Motion Picture Producers and Distributors Association of America.[16] But the enormous buildup given the film led to a lukewarm critical response.

> Many harsh words might be written of *Check and Double Check* were it not for the fun furnished by that radio team "Amos 'n' Andy." *Check and Double Check* as a story is a little too wan to stand up against criticism.[17]

On the other hand, the picture drew plaudits from the influential *Photoplay* magazine.

> Fifty million Amos 'n' Andy fans are going to mob the theatres to see their idols for the first time. And they will not be disappointed. Big, hulking Andy and browbeaten but rebellious Amos materialize on the screen without losing the quality that made them famous as voices. In many ways, their first picture is a brilliant job.[18]

Viewed today, *Check and Double Check* is, to say the least, deeply flawed. The appearance of the stars is the first obstacle to be overcome—and for many modern viewers, it may be insurmountable. Correll and Gosden appear not in stylized minstrel blackface but in an attempt at realistic Negro makeup. However, the makeup is poorly applied and serves only to accentuate their obviously Caucasian features. Correll also wears obvious lifts in his shoes to compensate for the fact that, although he might have matched Andy's envisioned girth, he fell considerably short of the character's imagined height. Neither performer appears comfortable before the camera, and they are further undercut by the plodding direction; dry, dead cinematography; and leaden pacing common to practically all early talking pictures.

But even more damaging to the film is the script. Screenwriters Bert Kalmar and Harry Ruby were veterans of musical comedy and were much more at home dealing with cartoonish song-and-dance comedians like Bert Wheeler and Robert Woolsey or Bobby Clark and Paul McCullough. The story they devised casts Amos and Andy as comedy relief to the main plot involving a romantic match between Richard Williams—the son of the owner of the farm on which Amos and Andy had once worked—and a high-society girl. A cardboard villain, a trite find-the-missing-deed plot, and an embarrassing haunted-house sequence further sabotage the picture, as does the imposition of an uncomfortable "yearning for the old plantation" undertone in Amos and Andy's dealings with Richard Williams, a minstrel-show cliché that was conspicuously absent from the radio series. Kalmar and Ruby's attempts at capturing the mixture of subtle humor and sentiment that characterized the radio program are heavy-handed at best—and, indeed, the only Amos 'n' Andy scene that really stands up is a pastiche of the various "telephone conversation with Ruby Taylor" sequences that had already proven themselves on the air, and which Correll and Gosden had already used to considerable success in their stage appearances. Even the showcased presence of Duke Ellington's Cotton Club Orchestra, performing several selections in a party scene, including the jazzy "East St. Louis Toodle-oo" and the Kalmar-Ruby pop perennial "Three Little Words," cannot save the picture.[19]

For Correll and Gosden, *Check and Double Check* was a crushing disappointment. "Dad thought it was the worst film ever made," comments Freeman F. Gosden, Jr., who was two years old when the picture was shot. "He never let us see it. It wasn't until about ten years ago that I got my hands on a copy. After I finally saw it I could see what he meant. He felt neither his acting nor the story line was up to par." Charles Correll sensed the insurmountable problem connected to the visualization of characters whose appearances depended entirely on the imagination of each individual listener. "We realized right there all we could do was disillusion everyone. Everyone had their own idea of what Amos and Andy looked like," he recalled in 1961, and as long as this was the case any single visualization of the characters was bound to conflict with the images built up in the minds of millions of listeners. The obvious artificiality of Correll and Gosden's makeup in the film only served to further emphasize this discontinuity. However listeners visualized the characters, they visualized them as genuine African Americans, not as white men in greasepaint. "As soon as we put on black face," Correll continued, "we became just a couple of minstrels."[20]

But Correll and Gosden's objections to the film notwithstanding, and despite the mixed reviews, *Check and Double Check* was a box-office smash—proving to be RKO's biggest hit of the 1930–31 season, grossing a total of $1,751,000 against a negative cost of $967,000. Once the costs of prints and promotion were deducted, the film realized a net profit of $260,000.[21] Although the high salaries of the performers—$250,000 plus a percentage of the gross—and the cost of paying for their nightly broadcast line for the 65 episodes aired during the team's stay in Hollywood cut into RKO's return-on-investment for the picture, the studio felt confident enough in the value of *Amos 'n' Andy* as a screen attraction to offer Correll and Gosden a multi-picture deal—which they immediately rejected.[22]

Correll and Gosden instinctively understood that they were a *radio* act—and, indeed, it was on the medium of radio itself that their influence proved the most significant. Fifteen-minute comedy-drama serials quickly became the fastest-growing format in radio, usually featuring dialect characters. Some were blackface acts. In San Antonio, Texas, in late 1929, the team of George Fields and Johnnie Welsh created *Honeyboy and Sassafrass* at station KSAT, a serial in which the two charac-

Correll and Gosden were sabotaged by a poor script and insensitive direction in their only starring feature film, *Check and Double Check* (RKO, 1930). The making of the film marked the performers' abandonment of minstrel-influenced makeup in favor of a more realistic style — but even that change failed to bring the images from the film into line with listeners' expectations. By the following year, Correll and Gosden discontinued all use of blackface in their stage performances and would make only three subsequent appearances in makeup over the rest of their career: a cameo appearance in *The Big Broadcast of 1936*, and CBS photo shoots in 1939 and 1942.

ters operated the "Black Panther Detective Agency" while seeking the favor of "the comely Peaches," proprietress of the "Black Kitten Cafe." The characterizations in *Honeyboy and Sassafrass* were far cruder and more heavily stereotyped than even the crudest work that Correll and Gosden had done in *Sam 'n' Henry*, but by 1934 the imitators had managed to ride *Amos 'n' Andy*'s coattails to a spot on NBC, running into 1937 as a daytime feature.[23]

Other black dialect programs grasping for a piece of the *Amos 'n' Andy* craze followed and were created and presented by African American performers. The pioneer of black radio in Chicago, Jack L. Cooper, created and portrayed both of the title characters in *Luke and Timber*, a comic serial about two young black men from Tennessee seeking their fortunes in the North.[24] Another African American dialect performer, Clifton Newton Moore, presented a similar feature at another Chicago station, under the title *Ephus and Mr. Bodilly*.[25] And in 1931, two legendary names in black musical theater—the team of Flournoy Miller and Aubrey Lyles—came to CBS to try their hand at broadcasting by performing selections from their repertoire of blackface stage routines.[26]

Other performers chose different dialects—or no dialects at all—but the imitation of *Amos 'n' Andy*'s format was just as overt. The performers who had attempted unsuccessfully to continue *Sam 'n' Henry* after Correll and Gosden's break with WGN, Henry Moeller and Hal Gilles, created a German-dialect serial, *Louie's Hungry Five*, which WGN eventually attempted to syndicate through recordings.[27] In November 1929, author/actress Gertrude Berg sold NBC a Jewish-dialect serial called *The Rise of the Goldbergs* and also played the lead role.[28] In early 1930, the San Francisco–based team of Johnny Patrick and Helen Troy began syndicating their comic serial about a teenage couple, *The Funniest Things, with Cecil and Sally*.[29] Maine native Phillips Lord created two major "Down East" dialect serials for NBC—*Uncle Abe and David*, and *The Stebbins Boys*, both featuring fellow Yankee dialect specialists Arthur Allen and Parker Fennelly.[30] And two young college men from Mena, Arkansas, named Chet Lauck and Norris Goff walked into station KHTS in Hot Springs one day in

Chester Lauck and Norris Goff, creators of **Lum and Abner**, pose with Correll and Gosden, along with Stan Laurel and Oliver Hardy, during a 1946 party at the Hollywood home of comedian Eddie Cantor. Lauck and Goff made their first venture into show business as direct imitators of Correll and Gosden, and the structure of their program in years to come would owe much to the format of *Amos 'n' Andy*.

1931 to begin a 22-year run as the "lovable old fellows from the hill country," Lum and Abner.[31] But none of the imitators, black or white, whatever the dialect, ever matched the appeal—or the audience—of the originals.

The impact of *Amos 'n' Andy* on radio itself went far beyond outright imitation. Beyond the fact that *Amos 'n' Andy* inspired the creation of an entire radio genre—which would eventually give birth to both the situation comedy and the soap opera—the program had a profound impact on the evolution of the most basic techniques of dramatic radio itself. Correll and Gosden proved to be the first great radio actors, perfecting a subdued, naturalistic approach to microphone acting that differed sharply from the broad manner that stage actors brought to the air—and their continued insistence on complete privacy while creating their scripts and broadcasting their episodes contributed to this manner of performance. Each afternoon, behind the locked door of their private office on the twenty-fourth floor of Chicago's Palmolive Building, Correll and Gosden used free association and improvisation to create their daily scripts. With Correll seated at the typewriter and Gosden pacing the floor, the performers assumed the personalities of their characters as they worked out each line and situation, often drawing from their own experiences to shape the narrative. "They are four distinct people, not two," observed Louise Summa. "From the minute that door closes behind them, they stop being Correll and Gosden and become Amos and Andy. Sometimes they write a script in an hour, sometimes it takes four, but during that time they never for a moment step out of character. They usually take off their shirts, collars, and ties, and often when they get through they're wringing wet. They live everything that goes into those scripts."[32]

The improvisation was not random. The performers approached each day's script as an extension of the one that came before, making the flow of one episode into the next a natural rhythm. "We'd just get together and say, 'well, what did we do yesterday?' and talk about that for a minute or two, and go from there," Correll recalled in 1972. "Freeman would walk around our office doing lines ... he'd do a line, then look at me to see if he could tell in my face whether I thought it was funny or it belonged in there or what. Once in a while maybe I'd contribute a line, I'd think of something, an answer to what he'd say."[33] No matter where Correll and Gosden were, at home in their Chicago office or in a hotel room or theater dressing room on the road, this routine was never allowed to vary over the 15-year run of the serial program.

Just as the scripts were prepared behind locked doors, so too were the broadcasts themselves. When WMAQ moved from the LaSalle Hotel to specially constructed quarters on the twenty-first floor of the Chicago Daily News Building in September 1929, a private studio, designated Studio D, was constructed to Correll and Gosden's specifications—a simple 14' × 14' square room with curtains that could be drawn over the windows to shield the performers from view. When WMAQ was purchased by the National Broadcasting Company in late 1931, another custom-built studio was prepared for Correll and Gosden in the network's Merchandise Mart headquarters—and in May 1932, the performers gave their first broadcast from the comfortably furnished living-room-like Studio F. Regardless of the location, however, spectators were strictly prohibited—and even announcer Bill Hay and the members of Joseph Gallicchio's orchestra were required to work from a separate studio. "It's not that we have any self-consciousness," explained Gosden, "but while visitors are looking at us there is almost an unavoidable tendency to play up what we say and do to the ones we can see listening, rather than to the audience we must please beyond the range of our eyes."[34] The privacy of the closed studio also allowed Correll and Gosden the freedom to fully absorb themselves in their characters—to feel what the characters were feeling to the extent that Gosden often became emotionally exhausted after an especially stressful scene.

Alone, in a small, secured studio, and always mindful of the unseen audience, Correll and Gosden never declaimed, never emoted, never engaged in broad theatricality. They understood, instinctively, that radio demanded a more intimate brand of acting. They understood that with radio there was no balcony one had to reach, there was no need to project one's voice to the furthest rows of a large auditorium—and there was no need for the exaggerated vocal gesturing necessary to make an impression on a large live audience. They also understood that radio acting required an entirely new set of techniques, involving careful modulation of the voice, sensitivity to pacing, and a thorough understanding of the microphone's directional characteristics. The slightest motion of the head away from the microphone, the slightest hitch in the voice could help define the meaning of a line of dialogue and the personality of the character delivering it. Tiny vocal quirks that would have been lost on the stage—Andy's weary drawl, Amos's nervous stammer—were magnified by radio, and could underline the emotional power of a word or phrase. "Intimacy, I decided, was the keynote of radio acting," recalled veteran radio actress Mary Jane Higby. "Mother had another suggestion. I want you to study *Amos 'n' Andy*—especially the way Amos carries on a one-sided telephone conversation. You can tell exactly what a person at the other end of the wire is supposed to be saying....' It was in this type of imagination that the top radio people excelled—and no one ever set a scene vocally better than Amos 'n' Andy."[35]

Primitive experiments in aural drama had been going on in American radio since 1922, but these early plays remained stagebound in both their technique and in their vision.[36] Correll and Gosden broke entirely with the techniques of the theater and turned radio's greatest limitation—its lack of a visual element—into its most powerful advantage, creating out of their own voices an entire self-contained fictional world in which characters grew and developed from one night to the next. This technique, in turn, encouraged the development of an intimate emotional bond between the characters and the listeners, who could easily imagine that Amos and Andy were talking directly to them, that they were *there* in the taxicab office or the rooming house or the lunchroom *with* Amos and Andy, listening in on the conversation of friends. Listeners didn't simply observe Amos and Andy's world—for 15 minutes each night, they became a *part* of it. "Read the manuscript of their daily skit and it is the driest of pointless drivel," commented O.O. McIntyre, "and yet in their hands it pulses with pathos, glows with an understanding sympathy, and you suddenly become conscious that it is the warp and woof of the phenomena called life. You want to hear more."[37]

Like McIntyre, another prominent critic of the popular culture of 1920s and 1930s America grasped the essence of Correll and Gosden's appeal, marveling at their ability to create an entire world from the fabric of their voices and their listeners' imagination. "Out of these characters a sort of bubbling of activity arose, surrounding the principals," observed Gilbert Seldes, "and these two, using the drawl and the slow take and the occasional pretentious language of the stage Negro, gave a pace and rhythm to their show which was almost the true beat of life."[38]

Correll and Gosden's work drew praise not only from the popular critics and columnists of the day but also from some of its more radical thinkers. In 1931, the iconoclastic journal *The Debunker*—hardly a bastion of small-town orthodoxy[39]—devoted several pages to an examination of the program by noted scientist/humanist scholar/Socialist philosopher Maynard Shipley. While conceding that "we may patronize [Amos] because his skin is black and he does not spell properly," Shipley believed the program's true appeal stemmed from deeper roots.

> When Amos loses his engagement ring and rings are sent to him from all over the country; when a lawyer turns off his radio because Amos is on the surgeon's table and he cannot bear to hear Amos suffer; when letters pour in advising Amos to accept an offer of a position where his money will be his own, there is evidence that to many thousands of persons this has ceased to be a piece of radio entertainment and has become the real story of real persons, what a well-known philosopher has described as "a bit of life as simple as a folk song." I have never heard of an act on the stage, in the movies, or over the radio, that had just this particular effect of veridity.... The conditions and limitations of radio have undoubtedly assisted greatly in this achievement; I have an idea that the coming of television will put an end to Amos 'n' Andy as we know them today. But for the present they have built up a characterization which has many imitators but which is itself unique. The "sirology" behind the accomplishment is interesting. Most interesting of all, however, is the emergence from a mere bit of radio foolery, panoplied in advertising and ballyhooed like all the others, of what is becoming a sort of oral American version of an actual "Comedie Humaine."[40]

Even as the *Amos 'n' Andy* craze swept the country during the winter of 1929–30, the program never wavered in its focus on the common experiences of common people. Following their relocation from Chicago to New York, Amos and Andy settled into a rooming house on East 134th Street in Harlem, between Park and Madison Avenues, and opened an office for the Fresh Air Taxicab Company on West 135th Street, just around the corner from Lenox Avenue.[41] While Andy dreamed up grandiose plans for cornering the taxicab market in the East, Amos was torn between feeling happy that the move brought him closer to Ruby Taylor, who was attending a private boarding school in that city, and feeling overwhelmed by the sheer enormity of the city and the challenge of earning a living in his unfamiliar new surroundings.

>   Andy---Amos, whut is de matteh wid you?
>   Amos---I'se just gittin' homesick, Andy. I'se gittin' un-couraged.

Andy---Dere you is. Standin' heah in New York City right on Broadway wid thousan's o' people goin' by heah ev'vy five minutes --- talkin' 'bout you gittin' homesick. Look at de people 'round heah. Mo' people dan you eveh seed befo' in all yo' life --- you talkin' 'bout gittin' homesick.

Amos---(sadly) It's mo' people all right but whut diff'ence do dat make to me? I don't know none of 'em. I'd be better off to have two -- three good friends in some itty bitty town dan I would wid all dese people 'round me dat I don't know. Look at 'em. Dey's rushin' up dis way -- an' dey's rushin' down dat way.

Andy---Dey is in a hurry -- dat's why dey rushin'.

Amos---Well Andy, I tell yo' one thing --- de way I feel tonight, I'se down in de dumps, yo' know it?

Andy---Now listen Amos --- wait two -- three days till we kin git dis taxicab comp'ny goin' heah an' we'll make a lot o' money an' we'll run all de rest o' dese taxicabs out o' business. You kin drive de taxicab an' I'll stay in de office ----- when we git one --- an' figgeh up how you kin make a lot o' money [Episode 442, 8/23/29].

The romance of Ruby Taylor and Amos Jones was the linchpin of the series during most of its first decade—even though seven years went by before Ruby ever spoke a word on the air. This simple love story brought out the best in Correll and Gosden's characters—Amos fought back his natural shyness to stammer out his feelings, while Andy muttered sarcastic asides (which by their very tone revealed his own loneliness).

Amos---You don't see her, do yo'?

Andy---Amos, yo' can't miss her. De minute she git out dat do', you goin' see her.

Amos---I'se so happy dat I feel bad. I just can't believe she's comin'. Just seem like to me it's too good to be true, yo' know it?

Andy---I ain't neveh heerd nobody raise so much Cain oveh somebody comin' to town.

Amos---I certn'y do hope she's on dat train. I wonder if I'se waitin' at de right place.

Andy---DERE SHE COME!

Amos---Where?

Andy---Right dere --- see her comin' down dere?

Amos---RUBY! OH Ruby! (fading out)

Andy---(to himself) Dere he go --- he gone crazy ---- look at him ---- kissin' each otheh --- Love -- I'se regusted [Episode 495, 10/24/29].

Probably no writers in all of radio were more skilled at expressing basic human emotion in their scripts—as epitomized by Ruby's near-fatal bout with pneumonia in the spring of 1931. Correll and Gosden had viewed Charles Chaplin's then-current film *City Lights* several times during early 1931 and were impressed with its effective use of pathos. Two years earlier, a supporting character in *The Gumps*, the innocent young woman Mary Gold, had died a lingering and tragic death, which inspired nationwide mourning among the strip's millions of readers. These influences are clearly evident in the story of Ruby's illness, which began as a barely noticed reference to Ruby coming down with an April cold and which gradually brought her to the brink of death.

> Amos---Did yo' say I kin see her?
>
> Doctor (CJC)---Yes, we'll take you in there right now. The only thing I want you to do is to be quiet and don't stay but a minute. The girl is very sick and we want her to see you.
>
> Amos---Alright doctor --- take me in dere den, will yo' please?
>
> Andy---We'll wait out heah in de hall.
>
> King---Well, dat's a tough job fo' Amos.
>
> Andy---I cert'ny do hope ev'ything come out all right. De crisis is bad, ain't it?
>
> King---I glad he got down heah 'cause it might help Ruby if she see him.
>
> Andy---Dere's two people dat love each otheh. I ain't neveh seed nobody in love like dey is, an' it's real love too.
>
> King---Ev'ybody dat knows 'em knows dat dey really love each other alright.
>
> Andy---'Course some time Amos gits down in de dumps an' wonder if she love him or not, but in de back of his head he know dat she do.
>
> King---If anything would happen to Ruby, dat would break de boy's heart alright. Yo' know, I like dat kid, Andy.
>
> Andy---Ain't but one like him in de world --- dat's him.
>
> King---De doctor told him not to stay in dere but a minute, but dat's goin' be a tough minute on him I guess.
>
> Andy---I thing de gal is worse off den dey is sayin'.
>
> King---Wait a minute, heah he come.
>
> (pause)
>
> Andy---Come on now Amos --- don't do dat.
>
> King---We is wid yo' Amos. Stop cryin' now.
>
> Andy---Come on --- walk down heah.
>
> King---Did yo' see her?
>
> Amos---She opened her eyes an' looked up at me, an' said "Sweetheart whutever happens I want you to know dat I'll always love you," an' den she closed her eyes an' I couldn't see her breath (sobs) [Episode 971, 5/4/31].

The hospital sequence revealed Correll and Gosden's mastery of radio technique, not just in the sense of acting but in the sense of presentation. Normally the episode-ending fade-out would be followed by Bill Hay's closing commercial for Pepsodent—but on the evening of May 4, 1931, Amos's sobs faded to a long silence. No commercial followed. Instead, Joseph Gallicchio and his Orchestra played a slow, mournful rendition of "The Perfect Song," to fill out the broadcast period. This striking departure from established format underlined the powerful impression of Amos's grief, and the deliberate ambiguity of the ending—with no concluding words of reassurance from Hay—left listeners to draw their own conclusions. *New York Times* radio columnist Orrin E. Dunlap, Jr., described the aftermath of the broadcast.

> And when Amos 'n' Andy signed off last Monday night many listeners believed that Ruby had passed through the golden gates of the great beyond. It was a sad evening for the invisible audience. Many admitted tears. Children in the streets called that "Ruby Taylor is dead." It was a great piece of radio acting that revealed how an emotional appeal can be stirred up in an unseen audience. It showed the vast possibilities in radio drama, and proved that Amos Jones and Andrew Brown are real actors."[42]

The following night it was revealed that, with her father at her bedside and Amos waiting anxiously in the hospital corridor, Ruby survived the crisis—and millions of listeners settled back in relief. Andy, meanwhile, struggled in his romantic life; his blustering pretentiousness led him into constant trouble. His 1928 entanglement with Lulu Parker, an ambitious Chicago divorcée, led to a breach-of-promise suit[43]—and when Amos and Andy moved East, the stage was set for that scenario to repeat itself with the advent of the formidable Madam Queen, whose beauty shop stood just across West 135th Street from the taxicab office.

> Andy---Look 'cross de street dere. No, no, down a little ways dere. Right dere --- see where it says "Beauty Shop?"
>
> Amos---Whut's dat otheh name under dere on de glass?
>
> Andy---De name is Madam Queen --- see dere?
>
> Amos---Well, whut about it?
>
> Andy---Well, dis mornin' while you was out wid de taxicab, I was standin' out in front heah lookin' oveh de sichiation an' while I was standin' heah Madam Queen, dat runs dat beauty shop, walked out in front of her place, an' boy I wanna tell yo' right now --- dere is de best lookin' gal you done eveh seed in yo' life.
>
> Amos---You is always jumpin' on me 'bout having gals an' heah you is talkin' 'bout some Madam Queen dat runs de beauty shop.
>
> Andy---Dere's a gal I gotta meet.
>
> Amos---You ain't thinkin' 'bout fallin' in love wid nobody, is yo'?
>
> Andy---You know I ain't goin' fall in love wid nobody. But I wanna tell yo' one thing --- boy, dere is a gal [Episode 449, 8/31/29].

5. A Coast-to-Coast Hookup

```
Mon. May 4, 1931.              "AMOS AND ANDY"
                                      by
                               Correll & Gosden.

                     No. 971.     BILL HAY:--Please read this
                     Page one.    sofe and seriously. Make it
                                  real.   Chas. & Freeman.
During the past twenty four hours Ruby Taylor's condition has become much
worse. Her doctor has called in two other physicians for consultation and
everything possible is being done. xxxxxxxxxxxxxxxxxxx She is running
a very high fever and occasionally during the past two hours she would
open her eyes and ask for Amos. No one except her father is allowed in
her room. The doctors informed her father that the crisis is at hand and
in response to her plea to see Amos her father has sent for him. As the
scene opens we find Andy and the Kingfish in the reception room on the
first floor of the hospital waiting for Amos to arrive xxxxxxxxxxxxxx
at the hospital. Here they are:--

KINGFISH STARTS.
King---Well Andy, how did you find out dat Ruby was so sick?

Andy---Well, I was sittin' in de taxicab office an' Mr. Taylor called up,
       wanted to git ahold o' Amos an' told him to have him call him heah
       at de hospital, but I couldn't git ahold o' Amos 'cause he was out
       wid de taxicab, yo' see, an' Mr.Taylor called back an' told me dat
       Ruby was worse off.

King---Well, where did yo' find Amos?

Andy---Well, I COULDN'T find him, so I had brotheh Crawford an' Lightnin'
       both togo out on de street an' look fo' him an' I just talked to 'em
       on de telephone----dey say dey found him an' he's on his way oveh
       heah.

King----Well, he ought to be heah any minute.

Andy---She's sick alright.

King---Whut did her papa tell you 'bout Ruby callin' fo' Amos?

Andy---Her papa say dat ev'vy time she wake up, open her eyes, she call
       fo' Amos, an' de doctor say it might be a good thing to git him
       oveh heah.

King---Well, I hope ev'ything come out alright.

Andy---Her papa say dat de crisis is heah.

King---You know whut dat is, dont yo'?

Andy---Yeh, he 'splained it to yo'----I wish Amos would hurry up an' git
       heah.

King---I tell yo' whut I better do-----I better call up my wife an' tell
       her. She think a lot o' Ruby.

Andy---De only thing is, since she been gittin' worse in de las' 24 hours,
       dey wont let nobody see her 'cept her pappa.

King---I better call de old lady anyway an' let her know whut's goin' on.
```

The May 4, 1931, episode of *Amos 'n' Andy* touched a nation—and nearly cost Amos the love of his life. Note the careful instructions to announcer Bill Hay at the head of the script.

The Madam and Andy carried on a whirlwind romance through most of 1930—until New Year's Eve, when Andy tried to back out of his ill-advised marriage proposal.

Amos---...Whut in de world did you say to Madam Queen?

Andy---Well --- somebody says it's a minute to 12 --- I stahted thinkin'. 'Fore I knowed it I heerd some bells ringin' --- ev'ybody was hollerin' "Goodbye 1930, Hello 1931 --- Happy New Year," so I whispered in Madam Queen's ear, I say "Sweetheart, come oveh heah in de corneh, I wanna tell yo' sumpin'."

Amos---Of all de tricks you done ever pulled, dat was de worst one.

Andy---Den I say to her --- I fo'git zactly whut I DID say, I was kind-a nervous, but I remembeh sayin' sumpin' like "Honey I don't see how we goin' git married tomorrow." She say "Whut yo' mean?" I say "Honey we goin' have to put off de weddin' 'cause mama told me neveh to git married on a odd year like 1931," an' I looked at her an' her eyes was gittin' as big as saucehs. She ast me again if I was foolin' an' I said "Honey to tell you de truth, I just can't git married tomorrow." Den I wished her a happy New Yeah.

Amos---I looked over in de corner an' saw yo' talkin'.

Andy---Den she kind-a backed up lookin' at me, an' while she was lookin' at me I heard her call fo' her sisteh. Dat's when I left.

Amos---Well, whut did yo' run away fo'?

Andy---Well, I wasn't goin' git in no argument wid both of 'em, 'cause if both of 'em jump on me, it was goin' be too bad.

Amos---If you could just see yo'self right now sittin' dere wid dat paper hat on yo' head an' dat red ribbon 'round yo' neck ----

Andy---I didn't even know I had de hat on. I left my otheh hat oveh dere.

Amos---Well Andy, I don't know whut's goin' happen to yo' son.

Andy---Oh, sumpin's goin' happen --- I kin feel dat in de air.

Amos---You know she fainted --- I told yo' dat. After she had dat catnip fit she just fainted right away. We put acrobatic spirits of pneumonia under her nose --- dat didn't he'p none so we got a doctor.

Andy---Ain't nuthin' else happened oveh dere, is it?

Amos---When she come to she was callin' "Andy -- Ducky Wucky --- Andy."

Andy---Dat was de wrong time to tell her alright -- I ought to told her last week.

Amos---De Kingfish's wife is mad wid yo' too. She said yo' ruined de party.

Andy---Well, ev'ybody didn't have to git mad wid me. Dey could-a stayed dere an' had a good time.

Amos---How was dey goin' have a good time wid Madam Queen screamin' 'round dere an' ev'ything after you told her dat?

5. A Coast-to-Coast Hookup

Andy---Well Amos, I was wrong. I done spent a lot o' New Year's eves in my life but I ain't neveh had one like dis one.

Amos---You cert'ny did spoil it fo' ev'ybody.

Andy---Wait a minute --- who's dat comin' down de hall?

Amos---I don't know -- I hear somebody comin'.

Andy --- Listen, dat might be Madam Queen. (fades) I goin' git undeh de bed. Tell 'em I ain't heah.

Knock at door.

Amos---Come in. Well, hello brother Crawford.

John---Hello Amos. I could not help but come over to see Andy, but I see he's not here --- an' it's just as well.

Amos---Whut's de matter?

John---Well, I wanted to tell the brainless wonder what I thought of him.

Amos---Well, I guess Andy's a little worried right now, so you kin see him tomorrow.

John---I wanna sit down on the side of the bed though Amos, and tell you a few things about that numbskull.

Amos---Is Madam Queen alright now?

John---She's sick in bed an' we've had to call the doctor, and my wife is gone crazy. She acts like she blames me for it, and it wouldn't surprise me if I would have to spend the night here with you. I don't know I'll be able to sleep at home.

Amos---Well, you better go home though once more an' see if ev'ything's alright 'fore you stay here 'cause dey might wanna see yo'.

John---Well, I could phone home and just stay right here. There's a phone out in the hall, isn't it?

Amos---Dere's a phone in the hall, but the landlord don't like yo' to use it after 12 o'clock at night, so you better go on over dere.

John---Well, Amos, I wanna say one thing to you before I go about Andy. I've often said to my wife that I didn't think Andy had a lot of sense. Now I KNOW he doesn't have any sense. He is without a doubt, the biggest blockhead I've ever seen, an' he showed it tonight.

Amos---Well, I guess he was a little nervous.

John---He has spoiled everything for everybody else, and the last thing that Madam Queen said before I left the house was that she would get him for this.

Amos---Well, I guess ev'ything'll work out alright.

John---Well, it wouldn't work out alright if Andy's got anything to do with it. He's made my wife very unhappy, and when I see him I intend to tell him a mouth-full.

Amos---Why don't you git on over to de house and see if ev'ything's alright, Den come back.

John---I might as well take my clothes off right now and go to bed.

Amos---You better go over dere an' see once more though.

John---Well, I'll take your advice and do so. I'll be back in 15 minutes, 'cause I wanna see Andy when he comes in anyway.

Amos---Alright.

John---And you tell that blockhead when he comes in that I'm coming back to tell him that he can't treat my sister-in-law that way. I'll be back in a little while. Amos. (fading) Happy New Year.

Amos---Same to you. I'll be waitin' heah fo' yo'. (pause) Come on out, he's gone.

Andy---(fading in) Well, dere's a pal fo' yo'. Dat just goes to show yo'.

Amos---An' de funny part of it is dat he's right. A fine start you got on 1931 [Episode 865, 12/31/30].

The story line carried on for 13 weeks from that auspicious beginning.[44] All through January and February of the new year, Correll and Gosden slowly unfolded the story of Andy's legal dilemma, and in doing so demonstrated that they understood the need for careful balance between humor and drama, between suspense and comic relief, between buildup and climax. Over the course of the breach-of-promise story line, every comic indignity suffered by Andy was balanced by the realization that with each setback he was being pushed deeper and deeper into serious trouble. The humorous aspects of the story line—Andy's experiences with the hopelessly inept private investigator Brother Snoop, or his unfortunate encounter with Mrs. Crawford's umbrella—only added to the sense of events careening out of control and actually served to heighten the suspense as the plot developed. "Breach of Promise" unfolded in real time, with each passing day adding to the crisis facing Andy, and new crises piled inexorably onto the old.

Further contributing to the sense of realism in the story line was Correll and Gosden's attention to detail, particularly in their depiction of Madam Queen's legal action, which began with a letter from a lawyer, followed by a registered letter from that lawyer, and finally by a summons. Gosden and Correll were advised throughout the writing of the breach-of-promise story line by NBC's general counsel, attorney A.L. Ashby, who provided them with a detailed summary of how breach-of-promise litigation was handled under New York State law, along with specific instructions on trial procedure. As a result, the courtroom scenes during the trial sequence were compellingly realistic, amplifying the tightly developed drama that dominated the climactic two weeks of the story line—a tension that built steadily until one night in March, when Correll and Gosden snapped the story to a sudden climax.

5. A Coast-to-Coast Hookup

Collins (CJC)--You honor, I would like to ask the court again please for permission to place Amos Jones on the witness stand.

Judge (FFG)--This request has been refused, and is now being refused again. Please be quiet in this court room back there.

Bailiff (CJC)--You folks in the rear sit down.

Judge (FFG)--Go ahead Mr. Smith.

Smith (FFG)--Gentlemen, I have presented to you one of the most complete cases, and one of the most one-sided cases ever recorded in any court in the United States. (aside to Judge) Your honor, would you ask Attorney Collins and Amos Jones to extend me the courtesy of being quiet during my talk to the jury?

Judge (FFG)--Mr. Collins, if you have to talk to your witness, take him out in the other room --- we must have it quiet in here.

Collins (CJC)--Your honor, I realize that it is not in order to put a witness on the witness stand after the case is practically closed. You and the jury are here listening to this case to ascertain one thing, the truth --- and if you do not permit me to put Amos Jones on the witness stand for a short time to tell a vital fact, you will have been wasting the time of THIS court and will only cause us to take an appeal, therefore wasting the time of another trial.

Judge (FFG)--Your witness has been on the stand, hasn't he?

Collins (CJC)--Yes, your honor, he has --- but since that time, he has been working to help you, and those 12 men know the truth, and I beg of you to let him take the stand and tell what he knows.

Judge (FFG)--Put him on the stand and get it over with as quickly as possible.

Bailiff (CJC)--Do you swear that the testimony that you are about to give in this case is the truth, the whole truth, and nothing but the truth, so help you God?

Amos---Yessah.

Collins (CJC)--I will not examine you. I will just ask you to tell and prove what you know.

Amos---Well, de other day when Madam Queen fainted, I got respicious, an' I tried to find out why she fainted. I found out dat she fainted 'cause she saw sumpin'. She saw a woman and yesterday a woman fainted right out dere sittin' right about dere. Dis woman fainted 'cause she saw Madam Queen. I followed dis woman in de other room, I followed her home, and I got de whole story. Dis woman wanted to see Madam Queen lose dis case 'cause she hated Madam Queen, an' de reason she hated Madam Queen is because Madam Queen made dis woman's husband divorce her an' den Madam Queen married dis woman's husband --- and dis woman is mad wid Madam Queen because she took her husband away from her. I is done found dis man dat married Madam Queen. He is her second husband. Madam Queen is been married three times, an' I got dis man, her second husband, out in de other room wid a policeman, an' he'll tell yo' right now, if you'll git him in heah, dat him an' Madam Queen ain't never been divorced. An' if whut I'm tellin' yo' ain't de truth, why is Madam Queen fainted again? Look at her. She's cold.

Judge (FFG)--Quiet in this court room please. People, sit down.

Bailiff (CJC)--Everybody back in your seats. Quiet in the court room [Episode 924, 3/10/31].

In restaurants and movie theaters, in exclusive clubrooms and in front of street-corner loudspeakers, and in millions of American homes, the sudden and shocking outcome of the Madam Queen Affair marked the high point of the *Amos 'n' Andy* craze. But the adventures of Amos and Andy and their friends were only beginning.

6. MEET THE CAST

"To think that two people like them could have so many different voices..."
—Bill Hay

"WE TRIED TO MAKE OUR characters a cross-section of life," remarked Charles Correll—and so it was that as the program developed a rich supporting cast surrounded Amos and Andy: a gallery of recognizable human types that in the words of entertainment historian Richard Barrios, "offered support worthy of Restoration comedy."[1]

Early on, Correll and Gosden recognized that their lead characters required a strong foil, a memorable adversarial presence, and a character capable of acting as an external catalyst for new plotlines. During the run of *Sam 'n' Henry*, this role was filled by the Most Precious Diamond—Sam and Henry's manipulative sometimes-friend who headed the Jewels of the Crown lodge, and when *Amos 'n' Andy* began in 1928, the performers soon recognized the need for a similar character in the new series.

So it was that George "Kingfish" Stevens, the head of the Mystic Knights of the Sea, entered Amos and Andy's world in May of 1928. Portrayed by Gosden in the same rumbling bass voice that had been used for the Diamond, the new character was conceived as the very embodiment of every small-time neighborhood hustler, every scheming promoter that Correll and Gosden had ever met, cloaking his "deals" behind a mask of hearty fraternal affection—and the Kingfish embraced this role from his very first appearance.

> King--Well brothers, I brought two application blanks wid me an' if you brothers would like to come into de Mystic Knights of the Sea, just sign dese two application blanks an' gimme two dollars a piece down an' you kin pay de balance when you comes in fo' 'nitiation.
>
> Andy---Dat cost two dollahs down huh?
>
> King--Now heah is de two application blanks. Yo' landlord is a sardine an'

> he told me dat you two boys was alright so if you gimme two dollars a piece you will be a couple of fish.
>
> Andy---Say dat last thing again?
>
> Amos---Yeh, whut was dat las' thing again about de fish?
>
> King--I say -- fo' two dollars down, we will welcome you into de Mystic Knights of de Sea. I know --- speakin' fo' de brothers, de Mackerel, de Whale, an' de Catfish, I know dat dey will welcome you into our great fraternity where you shall meet wid de greatest bunch o' fellows in de world. You will den be able to meet all of de brothers an' join us in our great work -- to make de world safer an' to help us go forward wid a spirit of good fellowship [Episode 52, 5/25/28].

As had the Diamond before him, the Kingfish sought refuge from his difficult home life and troubled marriage in the sanctuary of the lodge hall, constantly proclaiming his interest in the welfare of the members of "that great fraternity," even as he kept a close eye on its treasury. And while Amos soon learned to be wary of his propositions, through his constant finagling the Kingfish quickly developed a thorough understanding of the weaknesses of his favorite target: Andrew H. Brown.

> King---Brother Andy, today I is makin' a personal tour to see all de brothers an' I is collectin' de 50 cents dat all de brothers is gonna put in to gimme de testimony dinner an' send me an' my wife to de World's Series, an' knowin' dat you is one o' my close personal friends, I knowed dat you would give de 50 cents widout arguin'.
>
> Andy---Oh yeh, how is dey kickin' in wid de 50 centses?
>
> King---Well, de returns is better dan we thought dey WAS goin' be, an' I know dat you an' Amos wanna do yo' share.
>
> Andy---Oh sho', we wants to he'p if ev'ybody else is goin' do it --- we don't wanna be a couple o' pikehs.
>
> King---Well, now, if yo' could lemme have yo' 50 and 50 fo' Amos, dat would save me a lot o' time cause yo' know de World Series opens tomorrow.
>
> Andy---Yeh, dat's right, it DO open tomorrow.
>
> King---I'se workin' as fast as I kin today an' I thought if you'd gimme a dollar I'd check you an' Amos in --- den you'll know dat you is done yo' share, an' you ain't no piker.
>
> Andy---Yeh --- I think I got a dollah heah. Dere's a two-dollar bill --- lookit dere. Is you got a dollar?
>
> King---I don't know if I is or not. You don't wanna double up on yo' money an' gimme two dollars instead o' one, do yo', by no chance?
>
> Andy---Well-a --- you is just goin' to de World's Series in New York, ain't yo'? You ain't goin' to Chicago too?
>
> King---No, but on de other hand, some o' de brothers is givin' a little more dan we is astin'. An', by de way, Pop Johnson give two dollars personal.

6. Meet the Cast

Andy---Well, you betteh not count on doublin' up on no money from me cause I ain't holdin' much right now, an' I'se goin' need dat otheh dollah.

King---Would yo' lend me de other dollar?

Andy---I would, but I can't.

King---Well, I don't wanna press yo'.

Andy---Well, heah's de two, gimme one.

King---Dere you is brother Andy. An' I want you to know dat dis money dat you dear brothers is givin' me, is puttin' new life in de Kingfish of de lodge --- it is makin' me work harder --- it is makin' me love my brothers even more dan I DID love 'em [Episode 1410, 9/27/32].

The Kingfish earned his living from the lodge and from a career as an "outside man" for various Harlem businesses—bringing in customers in exchange for a percentage. And he was a born promoter, always looking for that one big angle that would allow him to hit it big, and always willing to risk other people's money to make it happen.

King---Whut is ev'vy woman talkin' 'bout today? Whut is ev'vy man talkin' 'bout today?

Andy---De repression?

Amos---Whut is dey talkin' 'bout Kingfish?

King---Dey is talkin' 'bout reducin'.

Andy---Salaries?

King---No, no, I mean dey is talkin' 'bout losin' weight. De minute dat a gal bends her arm an' de muscles stick up, she say to herself, "I is gotta take off dat weight."

Andy---I believe you is right.

Amos---Yeh, ev'ybody's talkin' 'bout it. Ruby says she gotta lose weight, Aunt Lillian says she gotta lose weight.

King---My wife wants to lose weight, brother Crawford's wife wants to lose weight.

Andy---Well, whut kin I do 'bout it?

Amos---Yeh, whut is de deal yo' talkin' 'bout Kingfish?

King---Andy, me an' you an' Amos kin open up whut is knowed as de "Amalgamated Reducin' System," guaranteed to make 'em lose two pounds a week.

Andy---Who guarantees dat, me or you?

King---It's simple.

Amos---How yo' do it?

King---Yo' do two things. Yo' put 'em on a diet, an' we keep feedin' 'em so little dat dey falls off to nuthin' ---- dat's one way. De other way is, we gits dese boxes, an' builds a fire under 'em --- we put dese people in de box an' shut de door, start de fire goin' an' dey just melt off a pound or two while dey is in dere. You know dese boxes dat you kin stick yo' head through de top.

Amos---Oh, I done seed pitchers of 'em.

King---Now heah's de way we work it. If you could git Madam Queen to put in a branch in her beauty shop, she could handle de women folks over dere. We could take de readin' room at de lodge hall an' fix dat up fo' de men folks.

Andy---Dat don't sound too bad, do it Amos?

Amos---No it don't, to tell yo' de truth.

Andy---Whut would we charge, Kingfish?

King---We could figure dat out later on.

Andy---We might do it like de butcheh --- he charges so much a pound fo' meat, we could charge 'em, say 25 cent a pound to knock it off of 'em.

Amos---Yeh, dat might be good.

King---Dat ain't a bad idea --- pay by de pound. Yo' see when you gits 'em in one o' dem hot boxes an' turn de heat on 'em, dey is bound to lose [Episode 1255, 3/30/32].

The Kingfish was a man of many talents, wrapped in the soul of a petty hustler. As a child he had toured with a medicine show—no doubt the source of his glibness—and his way with words also netted him a second career that would for a time be kept a secret from his friends: under the name of Leroy LeRoy, he wrote a slick and sarcastic gossip column for a Harlem newspaper, using connections attained in his lodge work to further his own personal ends.

George Stevens had consciously chosen the hustler's life and was usually willing to accept the consequences of that choice in exchange for the freedom of living by his wits instead of by a time clock—but there were also moments where he sensed the essential insecurity of the course he had selected and wondered where it might one day lead. These moments gave listeners insight into the man behind the Kingfish's mask –and prevented the character from sinking into either the role of a pure villain or that of a simplistic stereotype. Listeners came to understand that, rogue though he could be, the Kingfish also had a human, compassionate side, which could lead him to drop his hustler's persona to commit sudden and surprising acts of kindness.

King---Well boys, I has all kind o' deals now an' den --- I ast yo' yo do a lot o' things dat sometimes yo' do an' sometimes yo' don't --- I don't wanna bother yo' TOO much.

Andy---We still on de suckeh list though, ain't we?

King---Well, heah's de deal boys --- yo' station was robbed of $105 --- de boy

6. Meet the Cast

dat took de money, dis boy Philip --- well, in de first place, Philip ain't no thief an' he ain't no kleptomaniac --- I know de boy's papa --- he lives a few doors from me, 'bout half a block away.

Andy---Yeh, I know he do.

King---Well, dis Prince Ali Bendo got dis boy comin' over dere, start tellin' his fortune, an' all dat stuff, an' he got de boy believin' ev'ything he say. Now in de next place, he told de boy a lot o' stuff he ought to do, an' he got dis boy to take de money.

Amos---Yeh, dat's right, 'cause de POlice told me dat --- de boy was never 'rested before in his life.

King---Well, dey is holdin' de boy down at de jail.

Andy---Yeh, dey got de boy an' de Prince too.

King---Well, I is knowed de boy's papa fo' a long time, an' I been over to see him—see if I could help him, an' heah's whut I wanna ast yo'.

Andy---Yeh, go ahead.

King---De way I git it, you was robbed of $105 --- you didn't know it but you lost $105.^{25}, 'cause dat's whut de boy took, 'cause de Prince told him to be sho' an' take ev'vy cent dat was dere. Now, de POlice give yo' back $75 --- dat means dat you lost $30.^{25}

Amos---Yeh, dat's right --- I didn't know 'bout de 25 cents though.

King---I got in my pocket heah --- heah 'tis right heah --- I got $30.^{25} --- de boy's papa gimme dis to give to yo'.

Andy—-Sho' 'nuf?

King---Now, de boy's papa is a honest man -- he's goin' pay back ev'ybody dat de boy took de money from, an' I told him dis ---- I told him dat I would go around an' talk to ev'ybody an' ast 'em not to press no charges 'gainst de boy, an' let's see if we can't git him out o' trouble, 'cause he's a good boy, an' if he ever git out o' dis, he done learned his lesson an' he ain't goin' git in no more jams.

Amos---Cert'ny I'll do it --- I don't wanna see de boy git in no trouble.

King---Well heah Amos --- you take dis $30.^{25} ----- dat means you ain't lost nuthin'. Now de boy's papa is payin' off de others, an' I think I kin git ev'ybody to be easy wid de boy an' see if we can't git him out of it. Den I figger dat if he ain't got no more respect fo' his papa dan to stay out o' trouble, den de next time he git in trouble he kin go to jail fo' life if he wanna --- but I KNOW dat when he git out dis time, he goin' stay.

Amos---Well Kingfish, dat's good o' YOU to do dis.

Andy---Dat's de best deal you eveh had, or eveh done.

King---Well, I feel sorry fo' de old man --- de boy too [Episode 2525, 2/19/37].

After Amos, Andy, and the Kingfish relocated to Harlem with the start of the Pepsodent-sponsored NBC series, Correll and Gosden found themselves faced with

During the summer of 1931, Pepsodent offered *Amos 'n' Andy* listeners these stand-up cardboard figures as a mail-in premium. The figures were also distributed by dentists to children participating in a school-sponsored dental check-up program.

the task of creating a new supporting cast from scratch. The helpful, earnest teenager Sylvester remained behind in Chicago, but his role in the series, as a confidant for Amos and a counterpoint to Andy, would eventually be taken over by a very different sort of character, the querulous John Augustus Crawford, known to one and all as "Brother" Crawford.

Introduced into the series as Madam Queen's upstate brother-in-law, and portrayed by Gosden in a high, unctuous, rather spasmodic voice, Brother Crawford moved to Harlem with his wife and two children in the fall of 1930, on the promise of a job with the Fresh Air Taxicab Company from Andy. Disgusted when this job failed to materialize, Brother Crawford developed an immediate and lasting dislike for his would-be brother-in-law, but found a kindred spirit in Amos, who shared his views on the importance of hard, honest work as the key to success. In November 1930, Amos, Andy, and Brother Crawford went into business together in the operation of the Big 3 Lunch Room on 136th Street, an enterprise that operated successfully for the next year and a half and that further defined the often-contentious relationship of the three characters.

> John---Well, I want to tell you that I'm having domestic trouble --- my wife told me today that she is not going to stand for certain things, an' it's not only Andy but it's you too Amos. I'm putting 100 percent of my time in de lunch room an' only getting 33⅓ percent of de money. Dose are de figgers.
>
> Amos---While I think of it, I might as well tell YOU sumpin' too brother

6. Meet the Cast

The backs of the figures feature tips on dental health. The constant repetition of the slogan "Use Pepsodent Toothpaste twice a day—see your dentist at least twice a year" by *Amos 'n' Andy* announcer Bill Hay is credited with creating the American habit of twice-yearly dental examinations.

> Crawford. Dat you waste more time runnin' over to yo' house to find out if yo' wife is happy ev'vy 5 minutes dan me an' Andy runnin' de taxicab comp'ny.
>
> Andy---Yeh, how 'bout dat?
>
> John---Well, I have to go home when my wife calls.
>
> Amos---Another thing, you took home 2 pork chops an' half a pound o' butter.
>
> John---I want you to know that I put tickets in de drawer fo' de pork chops an' de butter.
>
> Amos---I know you did, but I just wanna tell yo' dat we is runnin' a lunch room, not a grocery store.
>
> Andy---Yeh, dat's right.
>
> John---Well, if it reaches the point that I can't take a little butter an' a little meat home, an' charge it, den I must say dat dere is something wrong.
>
> Amos---De only thing wrong is, dat we got de wrong kind o' store fo' yo'. We ought to be runnin' a grocery store [Episode 887, 1/26/31].

Brother Crawford was a dedicated family man—but unlike the prosperous, well-adjusted Taylor family, the Crawfords were a picture of storm and strife. Mrs. Crawford was plagued by constant and sometimes violent mood swings, and she frequently took out her rages on her husband, who nonetheless remained devoted to the marriage for the sake of his two children. But the stresses of his life left him in a constant state of emotional agitation, which he tried valiantly to repress.

> Van----Well, my good friend Mr. Crawford.
>
> Andy---Sit down, whut's on yo' mind?
>
> John---I just spent 30 minutes on the battlefield with my wife. Mr. Van Porter, you have started something that I dislike very much and my wife is very unhappy.
>
> Van----Why, what is the trouble?
>
> John---Ever since you talked to my wife I haven't had one minute's peace an' now she's just told me dat unless I move to the bungalow with the roses and the fence and the beautiful yard, she is going to leave me and move there herself.
>
> Van----Well, I KNOW dat yo' wife was very much interested in the charming subdivision I showed her pitchers of.
>
> John---You told her something about the nice fresh air and up to that time everybody in my family had been very healthy but now my children are getting very pale and my wife feels a breakdown coming on [Episode 965, 4/27/31].

Henry Van Porter, the swaggering, backslapping real estate and insurance salesman, offered another sort of counterpoint to Correll and Gosden's lead characters. An oily social climber, Van Porter was portrayed by Correll in a loud, hail-fellow-well-met voice and filled an ambiguous role in the series. Occasionally, he could work as Amos and Andy's ally, and occasionally he might align himself with the Kingfish. But more often than not, Van Porter was out only for Van Porter—and Amos and Andy learned to step warily in his presence.

> Van----Now Amos, you is comin' to me out of a clear sky an' tellin' me dat you have a fire --- I walk in heah an' find de store partly burned -- dis all comes very quickly.
>
> Amos---I 'member you tellin' me dat dis insurance comp'ny pays dey're claims quick.
>
> Van----But dose are JUST claims.
>
> Amos---Well, dis heah's a just one too. ---- ain't you got some man dat you kin send 'round an' check up on de thing heah --- one o' dem insurance rejusters?
>
> Van----Yes Amos, but I don't wanna worry my company until I am sho' dat you have a claim.

Amos---Yessah --- well, I got a claim Mr. Van Porter, cause on de REceipt dat you gimme fo' $7.50, it says fo' fire insurance.

Van----You better mail dat receipt to my office.

Amos---I'll show it to yo', but I ain't goin' let it git out o' my hands [Episode 2209, 12/3/35].

Self-interest of another sort motivated another key character, introduced into the series in early 1933. Portrayed by Gosden with a grating, adenoidal voice, Frederick Montgomery Gwindell was career-driven—an arrogant self-declared efficiency expert, business consultant and advocate of "Technocracy" who sought to enforce his will on anyone who happened to fall into his path. His dalliance with Madam Queen led to a disrupted wedding, a lawsuit for alienation of affection, and most of all an enmity with Andy that persisted for years. And as a result of that conflict, Gwindell never missed an opportunity to make Andy squirm.

Andy---Mr. Gwindell-a --- whut I wanna recuss wid yo'is-a -- sal'ry an' my POsition heah at de grocery sto' --- now-a ----

Gwin---Well now, I kin tell yo' dat right quick an' save you a lot o' time.

Andy---Yeah.

Gwin---First o' all, yo' salary is as high as I kin make it cause in de first place we can't 'ford to pay no more dan $3 a week, an' dat's whut we'se payin' -- an' to tell yo' de truth Andy, you ain't worth DAT much ---- now 'bout yo' position wid de grocery store --- I know dat you think dat you ain't satisfied wid whut yo' doin' -- … --- to tell yo' de truth, neither is I --- now, you don't know whether you goin' quit, but I goin' tell you one thing, if you don't perk up an' git better dan you is, I goin' fire you 'round de first o' de month, so dat tells yo' 'bout 'yo sal'ry, an' yo' POsition at de grocery store --- now, whut else is on yo' mind? [Episode 2268, 2/24/36].

Gwindell eventually mellowed, taking on a long-term job with a Harlem newspaper. His abrasiveness faded with the years, but he and Andy always remained a bit wary of each other—and he never fully came to terms with another resident of the neighborhood, a sleepy-looking youth from Alabama named Willie Jefferson, whose drawling speech and slow-motion personality earned him the ironic nickname of "Lightning."

Undoubtedly the most troubling of Correll and Gosden's characters for modern critics, Lightning is on the surface a mere reiteration of the "dumb coon" stereotype of minstrelsy—a slow-moving, slow-talking comedy-relief figure, inspired likely by the success of film comedian Stepin Fetchit in the 1929 film *Hearts in Dixie*, and portrayed by Gosden in a high, slow Fetchit-esque drawl. But as is usually the case with Correll and Gosden's work, there is much more to the character than is visible at first glance.

While Lightning may seem at first to be a mere "slow, lazy, and shiftless" minstrel caricature, a closer look at the character as established during the serial era reveals a more textured personality. Seen from this perspective, Lightning becomes less a "lazy" character than one who puts out his best effort only for those he feels deserve it. Amos treats him with respect and dignity—and when working for Amos, Lightning repays that respect by giving his best effort in return. But Andy, in his abrasive, blustering way, treats Lightning as a dull-witted lackey --- and Lightning gives back exactly what he figures Andy deserves, his studied ineptitude taking on an undertone of passive resistance to Andy's pompous, authoritarian behavior.

> Andy---Well anyway, Lightnin', when yo' git in de sto', you is gotta show de people how de stuff works.
>
> Light--Yessah, I knows dat.
>
> Andy---Now, de fust gal dat walks in de sto', you walk up to her an' say, "Rescuse me, but I wanna show yo' sumpin' heah dat will make yo' good lookin'."
>
> Light--Ev'ybody dat I walk up to thinks I'm tryin' to flirt wid 'em.
>
> Andy---You say de stuff eat de paint off de woodwork?
>
> Light--Yessah, I ain't foolin'.
>
> Andy---Well listen Lightnin', befo' you kin sell de thing, you is gotta believe.
>
> Light--I gotta whut?
>
> Andy---You gotta BELIEVE in it.
>
> Light--I believe alright. I believe it would make a better shoe polish dan a face cream [Episode 480, 10/6/29].

The Lightning-Andy dance proved one of Correll and Gosden's most durable character bits, and as the series evolved, Lightning took a straight-faced delight in subjecting Andy to a variety of mental games—amusing himself by poking subtle holes in Andy's pretended omniscience, all the while keeping up a façade of wide-eyed ignorance.

> Light--(fading in) Mr. Andy, you ready fo' me?
>
> Andy---Yeh, uh---got yo' apple-cation wid yo'?
>
> Light--Uh, yessah, I done filled it out.
>
> Andy---Yeh, lemme see it.
>
> Light--Yessah, heah it is right dere.
>
> Andy---Sit down---take off yo' hat. Now lemme see heah---(to himself) Name---Lightnin'. Uh---whut is dis otheh stuff heah?
>
> Light--Well, I put down my nickname too. My nickname is Willie Jefferson.
>
> Andy---Wait a minute, wait a minute---Willie Jefferson? Dat's yo' REAL name. Willie Jefferson is yo' real name, Lightnin'. Yo' nickname is Lightnin'.
>
> Light--Uh, nosah.
>
> Andy---Well now don't tell me.

6. Meet the Cast

Light--All right.

Andy---Is I right?

Light--Nosah!

Andy---You goin' git fired fo' yo' start you keep on messin' wid me. Listen heah now --- I is tellin' yo' now dat yo' nickname is Lightnin'. Now dat is a name dat yo' took fo' a nickname. So any name dat yo' take like dat is a nickname.

Light--Yessah, Mr. Andy, yo' is wrong, 'cause people called me Lightnin' all my life an' I didn't have no otheh name --- so I took Willie Jefferson.

Andy---Oh.

Light--Bahhhh! [Episode 3033, 2/1/39].

Women played a vital role in Amos and Andy's world—but for the first seven years of the program's run, no actresses joined Correll and Gosden at the microphone. Correll and Gosden early on solved the problem of how to present female characters without having to attempt the voices themselves—the women were developed not through actual speaking roles but by being spoken about. One-sided telephone conversations and conversations about the female characters between male characters brought the women of *Amos 'n' Andy* to vivid life.

Andy---Well, I was sittin' dere in de beauty shop while de Madam phoned Sadie an' ast her to come oveh. Dat's when my heart started beatin' fast so I say to myself "I gotta git talkin' to Sadie befo' de Madam git her" so I say to de Madam I say-a, "Rescuse me, I is goin' walk down to de drug sto'," thinkin' dat I would meet Sadie out front or sumpin'. De Madam say "Why is you gotta go to de drug sto'?" I say "'Cause I wanna git some headache pills." She say, "Dat's alright honey, I got some right heah," so dat was dat.

Amos---Well, whut did you tell Sadie de reason was fo' you not comin' over dere fo' supper?

Andy---Dat was anotheh mistake I made. I told her I had de headache an' I was goin' home an' go right to bed.

Amos---Den you run into her again huh?

Andy---Well Amos, I say to myself, "I is gotta say sumpin' to Sadie 'fore she talk to de Madam," so I made up my mind I was goin' let her in de beauty shop when she got dere ---- so de do' bell rung an' just as de do' bell rung de Madam was walkin' 'cross de flo' headed fo' de do' anyway, so when I heard de bell tingle de fust ting, I jumped up in front o' Madam Queen, like to knocked her down. She ast me if I was playin' football. Den I 'splained to her dat I didn't want her walkin' all de way to de front do' an' wearin' herself out.

Amos---Dat must-a been sumpin' --- I'd like to been dere. Whut happened den?

Andy---Well, I got de Madam sittin' down, an' den I opened de front do' an'

>   'fore I had a chance to say to Sadie not to say nuthin', she hollehs out "Hello honey, whut is YOU doin' heah?" an' de Madam heard it.
>
> Amos---Hot dog --- dat was a mess dat WAS a mess. De Madam heard her call you honey.
>
> Andy---Madam Queen stood up an' boy she looked as big as a ox ---- I thought she was goin' hit me, but lateh on I revinced her dat Sadie called me "funny" 'stead o' "honey" or sumpin' like dat.
>
> Amos---Well did yo' tell Sadie not to say nuthin' 'bout nuthin'?
>
> Andy---I told Sadie, afteh she say dat to me, I say, "Don't say nuthin' 'bout me an' you," an' dat fathead come in de room an' 'bout 20 minutes lateh she say to me "Whut was dat you said to me as I was comin' in de do' 'bout not sayin' nuthin' 'bout sumpin'?" De Madam opened her eyes as big as saucehs, so I straightened dat out [Episode 808, 10/25/30].

While phone conversations and third-person description created vivid pictures of their female characters, Correll and Gosden often gave their women direct voices as well—not through spoken lines but through letters read aloud by the male characters. This technique allowed female voices to be heard in the series—even when they weren't actually heard—and allowed Correll and Gosden to develop exceptionally well-rounded characterizations for the women. Andy might have emphasized the domineering side of Madam Queen's personality in his descriptions of her activities—but in her letters, the Madam spoke for herself.

> Andy---"Dear Andy ---- I received yo' letteh an' I wanna thank you fo' writin' to me" --- sound like I'se de head man, don't it?
>
> Amos---Well, read de thing --- find out whut de whole letter say.
>
> Andy---Say heah, "It has been many months since I have had a letteh from YOU—an' to tell yo' de truth, I enjoyed readin' it" --
>
> Amos---Well, dat's nice of her.
>
> Andy---Den she say heah "I read yo' letteh oveh twice, an' I have been doin' a lot o' thinkin' ... Dat is de fust serious letteh dat you have eveh writ to me because when we were seein' a lot of each otheh, I did not heah from you except now an' den you would write me a crazy note."
>
> Amos---Well, dat's de truth.
>
> Andy---Den she say heah, "You tell me dat you love me --- why didn't you think of dat befo'? --- why didn't you know dat you loved me when you were goin' wid Señorita Butterfly? --- or have you had a fight wid her?"
>
> Amos---She's tellin' you de truth dere.
>
> Andy---She say heah "Since you have stopped seein' me an' started goin' wid dat Butterfly girl, you have acted very strange --- you don't know about de many nights I have sit heah an' cried because I was so lonesome."
>
> Amos---Boy, she's bearin' down on dat, ain't she?

Andy---Den she say "I stood it as long as I could --- I did nothin' but think of you ---- I thought of de many happy hours we had spent togetheh an' when I stopped to think about you bein' wid another girl, it almost drove me crazy."

Amos---I think she loved you at one time.

Andy---Dis is gittin' me Amos.

Amos---Well, go ahead.

Andy---Den she say heah "Afteh I re'lized dat you were in love wid someone else, I could not stand it any longeh ---- I made a date wid a fellow who had ast me many times because I thought bein' wid him would RElieve my mind. He has been very sweet to me an' very kind, an' now you write to me tellin' me of your great love."

Amos---Uh-huh.

Andy---Den she say "Love is not sumpin' dat you kin throw away when you don't want it, an' pick it up again when you feel like havin' it --- it is not dat way wid me an' I don't see how it could be wid anyone else, but you are just like all men Andy --- you wanna change an' try someone else, but when you find out dat someone else cares about your REAL girl, den you think dat you would like to come back, but it's not so easy. When you hurt the one who loves you it is not easy for her to forget de time you hurt her. So Andy, you are just like all men. When you find somebody else wants your girl, you want her again, but you can't do dat to me."

Amos---Um -- um -- ain't dat sumpin' [Episode 1843, 5/7/34].

The letters and telephone conversations also allowed Correll and Gosden to build Ruby Taylor into one of the program's most well-defined characters—a bright, poised young woman who took life seriously, and who avoided all of the prevalent stereotypes of female characters in popular entertainment. Ruby was neither a "dumb Dora" nor a shrew, neither an aggressive gold digger nor a shrinking violet. And, significantly, she also avoided the stereotypes common in popular portrayals of African American women—she was neither a "mammy" nor a "tragic mulatto." Ruby Taylor was comfortable with herself, confident in her own identity, and shared Amos's determination to succeed in the world, regardless of obstacles. Listeners came to know Ruby as well as they knew Amos and Andy themselves—and when in early 1930 she was called back to Chicago to care for her father during a severe illness, Correll and Gosden skillfully portrayed the profound grief both Amos and Ruby felt over their separation, in a scene that became one of the series' best-remembered sequences.

Andy---Where you been since de train left? De train left almost two hours ago.

Amos---I drove de taxicab over by de Harlem River an' I been sittin' dere fo' 'bout half a hour.

Andy---Whut you wanna sit by de river fo'?

Amos---Well Ruby gimme a letter before she left an' I wanted to read it by myself.

Andy---Whut kind o' letter?

Amos---I got it heah --- yo' want me to read it to yo'?

Andy---It ain't no sad letteh, is it?

Amos---No, it ain't sad. It's a sweet letter.

Andy---Go ahead, read it to me --- whut do it say?

Amos---She start out heah she say "My darlin' Amos --- I want you to read dis letter after I leave New York an' sweetheart, I want yo' to know dat ev'vy word in heah is true ----"

Andy---Go ahead.

Amos---Den she say -----

Andy---Wipe de tears out yo' eyes Amos.

Amos---Den she say heah "You have been so sweet about my goin' away dat I know you love me an' yo' sweetness has made me love you more dan I thought I could love anyone." Den she say "We have had a hard time tryin' to work things out so we could git married but sweetheart, remember dat I will always wait fo' you no matter how long it is." Dat's sweet, ain't it Andy?

Andy---Oh she love yo' Amos, ain't no two ways about dat.

Amos---Den she say heah "I want you to work hard an' be a good boy an' think of me often as I think of you. If you git lonesome Aunt Lillian will be glad to have you come out to her house."

Andy---You ain't goin' git lonesome Amos.

Amos---Den she say heah "I will write you ev'vy day unless I am so busy dat I can't an' I will wait fo' de mailman hopin' to heah from you ev'vy day too."

Andy---Yeh, you kin write each otheh lettehs.

Amos---Listen at de last thing she say heah Andy.

Andy---Whut is it?

Amos---She say heah "So sweetheart, I don't wanna tell you goodbye because it's not goodbye but I do want to tell you dat you have been so sweet an' lovely to me dat I love you more dan I do my own life an' as time goes on I know I will love an' want you more an' more --- so goodbye dear --- always --- Ruby."

Andy---Come on now Amos, come on. You gotta snap out of it --- you got me feelin' de same way.

Amos---Nobody'll ever know, Andy -------- [Episode 595, 2/17/30].

Other than brief attempts by Gosden to voice Madam Queen in one episode of the 1931 breach-of-promise story line and again in two November 1932 episodes,[2] no female character had a speaking role on *Amos 'n' Andy* until May 1935 when the performers engaged dialect specialist Harriette Widmer to play the role of Henrietta

6. Meet the Cast

Johnson, an attractive young woman acting opposite Andy in a community-theater production.[3] On December 25, 1935, young Chicago radio leading lady Elinor Harriot spoke Ruby Taylor's first line, saying "I do" in the long-awaited wedding of Amos and Ruby.[4] From 1936 to 1937, Harriot became the first cast member to share the microphone with Correll and Gosden on a regular basis, portraying Ruby along with several other female characters, including occasional appearances as the Kingfish's formidable wife, who had been a prominent off-mike presence since 1928 and who was finally given the name of "Sapphire" in 1933. Also in 1936, a young Chicagoan named Terry Howard briefly portrayed the orphan girl "Pun'kin'," a role taken over by Harriot after the program moved to Hollywood in 1937. Late in 1937, the Texas-born Madaline Lee joined the program as Genevieve Blue, Andy's endearingly dizzy secretary.

> Blue---Alright Mr. Broom. When you is ready for me, I'll buzz.
>
> Andy---Yeh, thank yo'.
>
> Amos---Whut'd she say she'd do?
>
> Andy---Well, dis buzzeh I got on my desk --- she presses a button when I want her, an' dis buzzeh buzzes --- an' we holleh back an' forth a few times an' finally get togetheh.
>
> Amos---She ain't got a buzzer on HER desk, is she?
>
> Andy---No, de buzzeh's out heah --- she's got de button.
>
> Amos---I told yo' you had dat backwards.
>
> Andy---She likes it dis way though --- poor gal's been shoppin' fo' four solid hours --- I bet she's tired.
>
> Amos---Yeh.
>
> Andy---Wait a minute -- I'll git her out here.
>
> Amos---Want me to go?
>
> Andy---No, I wanna show you de list of stuff dat she ordered while she was shoppin'. (calls) Miss Blue, will you buzz me!
>
> SOUND--Buzzer.
>
> Andy---(calls) Now, come out heah, will yo'?
>
> Amos---Dat's some 'rangement yo' got on dat buzzer.
>
> Blue---(fading in) Mr. Broom, I don't see how we ever got along widout dat buzzer.
>
> Andy---Great stuff alright. A -- did yo' git ev'ything on de shoppin' trip?
>
> Blue---Well Mr. Broom, I left my list o' stuff heah, an' I left my money here, so I didn't know whut to git. You told me dat de shoppin' would take about four hours, so after I got out an' found I left my list an' de money at de office, I didn't wanna disappoint you on de time, so I stayed out de four hours.
>
> Andy---(soft) Yeah. I think I'll ride around in de taxicab wid Amos fo' a while

an' git some fresh air --- I'se gittin' de headache. Buzz me when I git back an' we'll start oveh again.... [Episode 2732, 12/7/37].

In 1939, Correll and Gosden added their first regular African American cast member when singer Ernestine Wade joined the cast as Andy's sweetheart Valada Green. Wade, who had developed impressive multiple-voice skills talking to her dolls as an only child growing up in Jackson, Mississippi, would subsequently make an enduring mark on the series after taking over the role of Sapphire Stevens.[5] Finally, in 1940, the performers added one additional cast member—the Chinese-American child actress Barbara Jean Wong, who portrayed Amos's daughter Arbadella.[6]

These were the primary characters around whom Correll and Gosden built their stories, but over the 15-year run of the nightly serial, this core cast was augmented by hundreds of other characters—some of them voiced by Correll and Gosden, and others presented as background figures, their roles built up through discussions, phone conversations, and letters. And these characters, spoken and unspoken, offered Correll and Gosden a broad canvas on which to develop their plots.

There was the wealthy philanthropist Roland Weber, "one of the richest colored men in America," who entered Amos and Andy's world in 1934. More than 20 years earlier, Weber had been a struggling coal miner who was saved from death in a mining accident by Elijah Jones, Amos's father. Jones gave his own life to save Weber's—and Weber pledged that he would one day repay that debt by helping his friend's young son. Striking his fortune in the Texas oil fields, Weber tracked down Amos through a classified ad and became a mentor and surrogate father to him. But Weber's life was tragically cut short one September day on a Harlem street, when the millionaire was struck down by a reckless driver moments after pulling a small child out of the oncoming vehicle's path.

There was Weber's widow Annie—once a professional dancer billed as "Señorita Butterfly"—who was unprepared for the demands of sudden wealth, and who after her husband's death developed an obsession with Amos that led, in the summer of 1935, to a tense murder mystery. There were Mr. and Mrs. Charles Francis Van DeTweezer and Mr. and Mrs. George Washington—the setters of the Social Pace—and there were Lawyer Collins and Lawyer Henry Lucas, who proved effective counselors when Andy needed legal advice. And there was Prince Ali Bendo, a corrupt fortuneteller, whose pretended mysticism offered an ideal cover for a cold-blooded blackmail racket and whose ill-starred career ultimately ended with prison time.

There was Flukey Harris, a gravel-voiced handyman with a career on the side as an amateur prizefighter, and there was the Landlord, the sympathetic owner of the rooming house where Amos and Andy boarded. There was the Short Order Cook, who loomed large over the grill at the Big 3 Lunch Room, and there was "Pun'kin," a six-year-old girl left homeless by the death of her parents, who was taken in and fiercely protected by the kind-hearted Andy. And there was Pop Johnson, an elderly trustee of the lodge who surprised everyone by eloping with a 19-year-old flapper named Flossie White.

There was Mr. Hotchkiss, an executive at the Harlem bank where Amos kept his savings, who was always ready to offer sound financial advice, and there was Honest Joe the pawnbroker—the only white character in the recurring cast—to whom the Kingfish all too often had to turn when funds were running low. There was Roscoe Brownlee, a corrupt publicity agent exposed as a criminal by Amos's detective work and there was Miss Elizabeth F. Sanders, a bank auditor and classically trained violinist who fell hopelessly in love with Amos. There was Sadie Blake, who pined away for years over her unrequited love for Andy, and there was Dr. W.L. Dickinson, Ruby Taylor's employer, who was eventually appointed the head of a "colored" hospital in Richmond. All these characters, and many others, whether portrayed on mike or through third-person exposition, helped to give the world of *Amos 'n' Andy* a richness, a depth, and a sense of realism equaled by few other radio programs of the 1930s.

With the exception of a few celebrity guests appearing as themselves in the later years of the run, all the male speaking roles from 1928 through the end of the serial in 1943 were played by either Gosden or Correll, who between them voiced over 170

Freeman Gosden's "raw persimmon" expression is well displayed as he enacts the role of the Kingfish, in a scene touted as the first photograph ever taken during an actual *Amos 'n' Andy* broadcast. The date is August 22, 1935; the setting is NBC Studio F, Merchandise Mart, Chicago. In the background, Bill Hay reclines on the studio sofa, awaiting the cue for his closing words for Pepsodent.

distinct characterizations during just the first decade of the program. "Gosden is the most versatile in this respect," observed Bill Hay. "In addition to Amos, he enacts the Kingfish, Brother Crawford, and about 70 percent of all the other characters. I can't help smiling when Amos does the Kingfish. He screws his face up into the expression a man might make when eating a raw persimmon, leans back three feet from the microphone—and there we have it. For Brother Crawford, he keeps approximately the same distance but gets the peculiar spasmodic quality you know so well by pumping himself up and down in an armchair."[7]

Voice characterizations were the essential building blocks of any dramatized radio program, and Correll and Gosden were meticulous in the development of theirs, introducing new characters only after thorough experimentation with vocal techniques. "It's like a guy picking away on a piano," Gosden explained. "You keep working around with the keys until you hit a tune, and then you follow it. We keep doing the same thing with our voices until we find something that would make a character in the script. First we get the voice, and then the kind of person it will represent sort of comes naturally. The 'feel' of the voice suggests the character who would have it."[8] By the end of the 1930s, Correll and Gosden augmented these vocal experiments with the use of a recording machine installed at their office, allowing them to critique potential new characterizations as though they were listeners tuning in on the program at home, ensuring that new voices came over the loudspeaker as their creators intended.

"To think that two people like them could have so many different voices," Bill Hay mused in 1973. "The most remarkable thing about that was that they had some characters for whom the voices were very different.... There was ten or twelve of them, and they could do ... the lawyer, they would do him tonight, we'll say, and possibly for the two or three next nights. And then they would change the entire thing, and you wouldn't hear that voice for two, three or four months. But the minute it came on, the tone, the pitch, was exactly the same as when they had done it three or four months before."[9]

7. SPEAKING THE LANGUAGE

"You're going to go up North, and those people won't know what you're talking about!"

—Charles Correll to Freeman Gosden

THE DIALECT USED IN *Amos 'n' Andy* has long been a point of debate, by black and white listeners alike, and the issue is perhaps the most politically charged question revolving around the program. Critics of *Amos 'n' Andy* frequently count the "mangling of English grammar" by the program's characters as one of their leading complaints against the series. However, a careful examination of the language used in the original 1930s radio scripts reveals that, far from being a crude, random mangling of grammar for comic effect, the language used by Correll and Gosden in fact displayed an awareness of specific and clearly defined linguistic rules: the rules of a form of speech commonly referred to by linguists as "African American Vernacular English," "Black English Vernacular," or simply Black English.

There persists a belief among some commentators, academics, and cultural critics that so-called Black English was merely an invention of nineteenth-century blackface comedians and local-color-fiction authors, who, seeking to ridicule the characters they portrayed, garbled common white Southern English into a synthetic dialect that bore no resemblance to the speech patterns of any actual African Americans. But this belief has long since been discredited by sociolinguists like William Labov and J.L. Dillard, who have documented many parallels between the traits of African American Vernacular English and various West African dialects.

> Suppose a Negro saw a minstrel show, was impressed by the "invented" dialect, and carried it to his own group, where it immediately caught on; that from his own group it spread to the neighboring cities, counties, states, etc.; that visiting West Indians heard the same new "invented" dialect and were so delighted that they carried it back home

with them; and finally that a few found their way back to Africa, where it formed the basis of present-day Liberian Pidgin English, WesKos Pidgin of the Cameroon and Nigeria, Sierra Leone Krio, etc.! The idea is intentionally absurd—but it is not much more absurd than the original idea of a minstrel-show dialect created out of whole cloth. That minstrel-show writers may have been especially inept recorders of already existing dialects is, on the other hand, a distinct possibility.[1]

Clearly, the issue to be considered here is not "does African American Vernacular English exist as a genuine, distinguishable dialect," but rather, "how accurate a representation of that dialect, as it existed in the early 20th century, was the language featured in *Amos 'n' Andy*?" Critics of the series frequently contend that Correll and Gosden were at best "bastardizing" genuine African American speech patterns—and as early as 1930, letters from listeners in the fan press argued over the authenticity of the characters' speech.[2] Southerners often criticized elements of the dialect as being not authentic to their particular region of the country—reflecting the reality that African American Vernacular English is not itself a single rigidly defined dialect but is an umbrella term used for an amalgamation of many regional forms of speech that are drawn from many different linguistic sources, both African and Southern American, but that share common and identifiable characteristics.[3]

Viewed from a sociolinguistic perspective, African American Vernacular English is neither a mangling of Standard English nor is it slang. It is a recognized dialect of English shaped by clearly defined grammatical and phonological rules—but because AAVE is not considered a high-status dialect, serious study of this complex language form has long been hindered by misinformation, by political agendas, and by class- and race-related cultural prejudices. But as argued by the language historian Dr. Walter M. Brasch, such politically and socially driven interpretations of the issue cannot be linguistically supported. "The entire Deficit Theory [which holds that African American Vernacular English is an "unacceptable," "inferior," "sloppy," or "poor" form of speech] with its many subtheories and hypotheses, is often advanced by educators, by social scientists, and, to a certain extent, by journalists," Brasch writes in his 1981 study *Black English and the Mass Media*. "It is not a linguistic theory of language, and not based upon hard language data. In contrast, both the creolist theories and those of the dialect geographers are based on a detailed analysis of the language. Both theories argue that the language is not substandard or 'sloppy' English; Black English is an acceptable dialect or variety of speech with its own well-defined set of linguistic rules. They also account for the fact that Black English is not one but many varieties of language, that not all Blacks speak Black English, and that some Whites also speak it."[4]

As Brasch and Dillard indicate, although the roots of African American Vernacular English extend to West African languages as well as Southern English, the dialect is not spoken by all African Americans nor is it spoken exclusively *by* African Americans. As with any variety of speech, it is easily absorbed by those who hear it, white or black—and this is especially true of children. The phenomenon of "bidialectism" is well documented by linguists; this refers to the circumstances through which a child learns one variety of speech from parents or teachers and another variety of speech from playmates. The younger a child is when this phenomenon occurs, the more likely it is that that child is to become fluent in both dialects.[5]

Freeman Gosden's own background offers a textbook example of the sort of circumstances that produce a bidialectal individual. Throughout his childhood, Gosden's closest friend was Garrett Brown—a black youth who spoke African American Vernacular English as well as Standard English—and Gosden heard the speech of other African Americans daily in the streets of Jackson Ward. Hearing both AAVE and Standard English spoken around him daily, it was natural for Gosden to learn the basic structure of both forms of speech and to be able to switch between the two dialects at will. It is reasonable to conclude that Gosden learned to speak African American Vernacular English in the same manner as an African American child would have—by hearing it spoken regularly by people around him.

The scripts Gosden dictated to Correll for *Amos 'n' Andy* were very specific as to how the characters were to sound. Dialogue was spelled out phonetically, with the lines intended to be read exactly as written. These characteristics allowed the scripts to be used as an accurate guide to what was actually broadcast by Correll and Gosden—and the specific structure of the lines may be examined for recurring grammatical traits, indicating the authors' degree of awareness of AAVE grammar and phonology.

The following African American Vernacular English rules are commonly observed in the scripts, although, as will be detailed later, there are significant variations in linguistic characteristics according to the background and personality of each character. Not all characters display all markers at all times—but these rules are observed most often:[6]

PHONOLOGY
- Stopped initial fricatives (d- for th- as in "dis," "dat" for "this" and "that")
- Nasal Replacement ("going" becomes "goin'," "walking" becomes "walkin'")
- Absence of the postvocalic "r" ("here" becomes "heah," "sure" becomes "sho'")
- Absence of the postvocalic "l" ("help" becomes "he'p")
- Substitution of labiodental fricatives for interdental fricatives ("mouth" becomes "mouf," "both" becomes "bofe," "with" becomes "wid")
- Elision of unstressed initial syllables ("'bout" for "about," "'splain" for "explain." Hypercorrection may create fancified forms: "regusted," "repression")
- Consonant cluster reduction ("mos'" for "most," "des'" for "desk," etc.) is only rarely specified in the scripts, but surviving recordings reveal that this marker is frequently present in the performers' actual delivery of the lines

GRAMMAR
- Present-tense zero copula used where appropriate: whenever Standard English can contract "is" or "are" to 's or 're, African American Vernacular English allows the option of full contraction of the copula ("He is going" contracts to "He goin'")

- Auxiliary "Is" replaces "Have/Has" and variants ("We is got it," "Is you got it?")
- Existential "It" used in sense "There exists" ("It's two dollars in my pocket")
- Third-person present tense marker is absent ("He go" replaces "He goes," but hypercorrection is sometimes present in first-person singular: "I goes")
- Pronominal cross-reference markers used where appropriate ("Our friend Henry, he got a buildin' fo' sale")
- Perfective "done" in pre-verb position ("He done gone home," "Done had de inside painted up")
- "Come" used in semiauxiliary position ("He come tellin' me dat")
- Adverbial "like to" indicates "almost" or "nearly" ("I like to died laughin'")
- Multiple negation indicates emphasis ("Ain't nobody seen dat nohow!")
- Habitual "be" ("I be workin'" for "I am steadily employed" but not "I am working at this moment") used very rarely but correctly. Sociolinguist William Labov points out that the habitual or invariant "be"—taken as a definitive characteristic of current-day African American Vernacular English—did not attain that status until after World War II, a sign that Black English is a dialect in a continuing state of evolution.[7]
- Stressed durative "been"("He been out o' work" for "He is unemployed and has been unemployed for some time") used rarely but correctly
- Occasional semantic inversion ("He's a bad man wid de ladies")

Inexperienced minstrel comedians sometimes merely overlaid African American Vernacular English phonology—the "disses" and "dats" of the genuine dialect—on a Standard English grammar. Seasoned by malapropisms and broad delivery, this sort of pseudodialect endures even to the present day in attempted imitations of AAVE by those who do not actually speak it. But the dialect used in *Amos 'n' Andy* clearly did not fall into this class. Although Gosden had no formal sociolinguistic training, it is evident that he had absorbed a great deal from the speech patterns of the African Americans who had surrounded him during his childhood in Richmond. It is also evident from the skillful use of early-twentieth-century AAVE grammar in the scripts that, far from being an inept minstrel-show imitation, the basic dialect Gosden incorporated into *Amos 'n' Andy* reflected a form of speech of which he was, in fact, a native speaker. Indeed, Charles Correll once noted that when he first met Gosden, the Virginian tended to speak with such a thick accent that he was difficult to understand. "If he wanted to say 'the score on the scoreboard is fourteen to four,'" Correll recalled, "he'd say 'de sco' on de sco'bo'd is fo'teen to fo'!' I said, 'Now, you're going to have to pronounce 'r's. You're going to go up North, and those people won't know what you're talking about!"[8]

Aside from the basic phonology and grammar of African American Vernacular English, Gosden understood and integrated into the series other distinctive speech traits. The use of malapropism and hypercorrection by certain characters, most notably Andy and the Kingfish, is one of the most controversial aspects of the dialect used in *Amos 'n' Andy*. While Correll and Gosden appreciated the humorous effect of malapropial and hypercorrected speech, they did not simply exploit these traits randomly for the sake of isolated gags. During the program's serial years, extravagant speech was most often used by Andy—and such speech was used not simply as a source of humor but as a way of carefully outlining the pompous, self-important, and vulnerable elements of his personality. A close examination of context reveals that Andy used pretentious language as a shield behind which he could safely conceal his insecurities.

> Amos---Well, read me de REport yo' goin' send to de lodge.
>
> Andy---Well, I done told yo' how I started out de otheh day 'bout de ex-zeck committee an' all dat --- dear brothehs ----- den I say heah "De Kingfish REpo'ts to me dat you want a REpo't, so enclosed on dis piece o' papeh is de follows" ---- I thought I might as well be all bizness wid it.
>
> Amos---Yeh, if dey lost money over dere dey can't hold yo' fo' it, kin dey?
>
> Andy---Dey THINK dey kin hold me, but I'se tellin' 'em heah.
>
> Amos---Go ahead, read it.
>
> Andy---Den I say heah "Disregardin' de money dat was lost, I has dis to say --- I don't know nuthin' 'bout nuthin' or nuthin' else 'bout de money, an' as chairman of de financh committee, I will he'p you look fo' it, but I kin tell you now I don't know where 'tis. An' moreoveh, an' nevah-de-less, I ain't neveh seed it, an' besides dat I resigns as de chairman of de financh committee hereafteh stated above," an' boy I wanna tell yo', when dey git dat, dey got sumpin'.
>
> Amos---Yeh, dey got sumpin' to figger out, I guess [Episode 895, 2/4/31].

While the frequent uses of hypercorrection and malapropism in *Amos 'n' Andy* are often criticized, it is incorrect to assert that these habits are solely derived from minstrelsy. Sociolinguists acknowledge that such habits are not without precedent in certain forms of historical African American speech—a point emphasized by Dr. Walter M. Brasch in his discussion of the program.

> The extensive use of malapropism by the star characters ... may have been humorous to a White American audience which, through ignorance, may have believed that the English spoken by Blacks was a substandard or inferior language. But it was still a part of the Black's Afro-American heritage. It was a pidginization of language; it was taking the rules of an African language experience, an experience passed by oral tradition from generation to generation, and trying to adapt them to an American language. Soon, there was even a "backwash" effect as Americans, fascinated by the hypercorrection, by the "sweet talk," by the distinctly African syntactic and phonological language characteristics, began to imitate, then adopt the language of the characters in the series.[9]

While the basic structure of the dialect used in *Amos 'n' Andy* stands up well under analysis, there are certain recurring traits that are more difficult to authenticate. For example, the substitution of "re-" at the beginning of various words is common, especially in Andy's speech. This is not a random habit nor is it an instance of malapropism inserted for comic effect. Rather, the practice follows a consistent pattern—the elision of an unstressed initial syllable from a multisyllabic word and the hypercorrected reconstruction of that lost initial syllable. In a typical example, "disgusted" is elided to "'gusted" and then hypercorrected to create the form "regusted." As is often the case with hypercorrected forms in early African American Vernacular English, "regusted" projects emphasis: "I'se regusted" expresses Andy's feelings with considerable force, much more so than would the elided "'gusted" or even the standard English "disgusted." While there is documentation for this habit in historical studies of AAVE,[10] some Southern listeners felt that the trait occurred too frequently in Andy's speech to be realistic.[11] The frequent substitution of "l" sounds for "s" sounds in Andy's speech—"propolition" for "proposition" being the best-known example—is of more uncertain origin, although it was probably intended as a form of hypercorrection. There is some suggestion that Garrett Brown may have been the source for some of the more unusual linguistic quirks encountered in *Amos 'n' Andy*.[12] It may also be that, in some cases, Correll and Gosden were specifically trying, through frequent repetition, to come up with unique catchphrases that could easily be identified with the program. Indeed, both "regusted" and "propolition" entered the lexicon of popular culture during the Depression years, ensuring that these constructions would endure in *Amos 'n' Andy* scripts for years to come.

In addition to pronunciation and grammatical structure, the dialect featured in *Amos 'n' Andy* often incorporated bits of distinctively African American idiom and slang. Phrases like "check and double check," "that's a dog," "cold turkey," and "sounds kind-a jaily" (referring to a venture of dubious legality), plus Andy's mid–1930s habit of using abbreviations ("dat's N.G." for "that's no good") and the frequent use of "brother" as a form of address all offered an additional touch of authenticity to the dialogue. But consistent with both the age and the rural background of the characters, there is no evidence of "jive" in their speech.[13]

Just as they reveal the use of a consistent form of African American Vernacular English phonology and grammar in the program, the *Amos 'n' Andy* scripts also reveal that Correll and Gosden were well aware of a fact that often escaped white authors of dialect fiction in the 1920s and 1930s: that AAVE is primarily a working-class language form, with the middle and upper classes often emphasizing a precise Standard English grammar and pronunciation. So it was that not all characters in *Amos 'n' Andy* spoke in dialect—and reflecting real life, the use of dialect is closely tied to each character's social status within the African American community portrayed in the series. The role of William Taylor, for example, was invariably written in a strictly Standard English style, appropriate for an educated, professional character. Indeed, surviving recordings reveal that Gosden portrayed Taylor with an authoritative, resonant voice—dignified, but not stuffy, and without resorting to dialect to convey the image of the character's race.[14] Other educated characters, like Ruby Taylor and Lawyer Collins, display similar speech patterns.

Collins--Well now, Andy, I want you to do me a favor. Otherwise we're not going to get anywhere. I want you to stop talking about this thing and hereafter if anybody wants any information if you'll send them over to me I'll be glad to give them everything that we should give out at this time.

Amos---Andy just tell ev'ybody ev'ything.

Andy---Hereafteh though I ain't goin' tell nobody nuthin'.

Collins--You realize that Madam Queen's lawyer can use that story as evidence and if necessary, he can bring that reporter in court and testify that you said what he printed.... I want you to promise me one thing, that you're not going to talk any more --- and if you do, I'm not going to be able to handle the case.

Andy---Oh, I ain't goin' say no mo'. I just say one thing to 'em. "See Mr. Collins, see Mr. Collins" -- dat's all I goin' say.

Amos---You ought to said dat in de first place [Episode 900, 2/10/31].

Sociolinguists treat the use of types of languages in cultural groups as a continuum, rather than as strictly defined categories. The ends of that continuum are defined by the most prestigious, standard form of speech—the "acrolect"—on one end and the lowest prestige form of speech—the "basilect"—on the other. The speech of specific individuals may fall anywhere along this continuum, becoming more and more "standard" as it moves toward the acrolect position. The linguistic continuum represented in *Amos 'n' Andy* may be represented thusly.

ACROLECT [HIGH PRESTIGE] ←←←←←←BASILECT [LOW PRESTIGE]

Mr. Taylor   Henry Van Porter   F. M. Gwindell   Andrew H. Brown

Ruby Taylor Jones   Brother Crawford   Amos Jones   The Kingfish   Lightning

Indulgence in "sweet talk" or "fancy talk" by bombastic characters like Andy, the Kingfish, and Henry Van Porter contrasts with the slow Alabama drawl of Lightning or the mild-mannered, businesslike diction of Brother Crawford, who usually spoke an unctuous sort of Standard English, but shifted into dialect when agitated—a trait that suggests that Gosden was aware of and understood the practice of "code-switching" by many speakers whose speech patterns bridged both ends of the dialect continuum. And Amos's speech patterns act as an audible index of his social evolution: when he arrived in Chicago in 1928, his dialect was similar to Andy's, even down to repeating some of his friend's distinctive speech habits, especially in the use of hypercorrected "re-" prefixes. But there were always subtle differences: Amos usually sounded the final "r" in words like "dollar" while Andy usually dropped it. By 1933, Amos's speech had improved somewhat, as the character himself had taken on a new depth and maturity. By 1939, Amos's dialect was much subtler than Andy's and it often approached Standard English.[15] After considering all of these factors, a strong case can be made that the language used in the serial version of *Amos 'n' Andy* was neither "mangled English" nor a mocking caricature but an attempt to accurately portray recognizable characteristics of a living form of speech.

8. TALES TO TELL

"We always try to introduce something that is common and happens to everybody."

—Freeman Gosden

THE SUCCESS OF *AMOS 'N' ANDY* in the 1930s was constructed on a foundation of solid storytelling. By the dawn of the decade, Correll and Gosden's skills in the development of character and plot had advanced far beyond their rudimentary *Sam 'n' Henry* stories to stories that could grab and hold the attention of a vast audience on multiple levels. The open-ended serial format allowed the performers to spend weeks or even months exploring a single basic plot idea, all the while allowing multiple subplots to evolve in the background of the main action. But even as their plots developed, certain basic themes remained constant throughout the series' run as a nightly serial.

Most of the story lines during the program's prime years revolved around one of three basic themes: Amos's desire to settle down with Ruby Taylor, Andy's many romantic entanglements, or attempts to make money by engaging in various business enterprises. The performers were careful to keep their plots grounded in the reality of daily life—but in doing so, they were also well aware of an allegorical element in their storytelling.

During the Depression years, the "money" stories could be taken as a cautious parable about what had happened to the United States in the 1920s: Amos stood for old-fashioned economic values, believing that wealth had to be earned, while the Kingfish and his fast-talking cohorts like Pat Pending represented the Wall Street lure of "easy money." And Andy was caught in the middle: represented the sort of overconfident investor who allowed his pride and his desire for fast profits to override his common sense. "We always try to introduce something that is common and happens to everybody," Gosden told journalist Mark Quest in 1930. "For example, most of us are gullible, especially about our financial interests."[1] Again and again the lesson was hammered home in these stories—Andy inevitably reaped what he sowed when his ill-advised ventures collapsed, just like what was happening to America itself with the collapse of 1920s prosperity.

Perhaps the outstanding example of a "money" story line took place during the early months of 1930, when the Kingfish, his wife, and Pat Pending joined to form "The Great Home Bank," a home-based financial institution that would earn money for its depositors through stock market speculation and bets on horse races (this was a pointed satire on the speculation-driven economy of the late 1920s). "No matter what we say, we try to leave the right impression," Gosden explained, "so the lesson in those episodes was that you'd be better off if you put your money in a good sound bank than in any wild-cat or fly-by-night scheme in order to get rich." After careful consultation with Ruby Taylor and his friend Mr Hotchkiss at the local bank, when Amos sternly refused to deposit his $125 in savings with the Kingfish's enterprise, listeners applauded.[2]

> Andy---Dat man down at de bank is done ruined ev'ything.
>
> Amos---No he ain't ruined ev'ything. Dat man told me right, an' I goin' down dere an' talk to him too 'fore I do ANYTHING wid my money. When I finished talkin' to him, I told him how much I thanked him fo' it an' ev'ything, an' he 'splained to me dat dat was whut de bank was fo'.
>
> Andy---Whut yo' mean?
>
> Amos---Well, he told me dat de bank is not only dere to save yo' money fo' yo', but dey wanna he'p ev'ybody out dey kin wid doin' de right thing wid dey're money. Hereafter I goin' talk to de bank too 'fore I let go o' DAT $125 [Episode 571, 1/20/30].

"Much to our surprise after we had finished these episodes, we got letters from bankers all over the country praising our good work in showing the people the value of good, solid banking institutions," noted Gosden. "I guess the effect wasn't lost on the public either, because we got lots of letters from people who said they had sure learned a lesson from the Kingfish's bank and would know enough to consult their own bankers before they made any investment."[3]

Correll and Gosden were, with rare exceptions, careful to maintain a sense of political neutrality in their broadcasts, but even with these efforts, certain personal points of view could occasionally be glimpsed under the program's surface. The scripts consistently projected an attitude of skepticism and distrust toward the speculative "fast money" attitudes that prevailed during the 1920s, and which many in the early 1930s considered a major cause of the Great Depression. Criticism of these attitudes was often expressed through the voice of Amos, who was consistently used as an embodiment of traditional "hard work and common sense" virtues. But Correll and Gosden also expressed a powerful streak of compassion for the less fortunate, and during the most difficult years of the Depression, the characters repeatedly urged listeners to be mindful of those who had been hit hard by the economic crisis and to offer practical help wherever possible. For example, as unemployment and urban hunger mounted during the summer of 1931, Amos and Andy's lunchroom became, like many small urban restaurants in real life, a focal point for the distribution of food to Harlem's poor.

> Amos---We have a little scraps left over here an' some scraps left over dere an' instead o' throwin' de stuff away we ought to cook it up an' give it to de people 'round heah dat's hungry --- some o' dese poor people. We don't stop to think about it, but dere's a lot o' people walkin' by heah ev'vy day dat maybe dey ain't had nuthin' to eat fo' two days, an' if we could do dat two-three times a week, we'd be doin' some good.
>
> Andy---Yeh, dat's a good idea alright Amos. I know a fellow right now dat ain't had nuthin' to eat since yestidday mornin' [Episode 1056, 8/11/31].

The Depression affected the characters in very realistic ways—many episodes dealt with the difficulty of making ends meet, and the lessons of the times were forcefully driven home when Amos learned that Mr. Taylor had been wiped out in the stock market crash. Ruby had to leave school and go to work as a switchboard operator—eventually earning enough to resume her education, with hopes of becoming a nurse—even as Amos had to work all that much harder as the couple reached toward their goal of marriage. Meanwhile, despite recurring health problems, Mr. Taylor strove to rebuild his business.[4] The message to listeners was clear: even when faced with the hardest of hard times, Americans couldn't allow themselves to give up hope for the future.

With the advent of the New Deal, the program took on an even more optimistic tone. Correll and Gosden became strong supporters of the first Roosevelt administration and repeatedly used the program to promote the president's policies. Beginning in March 1933, Correll and Gosden wrote to White House press secretary Stephen Early to seek official permission to include pro-administration messages in their episodes.[5] On the night of Roosevelt's inauguration, Amos encouraged listeners to pray for the new president's success, and three nights later, the program devoted much of the dialogue to a discussion of the "bank holiday." Roosevelt's first action had been to close all banks to allow the banking system a chance to stabilize, and as a result, privately issued "scrip" was being used in place of money in some cities. Many citizens were worried about what this might mean and Correll and Gosden devised a script intended to ease those fears, with the Kingfish gently explaining the dangers of unfounded panic to the worried Andy and Lightning.

> King---Boys, I is older den you is, an' I know just whut's goin' through yo' minds. You is worried 'cause yo' listenin' to de boys on de corner talkin' 'bout somethin' dey don't know nuthin' 'bout. I was down standin' on de corner yesterday listenin' to one boy down dere talkin' --- 'bout 10 other fellows listenin' to him --- he didn't know whut he was talkin' 'bout -- he was guessin' wid ev'ything an' 'fore he finished wid dese boys, he had 'em believin' dat black was white an' green was red --- an' don't fo'git dis --- dem boys dat heard him, dey tells somebody else an' when dey tells it, dey add a little bit on it, an' dat keeps up till it gits around ten times as bad as it was when it wasn't nuthin' to begin wid.

Amos added further reassurance as the conversation continued. Having expressed his hope on the evening of Roosevelt's inauguration that all Americans would join him in praying for the new president's success, Amos offered a ringing endorsement of the new administration's emergency fiscal policy. After a visit to his friend at the local bank, Amos was more confident than ever that the worst of the crisis was finally over.

> Amos---Dis man say dat if anybody's got fear in dey're mind, dey is crazy. He say dat dis bank holiday was de best thing dat could be done, an' it's goin' bring back prosperity quicker dan ever. He say it's de greatest move dat's been made in recent years to git ev'ything goin' like it was. He say dat instead o' dis bank holiday bein' sumpin' to fear, he say it's de greatest move o' reconstruction dat's ever been made.
>
> King---Dat man's right, too.
>
> Amos---Here's sumpin' dat he told me. He say dat President Roosevelt talked to de governors an' he say de way dat money put in de banks kin be kept safe is fo' de banks to either keep de money in cash or put it in Federal Reserve banks or buyin' gov'ment bonds wid it, so de President of de United States is fightin' fo' mo' dan just 'mergency bankin' relief --- he is workin' out a plan to have a system in de banks dat will not only he'p 'em now but will he'p 'em fo' all time to come, an' dis banker say dat dat's 'zackly whut's goin' happen, an' Mr. Roosevelt means bizness an' he's gittin' action, an' so yo' see, dis bank holiday is really a great thing fo' de country [Episode 1539, 3/7/33].

Correll and Gosden subsequently received the personal thanks of the president for their help in calming a nation on the verge of panic.[6] Throughout the Depression years, the performers took advantage of the platform offered by their enormous nightly audience to present subtly didactic material within the larger context of their continuing story line, repeatedly stressing the cyclical nature of economic crises and encouraging listeners to keep up their hopes for the return of prosperity. Even as the Hoover administration floundered in the summer of 1931 in its efforts to spark economic recovery and national confidence flagged, Correll and Gosden used the figure of real-estate salesman Henry Van Porter to present a carefully structured, simplified lesson on the ebb and flow of economic cycles over the previous 80 years.

> Van----Well now, this line running right through the middle of the chart represents normal conditions ---- now we start back here in about 1855, we have what is known as the Credit Expansion Prosperity --- then in 1857 we had whut is known as the Panic of 1857. Now we go along and we have prosperity and depression ---- this is before our time, but let us get up to 1914. This chart shows here in 1914 and 15 we had what is known as a War Depression --- den in 16, 17, and 18 we had war prosperity ----
>
> Amos---Yessah.
>
> Van----Now, it shows that we're now in a depression.

8. Tales to Tell

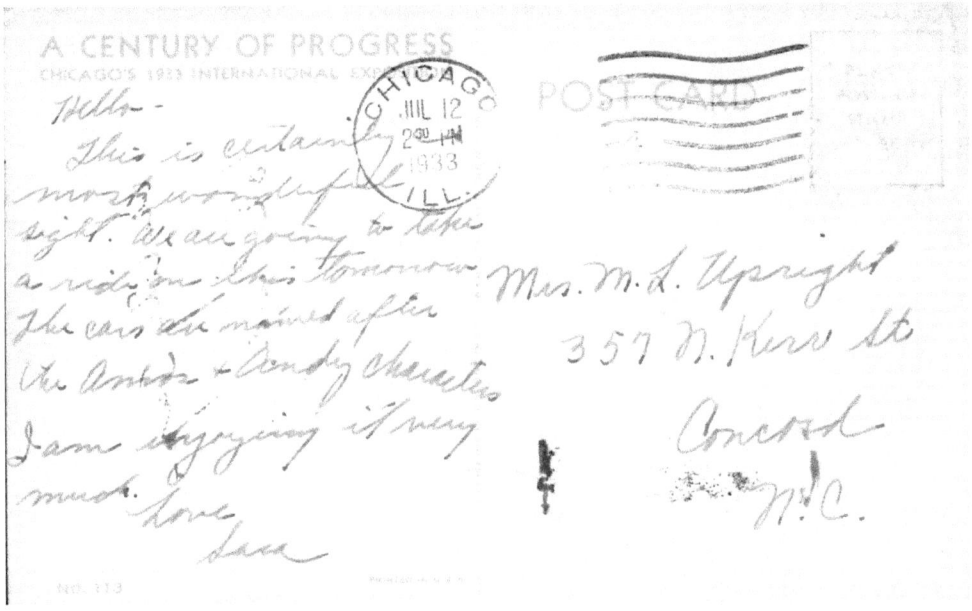

Correll and Gosden were closely involved with publicity and promotional efforts on behalf of the 1933 Century of Progress Exhibition in Chicago, sending Amos, Andy and the Kingfish on a two-week road trip to the Windy City where they toured the fair's attractions and offered detailed descriptions each night of what they saw and experienced. The Exhibition returned the favor by naming the twin towers of the Sky Ride—then the tallest man-made structures west of New York—after Amos and Andy. The cable cars traveling between the towers bore the names of The Kingfish, Brother Crawford, Madam Queen, Ruby Taylor, and Lightning.

> Amos---Yessah.
>
> Van----But the point of this whole thing that I'm trying to make clear to you, and which is not my idea, but based on actual figures of the past, regardless of what anyone tells you, according to past performance we are bound to come out of any depression that may exist at this time [Episode 1008, 6/16/31].

Material of this sort appeared frequently enough during the first years of the 1930s that, NBC president Merlin Ayelsworth brought Correll and Gosden to Washington DC in 1933 to testify before a congressional committee investigating questions of public service in commercial broadcasting, in doing so Ayelsworth praised the performers as "philosophers to the American people."[7] And, indeed, a careful examination of the content of *Amos 'n' Andy* during the Depression years reveals that Correll and Gosden took the treatment of educational themes in their program quite seriously.

While most of the didactic content of the program revolved around Depression issues and was played straight, Correll and Gosden occasionally used their characters as mouthpieces for their own views on larger world affairs. *Amos 'n' Andy* became one of the earliest American radio entertainment programs to directly attack fascism, when, in December 1934, Correll and Gosden used the series as the platform for a stinging satire of the very concept of dictatorship. Inspired by news stories about Mussolini and by reading a biography of Napoleon, the Kingfish seized political control of the small town of Weber City and was soon carried away by his own delusions of magnificence.

> King---I is gonna give my peoples de pleasure o' chippin' in an' buyin' me de high silk hat, which will be de emblem of me.
>
> Andy---Yo' want ev'ybody to chip in an buy yo' a hat?
>
> King---So dat my peoples will feel dat dey is doin' sumpin' fo' dey're great ruler --- now, comes de most reportant thing of de WHOLE thing.
>
> Amos---Whut is dat?
>
> King---De presentation of de silk hat to de dictator.
>
> Andy---Whut do dat mean, Kingfish?
>
> King---DICTATOR.
>
> Andy---Dictator.
>
> King---Knock dese ashes off dis seegar fo' me, will yo'?
>
> Andy---Yeh.
>
> Amos---Go ahead, Dictator.
>
> King---De PREsentation, boys, is dis --- lemme stand up heah, put one foot up on de chair. I kin think better ---- I'll rest my elbow on dis knee.
>
> Andy---I see yo' done cut some slits in yo' shoe dictator.

King---Yeh --- de dictator's feet is givin' him some trouble.

Amos---Yo' elbow is comin' out o' yo' coat too dere dictator.

Andy---Maybe yo' better switch dat hat fo' a suit o' clothes [Episode 1950, 12/5/34].

The Kingfish's wife believed that her husband had become mentally unbalanced and tried to convince him to see a psychiatrist; also, Amos took note of a "strange glow in his eyes." The climax of this unusual story line was eerily prophetic: after attempts at reasoning with the "dictator" failed, Amos and Andy were forced to resort to direct action.

King---Now wait a minute, young fellow, let me tell YOU sumpin'.

Andy---GIT YO' HAND OFF O' HIM!

King---Who you talkin' to Andy?

Andy---I'll show yo' --- (hits two or three times)

Amos---Wait a minute, don't hit him Andy --- don't hit him no more.

Andy --- Now lay down dere on de flo' --- an' startin' at 12 o'clock tomorrow we goin' keep second hand furniture in dis office, so git out o' heah. Come on Amos, let him lay dere [Episode 1954, 12/11/34].

The "Dictator of Weber City" story line had many possible interpretations for listeners in the winter of 1934. The activities of Hitler and Mussolini were attracting increasing attention in the American news media, while on the domestic scene, the bombastic anti–Roosevelt administration statements of Louisiana Senator Huey P. Long were the focal point of a powerful national political movement, which had attracted allies in other fringe political groups with overt Fascist leanings. And not coincidentally, Long himself was already well known by the nickname "Kingfish," which he enthusiastically appropriated from Correll and Gosden's character. But from whatever political perspective listeners chose to interpret the specifics of the story line, the essential point was hard to miss. Even in *Amos 'n' Andy*'s most broadly satirical sequences, common sense and the strength of the common man carried the day.

But political and social allegory made up only a part of *Amos 'n' Andy*'s appeal. Correll and Gosden were also skilled in the presentation of straight melodrama and by far the most compelling story lines in the series were those that placed the characters in real jeopardy. In late 1931, Amos and Andy and their friends saw their world disrupted by the arrival of Jack Dixon, a hard and enigmatic man who promoted investment schemes for women. The conflict between Amos and Dixon built steadily through the fall of 1931, with Correll and Gosden developing the plot slowly and gradually, allowing Dixon to ingratiate himself first with Aunt Lillian, and then through that connection attempting to develop a relationship with her niece Ruby Taylor. Amos was suspicious of Dixon's true motives from the beginning, but Andy allowed himself to be taken in by the newcomer's smooth talk and grandiose posturing until the partners found themselves nearly torn asunder by Dixon's machinations.

Finally, in November 1931, investigations begun by the Kingfish at Amos's suggestion revealed that Dixon was in fact a petty hoodlum from Philadelphia, who had come to New York with several henchmen to continue his criminal activities. Armed with these facts, Amos was able to abort Dixon's relationship with Aunt Lillian—an action that prompted an unexpected confrontation. Visiting the taxicab office one afternoon when he was sure that Amos would be there alone, Dixon finally revealed his true nature in a violent assault on the man who had foiled his plans.

> Jack---Somebody around here has been talkin' about Philadelphia, and they got a lot o' news around this town that I wasn't on the square in Philly, an' I think you're the guy that started that.
>
> Amos---WAIT A MINUTE --- Now, don't hit me Misteh Dixon.
>
> Jack---You heard me.
>
> Amos---Don't hit me now Mr. Dixon. I ain't goin' fight yo'.
>
> Jack---Well, yo' know what I do with guys like you that can't keep their trap shut?
>
> Amos---Nosah.
>
> Jack---(smack) That's whut I do wid 'em. (smack) An' that's whut I do wid 'em. Now if you'll git up off that floor I'll knock yo' down again. And you little shrimp, if you kin hear what I'm sayin', let that learn yo' to keep your trap shut. Now, lay there. And if you ain't got enough I'll come back over here and give yo' a couple more o' those [Episode 1150, 11/28/31].

Amos lay unconscious on the floor of the taxicab office for hours, until Brother Crawford discovered him and carried him across the street to Madam Queen's Beauty Shop for first aid. From there, Amos was taken to Harlem Hospital for X-rays, but to the chagrin of his friends he refused to report the assault to the police, insisting instead that he would take care of the situation in his own way. A week went by, and Amos's friends wondered what he meant by that remark.

Then, suddenly, on a cold December afternoon, word spread through the neighborhood that Jack Dixon was dead—murdered—his body found lying by the banks of the Harlem River with a 32-caliber slug in his back. And this news was rapidly followed by the greatest shock of all for Amos's friends and for millions of listeners, as two brusquely unsympathetic detectives took Amos into custody for the crime. Taken to police headquarters, thrown into an interrogation room, and denied sleep or food, Amos was relentlessly questioned for two days by the police, but he held fast to his claims of innocence.

> Man----Yo' know we've got proof that you said that you was goin' to get even with him, or you said you were gonna get him, an' you got him alright, but buddy, you're gonna pay for it.
>
> Amos---I never said I was gonna git him dat way though Mister---I never even thought o' dat.

Man----You love this girl of yours, don't yo'?

Amos---Yessah, I love her better dan I do my own life.

Man----He tried to take her away from you, didn't he?

Amos---Yessah.

Man----Well, if yo' love her better than you do your own life, you'd be willin' to do anything to help her.

Amos---Yessah.

Man----And you were jealous, an' you killed a man, and I want you to tell me.

Amos---I didn't do it.

Man----We've had you for two days and we're gonna keep you here for two more weeks if you don't talk.

Amos---I'll tell yo' anything you ast me Mister. I'se just so tired an' weak right now though dat I can't hardly keep my eyes open [Episode 1159, 12/9/31].

As Amos languished in jail, locked up with another accused killer, his friends rallied to raise the money for his bail. Mr. Taylor arrived from Chicago, offering to put up his property as security, and Pop Johnson agreed to do likewise. As the efforts to help Amos went on, his friends took turns visiting him at the jail in an effort to raise his spirits.

John---Well, I want you to know, Amos, that everybody is pulling for you.

Amos---Well, dat cert'ny is nice of 'em brother Crawford ---- I guess I need a lot o' people pullin' fo' me.

John---Ever since this thing happened, my wife is been very unhappy.

Amos---Well, thank ev'ybody fo' bein' so nice to me, will yo'?

John---Yes, I want you to know that we're all going to do everything we can to help you an' if Ruby's father can't get enough real estate owners to go your bail I think I can call on a friend of mine up the country who would do most anything I would ask him to do [Episode 1162, 12/12/31].

Finally released on $15,000 bond, Amos immediately secured the services of a well-regarded local attorney and began preparation for his trial. The case moved rapidly through arraignment and indictment—and by December 17, the trial was underway. From the beginning, it was evident that the prosecution held all the cards, and Amos's friends admitted to being worried about his chances of beating the charges, with Andy and the Kingfish venturing in hushed voices to wonder if, perhaps, in a desperate situation, even the gentle Amos might be capable of such a horrifying act.

Although much of the story line had a precedent in a 1929 sequence which led to Amos being falsely convicted of grand larceny, listeners were outraged by the murder charge, and complaints flooded into the Chicago offices of the Pepsodent Company, including threats of a boycott of Pepsodent products by the National Parent Teachers Association if Correll and Gosden dared to allow Amos to be convicted. Police officers were also outraged but for a different reason. The frank portrayal of Amos's brutal interrogation drew a formal complaint to NBC and Pepsodent from the National Association of Chiefs of Police. In the wake of this unexpected furor, the performers were summoned in mid–December to the office of Lord and Thomas president Albert Lasker. "The country's gone mad!" raged the beleaguered executive, and Correll and Gosden were told, bluntly, to find a way out of the story line.[8]

Finally, two days before Christmas, the trial reached its climax. Amos's friends clustered outside the courtroom, deeply worried about the fate of their friend. But the outcome was nothing anyone could have anticipated, as Correll and Gosden gave the story an audacious twist ending.

> Judge--Quiet in this courtroom please. Has the jury in this case reached a verdict?
>
> Foreman--Yes, your honor, we have.
>
> Judge--Will you hand the verdict to the court clerk. Now I will ask the court clerk to read the verdict. Mr. Clerk, will you read the verdict.
>
> (short pause)
>
> Clerk--We the jury in this case, find the defendant, Amos Jones ------
>
> (Alarm clock)
>
> Andy---Amos --- Amos ---- cut off dat 'larm clock.
>
> Amos---Awa ---- Andy!
>
> Andy---Git yo' arm from 'round my neck. An' cut off dat clock.
>
> Amos---Andy, where is we?
>
> Andy---It's 6:30 in de mornin' an' you is been kickin' me all night long.
>
> Amos---Andy, where is we?
>
> Andy---Amos, is you losin' yo' mind? Cut dat clock off. I'll cut dat thing off.
>
> Amos---Andy! I can't believe it!
>
> Andy---Listen, I ain't been 'sleep all night long, an' you is been kickin' me.
>
> Amos---Andy, I just had de worst dream of anything yo' ever heerd of in yo' life ... [Episode 1171, 12/23/31].

By snapping the story to a sudden finish—at the precise moment of the greatest possible tension—Correll and Gosden satisfied Lasker's demands for a clean ending to the story line without shattering the program's continuity. Whether they had intended this ending all along—or whether it was indeed an emergency expedient—will never be positively known. But the memory of Amos's ordeal became a part of the collective consciousness of Depression-era Americans and for the rest of their careers, Correll and Gosden found themselves apologizing for the "trick" ending. "It was a cheap thing to do," they admitted to an interviewer years later, "but we had to make the whole thing a dream. We had no other way out."[9]

Throughout the run of the *Amos 'n' Andy* serial, Correll and Gosden kept in mind an important truth: the secret to keeping a loyal following in broadcasting is to never wear out your audience. So it was that their heavier, melodramatic story lines alternated with light, humorous sequences. The comedy in the original *Amos 'n' Andy* often grew out of Andy's exploration of the fads and foibles of the day, creating sequences in which Andy threw himself wholeheart into whatever new trend had caught the interest of America at large: as, for example, his 1932 exploration of the Depression-era craze for personal advertisements with "matrimonial services."

> Light--All dese letters from girls dat wanna git married --- I can't git over it.
>
> Andy---Well, I got a few in dis pile right heah -- dese is from people dat wanna sell me diff'ent things --- dis fellow heah sells weddin' rings ---- dis fellow heah in dis letteh, if I send him 10 cents, he'll send me a book, de art of makin' love --- just think' o dat, it don't cost but a dime. Heah's a letteh from a --- de man says "send 50 cents fo' a bottle of our hair dye" --- den I got two-three heah from people, "how to keep from gittin' bald-headed." Heah's a funny letteh dat I just got dis mornin'. "Dear Friend number 972---"
>
> Light--Is dis one from a gal?
>
> Andy---No, dis is from a fellow heah -- listen to it -- he says "Dis ain't no letteh from no dame --- see --- I wanna sell you a hoss --- if you is got enough money to git married on, you is got enough money to buy a hoss ---- if you ain't got enough money fo' both, take my advice an' buy my hoss ---- I got married once --- I had $300 --- in two months I was busted, see --- so we quit --- I saves up my money an' buys a hoss -- a --- I starts in de hoss bizness ---- I answehs adds in de matrimony papeh an' sells men hosses --- take my advice pal -- don't git married, buy a hoss --- a hoss is a man's best friend --- I kin sell you a hoss fo' $95 ---- if you don't like hosses, do you wanna buy a used car or a good dog --- a dog is a man's best friend ---- so long pal --- let's heah from you ---- E.T. Harrison P.S. -- de hoss is a betteh buy dan de dog or de car, an' a hoss is a man's best friend."
>
> Light---You goin' buy de hoss?
>
> Andy---I'd like to buy dat hoss but I ain't got de money right now.
>
> Light--Whut would yo' do wid him Mr. Andy?
>
> Andy---I'd keep him in de back yard.
>
> Light--Well, whut would yo' use him fo'?
>
> Andy---Yeh, dat's right, ain't it? Yeh, come to think about it I don't need no hoss. I betteh git me some heavy underwear befo' I git a hoss.
>
> Light--Yessah, dat's de best thing [Episode 1416, 10/4/32].

This scene offers a prime example of the subtle, character-based comedy Correll and Gosden did best. There are no distinct jokes or punchlines, and yet the scene flows along as a droll parody of a Depression-era craze, drawing its humor from the audacity of E.T. Harrison's direct-mail salesmanship, Andy's utter lack of sales resistance, and from the clever way in which Lightning gently steers Andy away from making a potentially expensive mistake without ever directly challenging him. The scene illustrates the subtle personality traits with which Correll and Gosden endowed their characters. Lightning's perceptiveness in immediately sizing up the foolishness of the proposition stands in sharp contrast with Andy's usual image of him as a dull-witted lackey, but Lightning's desire to avoid confrontations at all costs prevents him from directly pointing out that Andy has no need for a horse. In a similar situation, the more assertive Amos would have confronted Andy directly—even though such a direct attack would have wounded Andy's fragile pride and would most likely have caused him to go ahead and buy the horse simply to prove Amos wrong. In presenting this brief comic scene Correll and Gosden succeed both in provoking chuckles and in demonstrating that they thoroughly understand the psychological motivations of their characters. Such subtlety contrasts with the broad "who was dat lady I seen you wid?" comedy of minstrelsy and even with the simple, wordplay-based humor of Correll and Gosden's earliest scripts.

Correll and Gosden were also gifted in the use of imagery as a complement to situational humor. Well aware of the power of the radio "mind's eye," and without the crutch of elaborate sound effects, musical settings, or descriptive narration, the performers skillfully used dialogue alone to guide and shape the visualizations of their audience: making their listeners full partners in the creation of the comedy.

> Amos---Well, I was heah at de garage dis mornin' an' a truck stopped out in front, an' I went out to see whut de man wanted an' he had a wooden crate on de truck an' he had a trained seal in de crate.
>
> Andy---Oh, I forgot to tell yo' dat de agent Kalinkowitz is goin' send de trained seal up heah, an' we goin' git a bath tub fo' de seal an' we goin' let de seal stay in de garage --- yo' know, dat's de seal we goin' use in de act.
>
> Amos---Yeh, well, dem plans is done been changed.
>
> Andy---Whut yo' mean, dey been changed?
>
> Amos---I told de man dat we ain't goin' keep de seal heah.
>
> Andy---You told de man whut?
>
> Amos---I told de man we wouldn't let de seal IN de garage --- told him not to even take de seal off de truck --- he started to argue wid me, I told him "I don't care, you kin argue wid me, but dat seal ain't comin' in de garage"— he called up de man dat owned de seal an' I talked to him on de phone.
>
> Andy---Listen Amos, you just messin' up ev'ything --- dat makes MO' trouble fo' me.
>
> Amos---You ain't goin' keep no seal in heah son. We done had a cow in de garage, but you ain't goin' git no seal in heah.

Andy---Dat is one o' de greatest trained seals in de world --- my agent, Mr. Kalinkowitz wanted me to git familiar wid de seal.

Amos---Well, you go someplace else an' git familiar wid de seal [Episode 1780, 2/7/34].

Throughout the run of *Amos 'n' Andy,* plots grew out of vivid characterization and as the series progressed, the characters grew and changed. Andy Brown gradually lost the more overt aspects of his arrogant, know-it-all attitude, as he came to realize through sad experience that he didn't know it all. But his head could still be turned by appeals to his vanity, and he never stopped dreaming the dreams of hitting it big that had brought him North in the first place. Andy might have seemed impractical at best—and insufferable at worst—but Charles Correll's carefully textured performance gave Andy an edge of real, human vulnerability that always seemed to bubble beneath his swaggering façade. Listeners soon came to realize that Andy's bravado stemmed from a deep sense of personal insecurity because he was afraid to acknowledge his own failings, ashamed of who he was and where he had come from, and envious of those who were more accomplished than he was Andy, therefore, sought refuge in an elaborate fantasy world where he wielded power and authority as Andrew H. Brown, president.

Andy---Listen Amos --- de trouble wid you is --- you think de man down at de bank is got mo' sense den I is. I knows things. I'se doin' dis fo' you as much as I is fo' myself. I'se just as big as anybody is.

Amos---Yo' want me to tell yo' sumpin'?

Andy---Go ahead.

Amos---De trouble wid you is Andy --- ev'vy since you was a little boy -- ever since I done known yo', you is done a lot o' talk --- even de boys down in Georgia dat you used to play around wid --- dey used to listen to you talk an' den laugh at yo' after you was gone. You is de kind o' fellow dat thinks you is sumpin' dat yo' ain't. No matter whut somebody else tell yo', you think dey is wrong. Now dat man at de bank is done been down dere all his life. He knows more about de bankin' bizness in one minute dan you'll EVER know. De thing fo' you to do is to listen to somebody sometime an' you'll git a-long better. Just 'cause you is president o' de Fresh Air Taxicab comp'ny don't think dat you is de president of de United States --- an' de sooner you find dat out, de better it's goin' be fo' ev'vybody.

Andy---I'se re-gusted [Episode 73, 6/18/28].

Deep down, Andy realized that his bluffing fooled no one—not even himself—but still he clung to the pretense, even when it opened him to easy exploitation by others who recognized and were only too willing to take advantage of his vulnerabilities. In Harlem, no more than in Chicago, none of Andy's extravagant bluster could earn him status in the community—and just as his long-ago Georgia playmates had dismissed him as a joke, so too did those who now surrounded him in the North.

In New York, as he had been in Chicago, and as he had been in Georgia, Andy remained, in his own words, "a square peg in a wooden hole." Despite constant disappointment, despite constant embarrassment, Andy continued to make claims he couldn't possibly support in a desperate effort to avoid having to face his reality. But there were rare moments of introspection where, for just a fleeting moment, he allowed the mask to drop.

> Amos---Yo' know Andy, if you would just say to yo'self dat yo' goin' put away one or two dollars a week, pretty soon you'd have some money, if you'd put it away.
>
> Andy---Yo' see Amos, when I got money, I don't figgeh dat I goin' eveh git nowhere savin' two dollahs. I figgeh I gotta have a big hunk o' money 'fore I kin git stahted.
>
> Amos---Dat's where yo' wrong though Andy.
>
> Andy---I know, but den on de otheh hand, it just seems like ev'ybody's afteh me fo' money. Ev'ytime de Kingfish walk in heah, I KNOW he got some big deal.
>
> Amos---I know I ain't got no sense Andy, but I tell yo' how I figger. De hardest thing in de world to say is "No."
>
> Andy---Well, if yo' tell somebody yo' can't do it, dey goin' think yo' cheap, an' dat's whut I don't want nobody to think, yo' see?
>
> Amos---It's alright to be a good fellow, but if yo' ain't got it, whut's de use o' tellin' 'em dat you is?
>
> Andy---Yeh, yo' right Amos. Yo' know, sometime when I'se by myself, I git to thinkin' an' I feel like dat I just done made a mess of ev'ything [Episode 755, 8/22/30].

The more hollow Andy's bluster, the more empty his boasts, the more listeners could see and sympathize with the essential sadness at the core of his personality. And yet, even in his frequent humblings at the hands of more polished, more successful rivals, Correll and Gosden never allowed Andy to become a figure of simple ridicule for the audience. Even in defeat, Andy Brown kept his personal dignity.

> Amos---Is yo' talked to G. Sampson Smith Jr. today?
>
> Andy---He went out a while ago, an' as he passed de desk he says "have my rooms cleaned up while I is out," an' I think he called me "boy."
>
> Amos---Maybe he didn't recollect yo' face when he looked at yo'.
>
> Andy---I don't want nobody callin' me "boy, do dis an' boy, do dat." My name is Andrew H. Brown [Episode 1392, 9/6/32].

Amos, meanwhile, emerged as the program's Everyman figure—a compassionate, occasionally heroic individual who epitomized decency, common sense and a gritty determination to overcome any obstacle life tossed into his path. Amos's father, a coal miner named Elijah Jones, was killed in a mine accident when he was very young, and his mother Sarah had been forced to work as a domestic before her untimely death left her only son to fend for himself in the world. In a 1934 episode, Amos recalled his tragic Georgia childhood in vivid detail.

> Amos---...We lived in a wood house wid 3 rooms. De house had a front porch an' a back porch. My papa, as well as I kin remember, was thin an' when I knowed him his hair was turnin' gray. He was not very tall, but he always looked tall to me because I was so little. We had one tree in de front yard dat was a big tree an' I remember one peach tree in de back yard. Dere was a little fence goin' 'round de front yard made out of pickets an' we had a high whitewashed fence around de back yard. We used to burn coal in de house when we could git it but when we couldn't git coal we burned wood.... I remember dat we had some straw carpet dat come in rolls but we didn't have it anywhere 'cept in de room where we used to eat. You ast me whut kind o' bed I used to sleep in. I did not have a bed but I used to sleep on a mattress on de floor as well as I kin remember. I do not remember much about my mama, 'cept dat people told me dat she was sweet to me an' I is always been sorry dat she ain't wid me now. She died right after papa went away. De reason I didn't know her better was because I think she worked for some people near Atlanta an' she only come home on her day off each week [Episode 1784, 2/13/34].

Without family, without formal schooling, young Amos refused to be beaten down by his childhood tragedies. He taught himself to read and write, applied himself to any job he could find, and eventually served in the Army during World War I. Though he might have seemed timid and deferential at first glance, Amos was far from a submissive, stereotypical Uncle Tom figure. Although he constantly battled feelings of insecurity and inadequacy that in their own way ran as deep as Andy's, Amos's strategy for coping with those feelings sharply contrasted with his partner's. Amos refused to allow his insecurities to dominate his life, and his soft-spoken demeanor concealed a steely determination to control his own destiny. Amos was fully able to rise above his inner conflicts and take a firm stand for his principles—and could only be pushed so far by Andy, by the Kingfish, or by anyone else, before fighting back.

> Amos---Well, whut we wanna do is just drop dis whole bizness. Now wait a minute 'fore yo' start talkin'. I just wanna tell yo' whut I done found out. I done been over an' talked to Susie's mama, an' Susie's mama told me in front of a fellow dat was wid me dat Susie ain't been sick --- dat you told her to go to bed.
>
> Jack---Say, where'd you heah all dat foolishness?
>
> Amos---...Now you done spent some time on dis thing writin' letters an' all dat mess -- an' heah's $5.00. We ain't got no bizness givin' yo' nuthin' but we goin' give you $5.00 an' den we goin' call ev'ything square.
>
> Jack---Now, just a minute ---

> Amos---Now wait a minute --- lemme finish --- now heah's de $5.00. Now if you don't wanna take dat an' call ev'ything square, just say so 'cause I been talkin' to a policeman an' he say dat if you don't wanna do dat to let him know an' he'll talk to yo' hisself. Now, dere's de five --- just lemme know whut yo' wanna do [Episode 673, 5/17/30].

Though Amos and Andy often bickered, both partners realized that their deep friendship transcended any differences they might have—and even in situations where he might have profited from walking out on Andy, Amos insisted on putting their friendship first.

> Gwin---You ain't never goin' git nowhere 'long as you is wid him. Now, you ast yo' wife if I ain't right.
>
> Amos---Well, dat's de funny part of it --- I talked it over wid Ruby last night, an' she kind-a understands me an' Andy, an' she knows dat we is close to each other an' all dat stuff --- I don't know --- well, I just don't know how I KIN bust up wid him.
>
> Gwin---Amos, he is holdin' you back [Episode 2270, 2/26/36].

Amos's relationship with Ruby Taylor gave his life a solid focus and a firm anchor; it provided the inner strength he needed to overcome any obstacle. With strength, integrity, and determination, Amos kept that focus for seven years, even as adverse circumstances repeatedly forced the couple into involuntary separations, as when Ruby's employer accepted an appointment as the head of a "colored hospital" in Virginia and asked her to accompany him South as a student nurse. For nearly a year, Amos and Ruby were apart, but even under such trying circumstances, their relationship endured and their love matured.

Finally, in the fall of 1935, with the economy in an upswing, the couple decided that they were finally ready to take the step they'd been planning since 1928. On Christmas night, 1935, with Andy as best man, Madam Queen as matron of honor, and Mr. Taylor giving away the bride, Amos and Ruby stood before a minister in a small Harlem church as their closest friends, and 20 million listeners, heard them exchange their wedding vows.

> Preacher--(continues) Will you, Amos, take this woman, Ruby, to be your wedded wife, to live together after the ordinance of marriage? Will you love her, comfort her, honor and keep her, in sickness and in health, in prosperity and adversity, as long as you both shall live?
>
> Amos---I will.
>
> Preacher--Will you, Ruby, take this man, Amos, to be your wedded husband, to live together after the ordinance of marriage? Will you love him, comfort him, honor him, and keep him, in sickness and in health, in prosperity and adversity, so long as you both shall live?
>
> Ruby---I will.

Preacher--Who giveth this woman to be married to this man?

Taylor--I do.

Preacher--What pledge do you offer that you will fulfill these vows? (softly, to Amos) The ring.

Amos---(to Andy) Andy, gimme de ring.

Andy---Yeh --- (nervous) Wait a minute --- I had it in heah --- oh, heah 'tis.

Preacher--What pledge do you offer that you will fulfill these vows?

Amos---(to Preacher) Dis ring.

Preacher--Do you, Ruby, accept this token of the same?

Ruby---I do.

AN AMOS 'N' ANDY RADIO EPISODE
"Amos' Wedding"

The Peposdent Company distributed over 1,000,000 copies of Correll and Gosden's 12/25/35 script to listeners who wrote in following the broadcast requesting it. The cover recycles old publicity photos from *Check and Double Check*.

Preacher--You will then, Amos, place it on the fourth finger of the left hand. You will now join right hands. These two persons having solemnly promised to live together in marriage according to the laws of this land, and having declared the same by joining their right hands, and by the giving and receiving of the marriage ring, I, by virtue of authority vested in me by the State, and in the name of our Father in heaven, pronounce them husband and wife. And whom Love hath joined together, let no man put asunder [Episode 2225, 12/25/35].

Amos and Ruby settled into married life, moving into a small but comfortable Harlem flat. Though money was always tight, the couple faced the future with confidence—and when their daughter Arbadella was born in October 1936, their friends in Harlem—along with millions of listeners—shared their joy.

Andy---Listen son --- I want you to know dat I don't care whut otheh people tell yo' --- whut I tellin' yo' now is right from my heart ---- I is just as happy as you is, an' I want yo' to know how glad I is dat ev'ything is alright --- I want yo' to know dat I goin' love dat baby as much as you do.

Amos---Well dat's sweet Andy.

A HISTORY OF AMOS 'N' ANDY

Things You Never Knew About Them Before

We are very happy to give you this history of Amos 'n' Andy. For, after reading it, we feel sure you will agree that the life story of these two young men is an intensely interesting one.

Freeman Gosden, now well known to millions of radio listeners as "Amos Jones," was born in Richmond, Virginia, on May 5, 1899. He began as a tobacco salesman, later sold automobiles. After the war he met "Andy," Charles Correll, with whom he became associated in the promotion and production of amateur theatricals.

Charles Correll, equally well known to radio millions as "Andrew H. Brown," was born in Peoria, Illinois, on February 3, 1890. He began as a newsboy, learned the bricklaying trade from his father, played the piano in moving picture theatres, then became a producer of amateur theatricals... meeting Freeman Gosden in Durham, North Carolina, while thus engaged.

After a short radio career on WEBH (one of Chicago's pioneer stations)... not as the now famous blackface comedians, but as Correll and Gosden, a vocal harmony team... in January, 1925, the boys were offered a job at WGN, Chicago, where they created "Sam and Henry"... the forerunner of their present act. This, incidentally, was the first radio work for which they were actually paid!

Three years later, on March 28, 1928, Correll and Gosden joined station WMAQ, Chicago, where they brought to life "Amos 'n' Andy." In the summer of 1929, The Pepsodent Co. decided that "Amos 'n' Andy" should be broadcast nationally, so they assumed sponsorship of the program beginning Aug. 19th, 1929, over the National Broadcasting Company network. A happy association that has been in existence for over six years!

It should be noted here that "Amos 'n' Andy" was the first 15-minute program broadcast and was also radio's first continued story with an episode broadcast nightly. In fact, their programs are now broadcast twice every night except Saturday and Sunday to assure all listeners a convenient listening hour. The first program, heard only on eastern stations, is on the air at 7:00 P.M. Eastern Time. The second broadcast is on at 10:00 P.M. Central Time which is also heard in the Rocky Mountains at 9:00 P.M. Mountain Time and on the West Coast at 8:00 P.M., Pacific Time.

Mr. Correll and Mr. Gosden write every line they speak. The average episode consists of about 1500 words. Their preparation is a fifty-fifty proposition, but it is no over-worked "Amos" who sits down at the typewriter to prepare the next story. It is "Andy" who does this, while "Amos" paces back and forth trying lines and dictating the dialogue. The only existing, complete set of episodes is in bound volumes closely guarded by "Amos 'n' Andy."

The one point to remember, however, about these episodes is that no one but "Amos 'n' Andy" themselves and the copyright office in Washington has ever before seen them! So you can see what a real treat it is to have a sample episode like this for your very own!

The boys themselves also take the parts of all the characters they introduce. For your information here is a list showing which ones each man does:

"Amos"— Freeman Gosden	"Andy"— Charles Correll
Kingfish	Henry Van Porter
Lightnin'	Landlord
Brother Crawford	And such straight characters
Prince Ali Bendo	as policeman, judge, etc.

The boys devote many hours a day to careful study of these characters. And, in their broadcasts no audience is permitted to observe them. For the world they have created around the "Fresh Air Taxicab Company, Incorpolated," the grocery store and their many other enterprises is so real to them that they must guard against any diverting, outside influence that might spoil the illusion. This devotion, no doubt, has been a great factor in helping "Amos 'n' Andy" attract the largest regular listening audience radio has ever known!

Many people have asked about the "Amos 'n' Andy" theme song. And the boys themselves say this melody, even after all these years, seems more lovely every time they hear it. It is called "The Perfect Song" — and was originally used in D. W. Griffith's moving picture, "The Birth of A Nation."

The premium script booklet also included this not-entirely-accurate miniature biography of Correll and Gosden prepared by the Lord and Thomas staff. However, the reference to Correll and Gosden carefully guarding their scripts from outsiders is quite correct.

8. Tales to Tell 113

> Andy---I know sometimes dat I say things dat you think ain't got no sense or no feelin' or nuthin', but right now, inside o' me, I is so happy fo' you dat I don't know whut to do [Episode 2440, 10/21/36].

Amos's tender Christmas Eve explanation of the Lord's Prayer at Arbadella's bedside, first heard in 1940 and repeated every Christmas Eve through 1954 may have been the program's most famous moment—and for Freeman Gosden, the annual presentation of the segment was an intensely personal experience. "Figuring the huge size of audience each year, it is probably safe to conclude that more people heard Amos' description of the Lord's Prayer than that of any one else in the world. There is no question that he felt this was his proudest lifetime achievement," recalls Freeman F. Gosden, Jr. "We would go to the studio and watch the show from the client's booth. Then Dad would bring the recording home and after dinner play it over and over again until midnight, with tears in his eyes."[10]

Even today, listening to Gosden's heartfelt reading of Amos's plea for everyday human kindness, set to the music of Alfred Hay Malotte, emphasizes just how different *Amos 'n' Andy* was from traditional "blackface" entertainment. Unlike the stereotype of the matriarchal broken home usually applied to mass-culture depictions of the African American family, the Jones family as portrayed in *Amos 'n' Andy* was solidly intact, built on a strong foundation of mutual commitment between Amos and Ruby—and Gosden's "Lord's Prayer" scene remains, more than six decades after its first presentation, one of the most powerful images ever offered in the popular media of the bond of love between a father and his child.

> Amos---...Now, de first line of de Lord's Prayer is dis: Our Father which art in Heaven. Dat means father of all that is good where no wrong can dwell. Now de next line is --- Hallowed be thy name. Now, that means, darling, that we should love and respect all that is good --- Thy Kingdom come, thy will be done in earth as it is in Heaven. That means, darling, as we clean our hearts of all hate and selfishness and fill our hearts with love, the good, the true and the beautiful, then this earth will be exactly like Heaven.
>
> Arbadella---Oh. That would be wonderful, Daddy.
>
> Amos---Then it says: Give us this day our daily bread. Now, dat means to feed our hearts and minds with kindness, love and courage, which will make us strong fo' our daily tasks. And then it says --- And forgive us our debts as we forgive our debtors. Yo' remember the Golden Rule?
>
> Arbadella --- Oh, yes sir.
>
> Amos --- Well, that means that we must keep the Golden Rule and do unto others as we would want them to do unto us. And then it says: And lead us not into temptation, but deliver us from evil. Dat means, my darlin', to ask God to help us do and to see and to think right so that we will neither be led or tempted by anything that is bad.
>
> Arbadella --- Uh huh.

Amos---An' then it says --- For thine is the kingdom, the power and the glory forever. Amen. That means, darlin', dat all de world and ev'ything that's in it belongs to God's kingdom—ev'ything—mommy, your daddy, your little brother, your grandma, you and ev'ybody. And, as we know that and act as if we know it, that, my darlin', is the real spirit of Christmas.[11]

9. BLACK AND WHITE?

"In 'blacking up,' you become a minstrel. You're not a normal human being. But these fellows in our radio show were human beings."
—Charles Correll

QUESTIONS OF RACIAL interpretation are inevitable in considering *Amos 'n' Andy*. Viewed solely through the lens of racial identity politics, no portrayal of black characters by any white authors—be they Correll and Gosden, DuBose Heyward, Thomas Nelson Page, Joel Chandler Harris, Mark Twain, Harriet Beecher Stowe or William Shakespeare—can ever offer an authentic construction of "blackness." But even acknowledging the inevitable cultural inauthenticity of their work, what were Correll and Gosden *trying* to do? What sort of impression were Correll and Gosden hoping to create in the minds of their listeners? How did the creators of the program see their own characters—and how did they want those characters to be perceived? Is there really any difference between *Amos 'n' Andy* and the caricatures of blackface minstrelsy? These questions can only be answered through a careful examination of the work itself.

Correll and Gosden set themselves apart from old-fashioned blackface early in their radio careers by deliberately avoiding "joke" comedy and by constructing their program on a foundation of solid characterization. This technique was a complete break from minstrelsy, with its interchangeable burnt-cork caricatures and its emphasis on snappy punchlines. Amos, Andy and their friends were distinctive personalities who experienced a full range of emotions—and indeed, in the works of Correll and Gosden, characters were rarely what they seemed to be at first glance. If the essence of stereotyping is the use of unchanging, generic personality types, of cardboard figures with no inner motivation for their actions—then the characters of *Amos 'n' Andy* were not stereotypes. A generic blackface character portrayed as "lazy and shiftless" for no reason other than the fact that he is a blackface character is a stereotype. Andy Brown, a three-dimensional figure whose behavior grew out of deep and well-defined personal insecurities, is not. While it must be acknowledged that many of Andy's traits do overlap certain common stereotypes, it is equally important to note that his character flaws are consistently presented as the personal shortcomings of Andrew H. Brown, stemming from his own particular inner weaknesses and not from "racial" traits. The same point can be made in considering the Kingfish, or Lightning, or any other *Amos 'n' Andy* character whose traits may seem at first glance to be a mere perpetuation of various minstrel clichés. In every case, Correll and Gosden gave their characters depth and substance beyond stereotyping.

It should also be noted that none of the characters in *Amos 'n' Andy* are rigidly defined by stereotypical behavior patterns. All of the characters in the series react to different situations in different ways, their behavior evolving with changes in circumstances. Amos is generally calm and level-headed—but everyday pressures occasionally push him into making significant errors of judgment. Amos and Brother Crawford both try to rein in their tempers, but occasionally they explode. Andy will sometimes step back to take a detached look at his life, to realize that most of his problems are his own fault. The Kingfish will from time to time stop battling with his wife long enough to acknowledge that deep down he really loves her. Lightning will on occasion set aside his distaste for confrontation to stand up for a principle. While the basic outlines of the characters remain the same from episode to episode, from story line to story line, there is also much subtle personal evolution as the characters cope with the pressures of everyday life. The changeless and carefree Sambo figure, a staple of minstrelsy, is nowhere to be found in *Amos 'n' Andy*.

Nor were all of *Amos 'n' Andy*'s characters of a single type—or even of a few types. Over the years, the *Amos 'n' Andy* cast portrayed all kinds of people that lived all kinds of lives. This was a notable rarity in American popular fiction, which usually relegated black characters to faceless servant roles or used them, as in the dialect stories of Octavus Roy Cohen, to broadly burlesque the conventions of the white world.[1] A common trope of academic discussion of *Amos 'n' Andy* is the assertion that the series presented the only significant representation of black characters on radio during the 1930s, but this is far from true. Minstrel-oriented characters like George Fields and Johnnie Welsh's "Honeyboy and Sassafrass," Pick Malone and Pat Padgett's "Molasses 'n' January," Katherine Tift-Jones's "Calliope" and Tess Gardella's "Aunt Jemima" were very much in evidence on network radio during the first half of the decade, alongside a veritable army of blackface comedy teams at the local level. Genuine African American performers like the comedy teams of Flournoy Miller and Aubrey Lyles, Ernest Whitman and Eddie Green, comedian Eddie Anderson, and the actor Clarence Muse were also featured on network programs during the 1930s—all of them portrayed a variety of stereotyped characters. Even an attemptedly straightforward dramatic series, the 1933 CBS serial "John Henry—Black River Giant," dwelled on the "exotic" nature of nineteenth-century Southern blacks, stressing "authentic voodoo lore."[2]

A prime example of how early radio tended to portray "real" African Americans—as opposed to characterizations offered in an acknowledged minstrel-show format—can be found in the earliest surviving recording of a broadcast to feature genuine African American talent. On May 15, 1928, the *Eveready Hour* program, presented by the National Carbon Company over the NBC Red network, dedicated its entire broadcast to a portrayal of the black inhabitants of "Needham's Grove," a small Southern town.[3] Headlining the cast was the famous Hall Johnson Choir, and members of that organization apparently took at least some of the dramatic speaking roles in the feature. The program opens on a church service, with the choir offering a rousing rendition of "Amazing Grace" and the preacher delivering a semi-humorous sermon. "De lion an' de lamb might lie down togeteh," declares the minister, "but when dey gets up, *where* is de lamb?" Sneaking out of the service to avoid the collection plate are two field hands identified as Sam and Mucus, who differ little in their manner or their material from typical minstrel end men.

> SAM: Dere's brotheh Low Down Brown -- so fulla corn likkah he jes' can't navigate!
>
> MUCUS: Well, he sells it! An' dat's one o' yo' main reasons fo' bein' a party at dis grand occasion!
>
> SAM: Yo' know I don' drink anything!
>
> MUCUS: Dat's jes' whut yo' do drink -- anything! Adams' Foot-Ease, hair oil, shoe polish -- anything!

Sam and Mucus soon encounter Albert Smith from New York City who is boasting, in a voice nearly free of dialect, to a group of women about the wonders to be found in that faraway place called Harlem. As Albert talks, a musical transition takes the listener to a typical Harlem nightclub, where blues singer Martha Copeland is introduced to perform a series of three musical selections in authentic low-down style. After her performance, the scene shifts to Albert and his girlfriend Sally at a nearby table.

> ALBERT: Sally honey, who is that fellow coming toward this table? His face is very familiar.
>
> SALLY: Oh my God, Al! That's Slick Wilson -- and he's drunk! Please, Al, don't say anything to make him mad. He's a bad actor when he's...
>
> SLICK: Now lissen here Sally, 'tain't no use try to hide because I see yo'! I been lookin' all over Harlem for yo', an' I find yo' jus' where I 'spected -- with some other guy!
>
> SALLY: I know, Slick. But I'm through with your games! He's a friend of mine from down home -- and he's willing to give me a break!
>
> SLICK: Oh, you're quittin', hey? Well get dis on yo' mind, ol' gal -- when you beginnin' to quit me, I jus' beginnin' to go wid you! Get up outa here befo' I break yo' jaw!
>
> ALBERT: No you don't hit no woman...
>
> SLICK: Whatta you got to do....
>
> (SOUND OF STRUGGLE)
>
> SALLY: Look out Albert—he's got a knife!

> SLICK: Yes! An' I'll use it too!
>
> VOICE (in background): Now put that gun down! What do yo' mean!
>
> ALBERT: That's what I mean!
>
> (GUNSHOT, SCREAMS)
>
> (MUSIC UP TO CLIMAX)

The *Eveready Hour* broadcast encapsulates the images of African Americans most commonly held by whites during the 1920s—the simple-minded, ambitionless Southerners, and the aggressive, hedonistic Northerners—who, despite a veneer of cultural advancement over their Southern kin, are hard-drinking brutes reduced to violence on the slightest provocation. For whites who held these views, black communities such as those found in Harlem or the South Side of Chicago were strange, exotic places populated by an even more exotic, dangerous race of people.

Alongside these other portrayals, the work of Correll and Gosden offered a sharp break from past conventions. In its depictions of both the South Side and of Harlem, *Amos 'n' Andy* presented a picture of a well-rounded, self-sufficient black community—a world free of exploitative exoticism and a world with distinct echoes of the vibrant Jackson Ward that Freeman Gosden had known as a child. That the central characters happened to occupy the lower end of the economic scale in no way prevented the series from acknowledging its upper levels, in pointed contrast to the various petty hustlers who frequented the lodge hall of the Mystic Knights of the Sea. Although the community portrayed in *Amos 'n' Andy* was unquestionably an idealization—for example, the performers failed to accurately portray the class-driven distaste with which many educated middle-class blacks viewed newly arrived Southerners like Amos and Andy—the mere fact that Correll and Gosden acknowledged the existence of a layered urban black community stands as a clear break from the minstrel past. Characters like William Taylor, Lawyer Collins, Pop Johnson, and Roland Weber—accomplished in business, respected, and prosperous—subtly told an audience accustomed to servile, irresponsible blackface caricatures that a black man could both succeed and excel. And far from the minstrel stereotype of the "loyal darky" who lived only to serve his "white folks," the dynamic, accomplished leaders of *Amos 'n' Andy*'s black world took care of their own.

> Amos---We ain't got no bizness readin' de man's mail, Andy.
>
> Andy---Ain't nuthin' pu'sonal in de things --- I done been oveh 'em once. Now listen.
>
> Amos---You is sumpin'.
>
> Andy---Dis fust one is from a place where dey keep colored orphans --- say heah "Dear Mr. Weber ---- we hardly know how to thank yo' fo' yo' check fo' $1000. It has been very hard to raise money lately, but due to yo' kindness our little colored orphans will not suffeh fo' a long time to come."
>
> Amos---Dat man do a lot o' charity work.

9. Black and White?

Andy---Den it go on to say heah 'bout --- a committee will call on him to thank him, an' all dat stuff. Heah's anotheh one --- look heah. Heah's one from El Paso, Texas. "Dear Roland ---- You kin reach Fred by addressin' him Gen'ral Delivery, El Paso, Texas. Yes, you are right --- he is up against it and I know $200 would see him through. Mighty nice of you to think of yo' old friends back heah. Take care of yo'self in New York, ol' fellow --- all yo' ol' Texas friends send dey're best regards --- signed Joe."

Amos---Dat man got a big heart in him, yo' know it?

Andy---Look heah, heah's a letteh from de George Washingtons.

Amos---I bet brother Crawford would be mad if he knowed dat he dropped dat mail over heah an' you picked it up an' read it.

Andy---Listen at de letteh heah from de George Washingtons. "Dear Mr. Webeh --- My husband joins me in tellin' me how sorry we are dat you could not come tea Friday. We will make it Monday instead an' please, please? Mr. Webeh, you really MUST come Monday, we want to know yo' betteh --- please do not fail us --- Yo' friends, Mr. & Mrs. George Washington."

Amos---Dat's from de George Washingtons, huh?

Andy---Ev'ybody's afteh him, ain't dey?

Amos---Dey sho' is.

Andy---Listen to dis one --- heah's a nice one. Say heah, "Dear Mr. Webeh --- Enclosed find post office money ordeh fo' $8.00 --- de hospital bill and ev'ything amounted to only $192, so I am REturnin' de amount left oveh. Thanks to you my husband is back at work again an' we is in de clear. May de Lord bless you" --- I can't read dat woman's name dat signed it.

Amos---He do a lot o' stuff, dat boy.

Andy---Now, heah's a letteh dat IS a letteh.

Amos---You know you ain't got no bizness readin' dat man's personal mail Andy.

Andy---If brotheh Crawford kin read 'em, why can't I read 'em?

Amos---Well, brotheh Crawford is workin' fo' de man.

Andy---Well, brotheh Crawford dropped de lettehs heah in de office an' I just picked 'em up. Now listen to dis one.

Amos---Alright.

Andy---Dis heah's from one o' de men dat work fo' Webeh down in de oil fields. --- Say heah ---" Deah Mr. Webeh ---- Number 16 came in yestidday --- anotheh gusheh --- nobody hurt --- we have got it tamed an' tapped an' are sinkin' in de casin' today --- it looks like anotheh 500 barrels a day --- this proved you guessed right again --- I am gettin' to work on numbeh 17 an' 18 --- you will hear from me --- befo' you close de deal fo' de ten acres adjoinin', I think we ought to hold off to see how number 17 an' 18 come out, don't you? Regards an' congratulations --- signed Walker."

> Amos---Listen Andy, give dat mail back to brotheh Crawford an' stop readin' it.
>
> Andy---De man is got a lot o' money Amos, an' I bet he throw it away to de birds.
>
> Amos---No, he don't, I goin' tell yo' whut he done. He had a pair o' rubber heels put on his shoes --- de fellow sent his shoes over, charged him a dollar --- he sent 'em back an' told de fellow to take 'em off, it was too much money --- den de fellow say it was 50 cents, an' Mr. Weber paid de 50 cents --- but heah's whut he done --- de boy dat works fo' de shoe REpair man was dressed up in kind-a ragged lookin' clothes --- you know, de boy dat brought de shoes back an' forth ---
>
> Andy---Uh huh.
>
> Amos---So Mr. Weber took him over an' bought him $15.00 worth o' clothes.
>
> Andy---Sho' 'nuff?
>
> Amos---Dat's whut he done. When he buys a newspaper, if de paper's three cents, 'stead o' throwin' a nickel out an' leavin' de nickel dere, he picks up his two cents --- even if he gotta wait dere 5 minutes fo' de man to give him de change --- but he'll go right out in de street an' if he see a blind man or somebody, he'll give 'em a dollar or two [Episode 1806, 3/15/34].

Correll and Gosden were meticulous in glossing over any depiction of overt tension between the races—and this is a characteristic of their work that often rings hollow for modern critics. But commercial radio in the 1930s was not the place to look for gritty depictions of stark realism, racial or otherwise. Commercial radio offered an escape from reality, not a documentary portrayal of it—and given the era in which they lived and the medium in which they worked, Correll and Gosden could hardly have been expected to portray in explicit detail the bleak realities of their time. Commercial factors made it necessary for *Amos 'n' Andy* to appeal to the widest possible audience—Southerners as well as Northerners, blacks as well as whites—and these considerations compelled Correll and Gosden to walk a very fine line in the portrayal of race relations. As a result, blacks and whites were rarely shown in direct interaction—even as the realities of the racially segregated world of the 1920s and 1930s could be depicted in only the mildest possible terms and with only the most veiled references. Controversy had to be avoided at all costs. Consequently, there is no reason to believe that any attempt at direct or obvious criticism of the racial codes of the day in a commercial entertainment program would have been permitted by the network or the sponsor.[4]

Despite those conditions, Correll and Gosden occasionally inserted understated scenes acknowledging to the careful listener that life was different for black Americans. In the very first episode of *Sam 'n' Henry,* a conductor at the Birmingham railroad depot directs Sam and Henry to take "any seat in that front car," a reference that black and Southern listeners would immediately recognize as pointing to the Jim Crow coach, which was always located closest to the locomotive. In a later instance, Amos expressed his frustration at the poor service he received in a clothing store—a scene that could have been taken by white listeners as a simple criticism of poor business practice, but which might have had special resonance for black listeners accustomed to rude treatment by white clerks.

> Amos---Well, in de first place, maybe it don't happen to nobody 'cept me, but anyway yo' have some money in yo' pocket, an' yo' go in a store, an' yo' know yo' wanna buy sumpin'. Well, de first store I went in, a man walked up to me, he looked like he was mad to start wid. He ast me whut I want an' I told him I wanna git a hat. Den he act like he didn't wanna wait on me. He ast me whut kind o' hat I want --- I told him I wanna git a new style hat, I didn't know fo' sure but I wanted to git one dat looked good on me if I could, an' he talked to me so funny an' he acted so funny dat he made me feel kind-a bad fo' comin' in dere. I know he didn't wanna wait on me --- so I went out de store --- 'bout 5 minutes lateh I went back in dere an' got another man dat was just as nice as he could be --- he sold me a hat in about 3 minutes ---- he act like he was glad I come in an' he act like he wanted to he'p me as much as he could ---- I goin' let him wait on me ALL de time too.
>
> King---I done had de same thing happen to me.
>
> Amos---An' de same thing happened when I was buyin' my underwear --- de man act just like he was mad 'cause I went in dere. He made me feel 'shamed o' myself 'cause I wanted to look at two-three diff'ent kinds, yo' see, I don't know nuthin' 'bout workin' in no store but if I WAS workin' in one I cert'ny would make de people feel like I was glad to wait on 'em [Episode 956, 4/16/31].

The most overt depiction of white racism in the entire run of *Amos 'n' Andy* is found in the interrogation scenes in the Jack Dixon Murder Case story line in December 1931. Over the course of three episodes, Amos is brutally questioned by two white detectives who treat their suspect with an unmistakable mixture of condescension and contempt. While the detectives, who assume Amos's guilt as a matter of course, try to extort a confession by physical and psychological intimidation, the exhausted Amos—raised in the Deep South during an era in which contradiction or open challenge of white authority by blacks often brought fatal results—respectfully but firmly maintains his innocence.

> Man----(softer) Listen boy, I want you to tell me how you shot this fellow. You shot him in the back too. And I want you to tell me how you did it.
>
> Amos---Mister, I didn't shoot him.
>
> Man----There's not but one way you could have killed him. You walked up behind him and shot him. A guy that'll shoot a guy in the back is a coward. Yo' didn't give him a chance.
>
> Amos---I didn't do it Mister.
>
> Man----Cryin' ain't gonna help you a bit. You've gotta take your medicine like a man.

Amos---I didn't do it.

Man----Sit still. (yells) Bill. ---- Come here. (softer) Bring that boy Andy Brown in here ---- tell him we don't want him to open his mouth. Just bring him here and let him say hello to this boy. That's all I want him to say.

Amos---Where's Andy, Mister?

Man----I just wanna let you know what kind of a friend you've got.

Amos---Is you got him down heah too?

Man----He's here, and he's talkin' plenty.

Amos---Yessah. Dere he is now. Hello Andy.

Man----I just want you to take a look at this guy.

Andy---Hello Amos.

Amos---Andy, tell Ruby dat I'se alright, will yo'?

Man----And you might as well tell her that he killed a guy for her.

Amos---But I DIDN'T do it --- don't tell her dat.

Man----Well now this pal of yours here has made up his mind that he's gonna tell the truth.

Andy---Mister, kin I talk to Amos a minute, please sir?

Man----You're goin' right back in the other room. Take him in there Bill.

Other man--(Gosden) (in distance) Come on.

Man----(softer) Now listen buddy, I want to give you another chance but I want you to tell me the truth. You know you were mad enough with that guy to do anything to him.

Amos---I was mad wid him, I tell yo' dat.

Man----You know you were mad with him over a woman.

Amos---Yessah, but den on de other hand, he come in de taxicab office an' hit me twice an' knocked me out.

Man----You wanna get this girl in trouble?

Amos---Nosah, Mister, nosah, don't git her in it. I'll take it myself, but don't git her in it. She's good.

Man----Well, if you don't come clean she IS gonna git in it. How would you like to see her sittin' behind the bars for five or ten?

Amos---Nosah mister.

Man----Well, if you don't tell the truth, she's gonna be there.

Amos---I'se tellin' you de truth Mister. If yo' just lemme lay down fo' 'bout a hour Mister I'll feel better.

Man----Well, you're not gonna lay down till yo' tell the truth.

Amos---Mister, I'se so tired I can't even think.

Man----Well you don't have to think. All I wanna know from you is why you shot him, an' when you shot him. And boy, you don't have a chance. You might as well come clean now. We've got a 32 gun with one bullet gone and Dixon was killed with a 32.

Amos---I didn't shoot dat gun Mister. I told yo' dat de fellow dat I took de gun away from shot de gun in de Harlem River to see if it was workin'.

Man----You got a pretty good alibi there son, and your friend told us that he shot the gun but that don't hold water in this place. And if you think your gonna find somebody to lie for you to get out of this you're wrong.

Amos---I ain't tryin' to git nobody to tell yo' nuthin' dat ain't de truth.

Man----You don't have a chance. We got it on yo'.

Amos---Mister, I know it looks bad fo' me, but I didn't do it.

Man----Well, you're gonna sit here till yo' tell me you DID do it [Episode 1159, 12/9/31].

Although Correll and Gosden had portrayed a similar scene in a 1928 sequence, the three December 1931 episodes describing Amos's interrogation were by far the rawest and most racially charged scenes in the entire series. They resulted in an official complaint to NBC and Pepsodent by the National Association of Chiefs of Police. During an era in which the story of the Scottsboro Boys was on the front pages, such a portrayal of abuse of a black suspect by white police officers may well have struck too close to home. In presenting these scenes, Correll and Gosden crossed a line they would not cross again.[5]

As circumspect as Correll and Gosden had to be in depicting the realities of race relations in the 1920s and 1930s, their decision to set *Amos 'n' Andy* in an essentially all-black world allowed the performers to go further than any popular media of their time in portraying black characters of genuine substance. By avoiding regular interaction between blacks and whites in their scripts, they also avoided the then-prevalent cultural conventions that required black characters to always be presented as subservient to whites. But even more important, the absence of whites from Amos and Andy's world compelled white listeners to identify with the African American characters as they followed the developing story lines. The absence of white characters meant there were no "me" figures against whom Amos and Andy could be assigned "not-me" status by the white audience—and, indeed, on the rare occasions when unmistakably white characters do appear for more than a line or two they are often marked by Jewish or other ethnic dialects. In this way, Correll and Gosden explicitly position these white characters as the outsider figures in these scenes, ensuring that listener identification remains fixed on the black Amos and Andy.

Through such careful manipulation of racial imagery, Correll and Gosden deemphasized the racial "otherness" of their characters even as they defined the characters as African American—and by doing so, they maneuvered and manipulated their listeners into identifying with characters who on the surface were very different from themselves. As a result, even a figure like the slow-moving Lightning could be presented not as a two-dimensional butt of jokes but as a sympathetic individual.

Correll and Gosden were entertainers producing their work for a mass audience, not social activists. It would have been easy, had they been so inclined, to simply follow the lead of a legion of blackface performers before them and to cling to the comfortable, shallow stereotypes. But instead, Correll and Gosden consciously encouraged their listeners to view the characters not as racial cartoons but as individuals whose color was merely one facet of their identity, and whose dreams, hopes, and fears were those of all people. In an era in which the literary African American was commonly defined by "exotic, primitive" characteristics, and black characters in popular culture were rarely more than pop-eyed servants, Correll and Gosden broke significant ground by consistently defining their characters by their humanity, not by their "blackness."

The performers made an even more dramatic break with minstrelsy in their personal appearances. Conscious from the beginning of their careers of the artificiality of blackface, Correll and Gosden worked to divorce themselves and their program as much as possible from old-style minstrel methods—and they did so by, both figuratively and literally, wiping off the burnt cork. While their early personal appearances as Sam and Henry were done in traditional blackface makeup, by the end of the 1920s, the performers were ready for a bold change. Rather than offering blackface as it had been presented on the minstrel stage since the 1830s, the performers chose to deliberately undermine that tradition with an act incorporating techniques that played havoc with rigid notions of racial characterization. During their Pantages tour of 1929 and their Publix tour of 1930, Correll and Gosden appeared in special makeup, which, when used in conjunction with special stage lighting, allowed them to switch instantaneously from black to white during their performance—a trick that invariably produced gasps of astonishment from theater audiences. They then concluded their act as two white men in formal evening dress, performing a routine in the voices of Amos and Andy. It was an act that, in the words of social historian Melvin Ely, caused Correll and Gosden to jump "across the color line in a manner both cavalier and surreal—indeed, in a way which caused the line, in the last moments of each show, to blur altogether."[6] In this "cavalier and surreal" disregard for the color line, Correll and Gosden pointedly symbolized their rejection of the minstrel mask and the generic minstrel characterizations that went with it.

During their personal appearance tours of the 1930s, Correll and Gosden continued their deconstruction of minstrelsy. For their 1933–34 coast-to-coast tour of the RKO Vaudeville circuit, they dispensed with blackface completely—performing their entire act in whiteface and ordinary street clothes and bringing Amos and Andy to life, as they did on the air, through their voices alone. Audiences attending these performances saw *Amos 'n' Andy* billed on the marquee but they saw Charles Correll and Freeman Gosden on the stage, thus allowing them to preserve in their own minds their own unique vision of what Amos and Andy looked like.

Knowing that they could never offer a convincing visual impersonation of char-

RAILROAD ILLINOIS TERMINAL SYSTEM

Take Advantage of Our Bargain Round Trip Rates Between Here and St. Louis To See

Radio's Greatest Stars

AMOS 'N' ANDY

— With —

BROTHER CRAWFORD, THE KINGFISH, LIGHTNIN', HENRY VAN PORTER, PRINCE ALI BENDO.

IN PERSON

IN A GIGANTIC EASTER WEEK STAGE SHOW FEATURING

6 GREAT ACTS!

— PLUS ON THE SCREEN —

"WOMEN IN HIS LIFE"

Otto Kruger, Una Merkel, Ben Lyon

WEEK STARTING FRIDAY, MARCH 30th

AMBASSADOR THEATRE
ST. LOUIS

Correll and Gosden's 1933 personal appearance tour took them coast to coast with an unusual stage presentation recreating the technique of their regular nightly broadcasts. Following a filmed introduction by Bill Hay, the curtain opened to reveal the two men in street clothes, seated at a table, performing a sample *Amos 'n' Andy* script. The technique proved so successful that it set the precedent for all of the team's subsequent live appearances.

acters whose images existed only in each listener's imagination, Correll and Gosden in their personal appearances—just as in their broadcasts—refused to reduce Amos and Andy to simple blackface caricatures. "In 'blacking up,'" Correll pointed out in a 1972 interview, "you become a *minstrel*. You're not a normal human being. But these fellows in our radio show *were* human beings."[7]

10. DISSONANT VOICES

"There is a positive disapproval of the exploitation of two types of Negro [sic] for the sole purpose of making money at the expense of a group of people who need every helpful influence it can get from every source possible."
—Editorial, *The Pittsburgh Courier*, 1931

"I think their programs have done more to help the white people understand us than all the books ever written."
—Rooming House Owner, Harlem, 1930

THE RADIO REVOLUTION OF THE 1920s was by and large a phenomenon of white America. Although a few African American performers were able to establish themselves as broadcasting personalities during the 1920s, radio listening among blacks remained a limited phenomenon, and as late as 1930 less than 8 percent of black families owned radios.[1]

Nonetheless, the impact of *Amos 'n' Andy* was felt in the African American community. Even before the program began its network run, blacks were aware of the series and the images that it portrayed. Correll and Gosden attempted where possible to reach out to the black community in Chicago, and took pride in a 1928 survey of members of the Chicago Urban League that endorsed their program. "Before the *Chicago Daily News* engaged us for the WMAQ feature," Gosden recalled in 1930, "they investigated that angle. They did not want to seem to condone anything that might be regarded as offensive to the colored people of Chicago. They made inquiries of members of the Urban club, where the intellectual leaders of the race belong. The Urban club endorsed our feature because they declared that we had never said anything that reflected on the least on the moralities of the colored people, and that we had always been considered as presenting a creditable side to the characters we portrayed."[2]

Correll and Gosden's efforts to forge a connection with Chicago's African American community extended back to the days of *Sam 'n' Henry*, with appearances at community functions organized by the *Chicago Tribune*, but these efforts moved into high gear when the team joined the *Daily News*, a paper that had taken the lead in encouraging healing in the city in the wake of violent racial tensions in the early 1920s.[3] Correll and Gosden appeared before meetings of the Chicago Urban League and other African American organizations and made a point of booking their stage act into the city's leading black theater, where they found themselves nearly overwhelmed by the positive response. "We put in our Amos 'n' Andy vaudeville act out at the Regal," Gosden related, "which is really a palatial theatre patronized almost exclusively by colored people. When we appeared on the stage we received such an ovation from the packed house that we didn't know what to do."[4]

Early publicity articles emphasized these positive reactions. "Amos 'n' Andy are perhaps prouder of the approval they get from Negro radio listeners than anything else," commented the *Christian Science Monitor* as the program approached its first anniversary on WMAQ.[5] But after the feature moved from chainless chain syndication to the NBC Blue network, other voices began to be heard: African American voices that took a more critical tone in discussing the program and the images that it portrayed. Some of these voices surfaced away from the hearing of the white press and public but others made mainstream impressions.

As the *Amos 'n' Andy* craze peaked in the early months of 1930, *Radio Digest* magazine presented a series of articles exploring every conceivable angle of the unprecedented phenomenon, including a surprisingly candid examination of how African Americans from all walks of life responded to the program. Correspondent A.W. Clarke was dispatched to Harlem and to the black district of Hartford, Connecticut, where he interviewed a cross-section of black residents about their feelings regarding the program, with the results published in the magazine's August 1930 issue.[6]

Clarke's article offered white Americans their first substantive insight into the diversity of opinions black listeners held toward the nation's favorite radio feature—and the assessments, examined today, come across as both candid and surprisingly free of press-agent slanting or promotional exaggeration. Clarke approached his interview subjects with two basic questions: "If Amos and Andy were Negroes, what do you suppose your attitude would be toward them? If you were white and they were Negroes, what do you suppose this attitude would be?" Most of Clarke's respondents were drawn from the African American middle-class—both professionals and merchants—and the replies ranged from guarded to forthright in their assessment of the positive and negative aspects of the program.

Supporters of the program emphasized that, in their view, Correll and Gosden were portraying real-life character types in a sympathetic or even constructive manner, even as they acknowledged that these opinions were by no means universal in the black community. "With certain types of colored people even in our day, the Amos and Andy stuff is natural, though as a whole we are growing away from it," commented Dr. F.A. Hinkson, a Hartford dentist. "The younger generation naturally considers itself above that and cannot appreciate it. Yet Amos and Andy are harming no one."[7]

A Hartford barbershop patron was emphatic in his endorsement of the program, dismissing suggestions that Correll and Gosden offered a demeaning portrayal of their characters. "If they were attacking the colored people, their entertainment would have died long ago," he contended, "but what they are saying is so humorous and free from the taint of prejudice I do not see how any person, white or colored, can take it in a personal way." This respondent went on to suggest a candid explanation for opinions contrary to his own. "The modern Negro is too self-conscious," he declared. "To give you an example of what I mean, I have a friend who owns a radio. He never misses *Amos 'n' Andy* when home among his family, but when in the presence of white people he just cannot stand to listen to them. I will listen to *Amos 'n' Andy* in any place among any crowd. *Amos 'n' Andy* have this race down pat, I am telling you."[8]

Other black *Amos 'n' Andy* enthusiasts focused their responses on the program's dramatic appeal in explaining their enjoyment of the series. An African American police officer from New York City's 32nd Precinct was among the most enthusiastic listeners questioned by Clarke. "My post is in the heart of Harlem, and it gives me a good chance to watch my people and know what they like and dislike," the patrolman maintained. "With very few exceptions, everyone I come in contact with is a rooter for *Amos 'n' Andy*. I like the program myself, and when I am on duty from four in the morning until midnight, I will say positively that every radio on my beat is tuned in on those two boys at seven o'clock. That pair certainly know their stuff, and it is marvelous to me that they play all those different parts, but I think the best acting was done by Amos when Ruby Taylor went to Chicago. I sure felt sorry for him. I couldn't help believing that his heart was breaking."[9]

Perhaps the most unusual response received by Clarke came from the owner of a rooming house on 134th Street in Harlem—the very neighborhood in which Amos and Andy themselves were said to live in Correll and Gosden's scripts. The woman emphasized the program's value less as entertainment than as a window allowing white Americans to catch a sympathetic glimpse of a world with which most of them had no real-life acquaintance. "Like everyone else in Harlem, I listen to *Amos 'n' Andy* every night," she declared. "Those white boys know how to play Negro parts better than any blackface comedians I have ever heard. For one thing, they do not belittle the Negro and I think their programs have done more to help the white people understand us than all the books ever written."[10]

But other responses gathered by the *Radio Digest* correspondent revealed a range of criticisms, ranging from mild annoyance to outright anger about the images portrayed in the program. A Hartford barber saw Correll and Gosden as simply the latest in a series of white performers capitalizing on black stereotypes for the sake of commercial gain. "If you want my personal opinion, here it is," he offered. "Amos and Andy are commercializing certain types of Negro characters, as they could not find anything among the whites to amuse the general public."[11]

A Hartford undertaker, one M.A. Johnson, interviewed by Clarke, dismissed *Amos 'n' Andy* as a burlesque but also suggested that the performers were exposing a side of African American life that was best not discussed within the hearing of whites. "No race likes to have its women exposed, and that is what Amos and Andy have done," he cautioned. "Here is what I mean: Madam Queen has a traveling salesman as her sweetheart. When he is in town, Andy must stay on the outer rim of things; when he is gone she calls up Andy and gives him his date. Of course, this is true to life among all races, but knowing some white peoples' attitudes toward the unfortunate side of Negro life, I should rather deplore this."[12] Like many middle-class African Americans of the 1920s and 1930s, Johnson evidently believed that in order for blacks to achieve social progress, it was necessary to not only adhere to the cultural standards expected of middle-class white America but, wherever possible, to exceed them too. For him, in the final accounting, *Amos 'n' Andy* stood less as a fictitious caricature than as a reminder of unpleasant social realities that stood as an obstacle to progress.

Other middle-class black professionals interviewed by Clarke shared this perspective. They distanced themselves and their own achievement-oriented culture from what they perceived as the retrogressive picture of working-class black life presented by Correll and Gosden. "Only the most illiterate type of Negro will speak as Amos and Andy do," was the emphatic comment of a Hartford attorney, "and that type is fast leaving us."[13] That opinion was seconded by F.L. Peterson, an English professor from Boston, who offered the most emphatic criticism recorded by Clarke. "If they were Negroes," Peterson declared, "I should think that they were making fools of the race."[14]

The *Radio Digest* article offered the first hint of controversy brewing around the program to appear in a mainstream publication, but the debate would take on greater significance during 1930 to 1931 in the pages of the African American press. As far back as 1928, Correll and Gosden had been praised by the *Chicago Defender,* then the nation's leading black newspaper, and had received additional favorable coverage from that publication in the years since. Their program had also received positive attention in the pages of several other African American papers during 1930, including the *Baltimore Afro-American,* the *Philadelphia Tribune,* and the *Kansas City Call.* But in December 1930, W.J. Walls, Chicago bishop of the African Methodist Episcopal Zion Church, and one of the nation's best-known black churchmen, sharply denounced *Amos 'n' Andy* in an article published in *Abbott's Monthly* magazine—a journal founded and owned by *Chicago Defender* publisher Robert Abbott. Walls was already noted as a crusader against jazz and other types of popular entertainment, music, and literature that he believed exploited the "primitive weakness" of the lower classes in black America—which he dismissed as "the unlettered and mentally imbecilic group of our race"—and he used his article on *Amos 'n' Andy* as a platform to second scholar and social historian Benjamin Brawley's overall denunciations of the "sordidness, realism, vulgarity, psychoanalysis, free verse, and staccato writing" that he felt characterized much of the literature by and about black Americans. Like Brawley, Walls had no use for any form of ghetto imagery in depictions of black America by black authors—and even less tolerance of such images when they came from white authors like Correll and Gosden. Walls's criticism of *Amos 'n' Andy* took particular aim at the lower-class characterizations, contending that they failed to show any evidence of "the highest intuitions of the civilized man" and that the "crude, repetitional, and moronic" dialogue of the program had a "somnolent effect upon the minds of many of our people, especially of the youth."[15]

Four months later, Walls's theme was picked up by Robert Vann, publisher of the *Pittsburgh Courier*, then the nation's second-largest black newspaper. In the spring of 1931, Vann and his chief editorial writer George S. Schuyler—a combative, choleric journalist widely known as "the colored Mencken," who shared Benjamin Brawley's outspoken contempt for representations of ghetto life—proclaimed the start of a nationwide campaign to drive *Amos 'n' Andy* from the air.

The *Courier*'s campaign began with an editorial in the issue of April 25, 1931, probably written by Schuyler, pointing out that Correll and Gosden were white men employed on behalf of white-owned business institutions and that therefore all financial gain resulting from the program accrued to whites. "But the people who are getting the black eye out of it all are the Negroes of this country, and of every other country where Negroes are found," the editorial maintained. And while the *Courier* did not argue or attempt to prove that Correll and Gosden's portrayal of African American life was a fabrication, the paper took as the main thrust of its attack the argument that the characters of Amos and Andy, as examples of "two types of Negroes to be found in the United States," were being, in substance, exploited by their creators and promoters solely for the sake of financial profit. "There is a positive disapproval of the exploitation of two types of Negro," continued the editorial, "for the sole purpose of making money at the expense of a group of people who need every helpful influence it can get from every source possible."

The *Courier* editorial went on to contend that as a result of the popularity of the series, white Americans were interpreting Amos and Andy not simply as "two types of Negroes" among many but as typical representatives of an entire race. "On the streets, in the banks, in the business places, Negro help is often referred to as Amos or Andy," claimed the paper. "Negroes are being put down as being one of two types. We are either Amos or we are Andy." The editorial concluded with a call to direct action—encouraging, without directly stating so, a boycott of both the radio program and its sponsor. "If we can continue the fight as started," exhorted the editorialist, "we may be able to persuade exploiters that we are not such fools as to spend our money to see ourselves classified below our own ideals. The fight is on."[16]

While the subject matter of the editorial stood out as an unusual topic for politicization, in its overall tone and presentation it bears a strong similarity to past *Courier* crusades—crusades that had served to sour the reputation of the paper and its editor among some African American leaders. While there is no questioning Robert Vann's commitment to the cause of black advancement, he was also a businessman, and, by the time of the *Amos 'n' Andy* campaign, the publisher was dismissed by many critics as an opportunist, with a history of mounting elaborate crusades and then dropping them just as abruptly when they failed to sufficiently spur the circulation of his paper. As black-media historian Dr. Patrick Washburn has observed, "In an attempt to get more circulation—and he had to have circulation because advertising was low at this particular time—he would run one position one week. The next week he would change and run another position, anything to get more circulation."[17]

Vann chose prominent targets for his crusades—five years before the *Amos 'n' Andy* campaign, the publisher had publicly and personally attacked prominent black leaders W.E.B. DuBois and James Weldon Johnson over their handing of certain funds entrusted to them by the NAACP. This crusade had ignited a furor in the black community and brought national attention to Vann and his paper, helping to spur circulation to nearly 55,000 copies per issue. The controversy boiled for nearly three years, but public opinion gradually shifted away from the crusading publisher, and in 1929, Vann publicly retracted his statements and issued a formal apology. At the turn of the 1930s, circulation of the paper wavered between 35,000 and 50,000 copies per issue—and the financial burden of a new printing plant, constructed in 1929, weighed heavily on the *Courier*'s account books. By the fall of 1930, the financial situation had deteriorated to the point where *Courier* employees were hit with massive pay cuts and key loans were going unpaid. By early 1931, the *Courier* was desperate for additional circulation and the additional revenue it would bring.[18]

The crusade against *Amos 'n' Andy* became a focus of circulation-building efforts for the *Courier* during 1931. Whatever Vann's exact motives were in mounting the campaign, the pages of the *Courier* were filled for nearly six months with anti–*Amos 'n' Andy* articles, editorials, and letters from readers. Petition forms were published, and readers were encouraged to circulate them, toward a final goal of one million signatures, with the progress of the drive tracked by a weekly front-page graphic. The campaign soon picked up the support of Bishop Walls, the National Association of Colored Waiters and Hotel Employees, and a number of African American fraternal organizations—the *Courier* had devoted particular criticism to the portrayal of "Negro Social Orders" in the series.[19]

As the campaign picked up steam through the spring of 1931, a *Courier* editorial attacked specific elements in the recent breach-of-promise story line. "The Negro lawyers Andy picked out to defend him were shown to be 'crooks,' and most unfit to practice the profession," declared the editorialist in the May 16, 1931 issue. "This was a slap at Negro lawyers, and Madam Queen's bigamy was an insult to all Negro women. There are intelligent lawyers in the Negro race. Why did not the pair select one to represent the profession? The Negro lawyer was presented to the listening world as a crook unfit to go in any court. And yet we sit still and allow this insult to be sent all over the radio world."

Many of the arguments raised by the *Courier* during its campaign were based on broad generalizations. Questions of perceived exploitation and of whether one takes personal offense at the program are not based on arguments of hard facts but on personal viewpoints. Whether one interprets Madam Queen's confusing marital history as a slander against all black women and the financial chicaneries at the Mystic Knights of the Sea as representative of all African American fraternal organizations or one views these portrayals as merely individual pictures depends on personal attitudes and perspectives that, in the end, have little to do with the radio program itself. But in accusing Correll and Gosden of showing "Negro lawyers" as "crooks," the paper raised a specific issue that can be checked against the surviving scripts. Did Correll and Gosden truly present "the Negro lawyer" to the listening world "as a crook unfit to go in any court?"

Although the *Courier* fails to elaborate on the specific characterization it intended to criticize in its editorial, it appears that the writer was combining the traits of two separate characters—neither of which ever represented Andy in the courtroom. The first of the two characters, one "Brother Snoop," was an enthusiastic but inept private investigator engaged by Andy to investigate Madam Queen's activities during January 1931, while doubling as a legal advisor. Although Snoop represented himself as an attorney, investigation of his credentials by Amos revealed that he was, in fact, merely an income tax investigator with no bona fide legal training or courtroom privileges.

> Amos---De thing fo' you to do right now is to git rid o' him. Don't give him a nickel. He ain't done nuthin' fo' you an' he ain't no real lawyeh.
>
> Andy---You don't mean to say he ain't no lawyeh.
>
> Amos---He THINKS he is, an' he try to make ev'ybody else think he is, but he ain't no lawyeh [Episode 881, 1/19/31].

Andy followed Amos's advice, and the character of Snoop disappeared from the story line at that point. At no time did Snoop represent Andy in the courtroom. Following Snoop's dismissal, Andy acted on Amos's recommendation and engaged professional, well-spoken Lawyer Collins, only to be sidetracked temporarily by the appearance of the fast-talking Johnny Cook, a friend of the Kingfish's, who attempted to insinuate himself into the case. Amos distrusted Cook from the start and finally convinced his partner to keep his case in Collins's hands.

> Amos---Don't you think in yo' own heart dat Mr. Collins is alright?
>
> Andy---Oh sho', he's alright.
>
> Amos---Don't yo' think dat he's gonna do ev'vything in de world dat he kin to git yo' out o' de trouble dat you is in?... Don't you think dat you would like to keep him as yo' lawyeh as long as he is done done all dis work on de case --- don't you wanna keep him?
>
> Andy---Yeh, I betteh do dat.

Amos then turned his attention to Johnny Cook himself and took decisive action to banish him from the case. Cook protested, but Amos stood firm, insisting that Andy would settle for nothing less than honest, reliable legal counsel.

> Amos--... Now, he got a lawyer --- you KNOW he got a lawyer an' now, he ain't goin' change so de thing fo' you to do is git out of' heah an' stay out o' heah. Now, wait a minute! I don't wanna even heah whut you got to say.
>
> Cook---Now listen ----
>
> Amos---I don't wanna listen, an' I want yo' to git out o' heah right now, an' I want yo' to let Andy alone.
>
> Cook---Andy, whut do you think o' dis?

> Andy---I ain't got nuthin' to say 'bout it. When Amos gits mad ain't no use to argue wid him.
>
> Amos---Now git on out heah, an' don't never put yo' foot back in dis office again. An' I don't want yo' hangin' 'round de lunch room! Now, git on out heah, an' let Andy 'lone [Episode 910, 2/21/31].

With Snoop and Cook dismissed from the scene, Lawyer Collins remained in place for the remainder of the story line as the only attorney to represent Andy. Correll and Gosden were careful to portray Collins as a black man in the same manner in which they identified the race of other nondialect-speaking black characters—through carefully placed contextual clues. For example, Collins's office was shown to be within close walking distance of Amos and Andy's taxicab office—locating it in the heart of Harlem, a location that Correll and Gosden consistently portrayed as essentially an all-black community, with the rare white resident portrayed in Jewish dialect. Collins, however, consistently speaks straight standard English, positioning him, within the context of Correll and Gosden's portrayal of Harlem, as a middle- or upper-class black. Additional confirmation of the lawyer's racial identity is found in a brief exchange in the episode of February 2, 1931, in which Andy suggests Collins as a potential romantic match for the divorced mother of one of his current girlfriends—a scene that managed also to indicate that Collins's status as a skilled professional clearly placed him in a higher social class within Harlem than that of Andy and his friends. Likewise, Madam Queen's attorney M. Smith, who, though flamboyant in the manner of old-school attorneys, is also free of dialect and is introduced into the story line as "the best lawyer in Harlem," a clear confirmation that, according to the established contextual rules of Correll and Gosden's story universe, Smith too is a black man.

Throughout the breach-of-promise story line, Correll and Gosden presented Lawyers Collins and Smith as figures of unquestioned ability—while presenting Snoop largely as comic relief and Cook as a potential villain. A close examination of the story line reveals no instance in which the two "pretend" attorneys were presented as typical examples of "the Negro Lawyer," despite the *Courier*'s assertions, while both Collins and Smith *were* clearly intended by Correll and Gosden to be representatives of the African American legal profession. This contrast between editorial exaggeration and the reality of the program's portrayals suggests that Vann and Schuyler were not above using straw men in order to generate talking points against the series.

Such hyperbole increasingly characterized the content of the *Courier*'s editorials during the *Amos 'n' Andy* campaign. As the protest advanced through the summer of 1931, the *Courier* promised its readers that a team of lawyers was preparing to file for an injunction in Cook County Superior Court in Chicago in order to halt the broadcast of *Amos 'n' Andy,* and that 5,000 clergymen would preach sermons against the program on a given Sunday in October.[20] However, none of these goals were met. No court action was ever filed. Although a number of ministers nationwide did preach sermons urging black Americans to develop self-respect on the designated Sunday, few appear to have mentioned *Amos 'n' Andy*.[21] So it was that far from gathering universal support, the aggressive tone taken by the *Courier*'s campaign contributed to its public repudiation by a broad cross-section of other black papers.

The most emphatic rejection of the *Courier*'s crusade against Correll and Gosden occurred in their home base of Chicago, where the performers had long since developed strong positive ties within the black community. As the *Courier* campaign neared the height of its activity in August 1931, the *Chicago Defender* pointedly invited Correll and Gosden to host the annual summer picnic of the "Bud Billiken Club" before an estimated audience of 35,000 black Chicagoans. Appearing in street clothes, with no character makeup, Correll and Gosden were greeted by tumultuous applause when they were introduced from the platform by a performance of their radio theme music by Duke Ellington's orchestra. "The crowd went wild—they did—they did," declared a front-page article describing the event in the *Defender*'s August 22, 1931, issue. "Amos 'n' Andy mounted chairs with megaphones, but you couldn't hear your ears." Unable to address the crowd over the tumultuous ovation, Correll and Gosden instead led the audience in a sing-a-long rendition of "Hail, Hail the Gang's All Here." "Amos 'n' Andy led the chorus, waving vigorously their megaphones," continued the *Defender*'s account. "It got so good toward the end that Andy jumped down from his chair and danced a jig. When it was over, the crowd let out a salvo of applause that could be heard for miles."

Although the *Defender* was the most prominent African American newspaper to oppose the *Courier*'s campaign, it was not the only black-owned paper to dismiss Vann and Schuyler's arguments against *Amos 'n' Andy*. The *Louisville News*, rejected the *Courier*'s call to action by declaring "[f]or every two Negroes that talk like Amos 'n' Andy there are twenty thousand Colored Americans far removed from them in intelligence, in speech and in character. Our white neighbors know this as well as we know it, and the race is not affected."[22] An even sharper rebuke of the *Courier*'s campaign came from Theophilus Lewis, entertainment columnist for Harlem's *Amsterdam News*. "The *Courier* campaign will serve one good end," Lewis wrote in his column of July 22, 1931. "When they complete their tally of signatures, we will know precisely how many halfwits there are in the race."

Perhaps the most elaborate direct response to the *Courier*'s campaign came from the largest African American newspaper in the Pacific Northwest. Over the course of three consecutive issues in the fall of 1931, the *Northwest Enterprise* of Seattle published a lengthy rebuttal to the *Courier*'s denunciation of *Amos 'n' Andy*. In a character-by-character examination of the series, the *Enterprise* contended that Correll and Gosden were merely holding up a mirror to African American life by portraying a wide range of authentic character types. Far from reckoning Amos as a caricature, the *Enterprise* recommended him as a role model for the aspiring African American entrepreneur. "Amos is a thrifty fellow, and energetic. He has tons of common sense, and really runs the 'Taxicab Business' and the 'lunch room,'" the *Enterprise* pointed out. "There are hundreds and hundreds of his type in everyday life—honest and thrifty, and who cannot be burned for fools. You will find many characters like Amos in real Negro life. And more would not hurt if they displaced the shrewd and cunning sharks who claim to be conducting business."[23]

The *Enterprise* saw Andy, by contrast, as both a parody of universal self-importance, and as a representation of a character type that, the paper argued, was far too common in the black community of 1931. Rather than expending energy to attack a radio program, the *Enterprise* maintained that a more appropriate course of action would be to publicly rebuke Andy Brown's real-life counterparts. "There are Negroes in business and in church who will promise anything when they know they have no way on earth to keep the promise," argued the *Enterprise*'s writer. "This runs true for the Negro preacher down to the Negro hot-dog seller. All this class wants is a scheme to get by, and they only get by because more worthy and misled Negroes help them by. Their pictures are ever in the paper. They thrive on publicity and spend their time and money 'dolling up' in 'fronts' for public praise, hoping to appear as prosperous business assets. Let Negro pulpit and press center on these Andys in real life, and they need not worry about Andy on the air."[24]

Unable to rally a majority of the black press in support of its cause, by late summer, the *Courier* was attempting to frame the protest along lines of social class and intelligence—and the paper's editorials took on a tone of desperation, denouncing black supporters of *Amos 'n' Andy* as harshly as they attacked the program itself. "Our protest has the sanction of all intelligent people, white and black," insisted a column in the *Courier*'s August 29, 1931, issue. "We do not expect ignorant Negroes and whites to be able to see the insult. We are not looking for the 'Amos 'n' Andy' Negro to join our protest. We are happy to have the intelligence of both races indorsing [sic] our program. It has grown beyond the proportions of a joke; it has reached the serious stage. We are going on—with the help of all, if possible, but without the help of the ignorant, if we must."

Despite those determined words, less than two months after that defiant editorial appeared the *Courier* without explanation abandoned the campaign. "We finally had to give it up," recalled Jessie Vann, Robert Vann's widow, "because seemingly we were not accomplishing anything, unless it was popularizing [the program], for the radio program continued to have just as many listeners as before, and among our own people."[25] No verified, independent count of petition signatures was ever made, but the paper claimed in October 1931 to have gathered 675,000 names in opposition to *Amos 'n' Andy*.

Robert Vann's campaign collapsed for a variety of reasons, not the least of which was the honest popularity of *Amos 'n' Andy* with many black listeners. But his arguments were further undermined by the shrill manner in which the campaign was presented, by his own somewhat dubious reputation among his colleagues in the African American publishing community, and by his inability to attract high-profile national support. Despite Vann's published claims, the national office of the NAACP never endorsed the *Courier*'s drive nor was there any consensus among local chapters: while an official of the Memphis, Tennessee, chapter of the organization proclaimed his support for the campaign, the president of the Casper, Wyoming, chapter denounced the effort as a publicity stunt for the newspaper—and endorsed *Amos 'n' Andy* as "good humorous entertainment."[26]

Correll and Gosden themselves followed the protest closely by means of newspaper clippings gathered from all over the United States, and they directly responded to one of Vann's harshest criticisms by abruptly dropping a story line that revealed that Madam Queen had committed bigamy.[27] However, the performers never publicly commented on the campaign, which proved to be the only organized protest of the series to arise until the NAACP condemned the television version of the program in 1951. Ironically, even then, the NAACP failed to formally condemn the radio program. And in the greatest irony of all, the television series received some of its warmest and most sincere praise from the radio-TV critic of the *Pittsburgh Courier*.[28]

11. THE LATER YEARS

"A national sponsor would be a fool to risk putting it on a network today.... Things have changed too much."
—Charles Correll, 1961

THE ADVENT OF WORLD WAR II meant changes for Amos and Andy and their friends. After the attack on Pearl Harbor in December 1941, Amos put the Fresh Air Taxicab in storage and took a swing-shift job in a local defense plant. Ruby and her mother filled their evenings with volunteer work for the Red Cross, and Andy and the Kingfish looked for ways to improve homefront morale and to promote the sale of war bonds. And Correll and Gosden themselves did their part by contributing their services to Treasury Department bond-selling campaigns.

> Arbadella---Mommy says lots and lots of stamps have swastikas on them now. When a country is defeated, the invaders don't print new stamps. They just print the swastikas on top of the old stamps.... Will our American stamps ever have swastikas on 'em, Daddy?
>
> Amos---Well, dat all depends, darlin'. If we win dis war, free men ev'ywhere will have dere own stamps. Dere own flags An' dere own religion.
>
> Arbadella---If we lost the war, would they let me keep on collecting stamps?
>
> Amos---Well, if enough of us collect de right kind of stamps, darlin', de war is not goin' be lost.
>
> Arbadella---Which kind should I save, Daddy?
>
> Amos---Well, I wasn't goin' say nuthin' 'bout dis, Arbadella, because I wanted to surprise you an' Mama. But I got de right kind right heah in my pocket. Heah dey is.
>
> Andy---Oh, yeh! Dat's dem DEfense Stamps I bin hearin' so much 'bout.
>
> Amos---Yeh, I got thirty-one of 'em. That's seven dollars an' seventy-five cents worth. Now, when I kin build dat up to eighteen dollars an' seventy-five cent, we kin git a bond.

Andy---Yeh. I think I'll git me one o' dem books.

Arbadella---Me too, Daddy! I can put my other stamps away until after the war. How long will the war be, Daddy?

Amos---Well, nobody kin tell yo' dat now, darlin'. But ev'y one of these DEfense Stamps anybody buys will help make the war shorter [Special script for "Treasury Star Parade," Program 71, week of 3/18/42].

But even greater changes were in the offing for *Amos 'n' Andy*. Times had changed, tastes had changed, and audiences had changed. In a busy wartime world, the era of the nighttime early-evening comedy-drama serial was drawing to an end. The program's ratings had declined sharply since 1939 even though the performers had by this time attained the status of being broadcasting's elder statesmen, with their work still drawing high praise from some of the industry's sharpest minds. "Amos and Andy are really the cleverest team in radio today," wrote comedian Fred Allen in 1941. "Their dialogue holds up better than any of the other shows which is really something when you realize that for over ten years they have been grinding out five shows a week. Their voice changes and the fading in and out of the characters as they come and go are uncanny."[1]

In January 1943, the Campbell Soup Company, which had replaced Pepsodent as sponsor in January 1938, advised Correll and Gosden that the wartime shortage of tin had forced them to cut domestic soup production by half—and consequently, the company could no longer afford the program's annual $1.8 million budget. Campbell proposed continuing the series as a weekly self-contained half hour, but the performers preferred not to make such a dramatic change in their format in the middle of the broadcast season. Instead, they ended their five-year association with Campbell, and announced their temporary retirement from the air.[2] So it was that on February 19, 1943, an older, wiser Andrew H. Brown announced that he had at last settled all of his outstanding debts and that he would be doing his part for the war effort by following Amos's example and taking a full-time job in a defense plant. With all plot threads thus concluded, Correll and Gosden signed off the final episode of the original *Amos 'n' Andy*. In the *New York Times*, radio columnist John K. Hutchens noted the passing of an era.

> Radio's past being a short one, the word institution has a relative meaning, but Amos 'n' Andy were and are an institution. They held their fifteen-minute spot against all comers, created names and phrases that went into the language, and had as much as anyone to do with creating the technique of the continued story on the air. As most serials do not, they worked in terms of character, in an easy, relaxed style, with good humor, and above all, an enthusiasm incredibly sustained throughout more than 4,000 episodes. Certainly they have earned a rest. Just as certainly, they must return, if only because a public institution has a civic duty.[3]

Correll and Gosden did return to the air the following October but in a radically different format. The steady, human flow of the nightly serial had been replaced by a half-hour weekly situation comedy. The friendly, contemplative mood created by two men sitting alone in a tiny studio, creating an entire busy world out of their own minds and voices, was replaced by a brassy, fully Hollywoodized production, complete with a raucous studio audience.[4] Where Correll and Gosden had written every word of the serial themselves, with the advent of the situation comedy format a team of gag writers was hired to translate the simple, honest characterizations of Amos, Andy, the Kingfish, and their friends into full-fledged comedy stars. A full cast of supporting actors was added as well—with the already-established Ernestine Wade

```
                                          INVENTING LOCK SHOW
                                                  SCRIPT #33
                                                  VOLUME # 4




                              RINSO

                             Presents

                     "THE AMOS 'N' ANDY SHOW"


    TUESDAY, MAY 13, 1946                    5:00 - 5:30 PM PST

    WHISTLER:     (RINSO WHISTLE)  (TWICE)
    AMOS:         Andy, you know what day this is?
    ANDY:         Certainly, Amos, it's Tuesday.
    AMOS:         Dat's right, and Tuesday means we're on de air for
                  triple-action Rinso.
    MUSIC:        ABOUT FOUR NOTES OF THEME
    ANNCR:        Yessir.  Rinso, the soap that gets clothes Rinso white
                  and Rinso bright brings you the Amos 'n' Andy Show, a
                  full half hour of entertainment with all the Amos 'n' Andy
                  characters, plus - Lud Gluskin and his orchestra.
    ORCH:         TWO OR THREE NOTES ENDING ON PITCH FOR DELTA RHYTHM BOYS
    ANNCR:        And those famous....
    DELTA BOYS COME AND SING IN SWING TEMPO:  Delta Rhythm boys!
                  (APPLAUSE)
    MUSIC:        PERFECT SONG FULL......FADE FOR:
    KADELL:       And now, Lever Brothers Company, the makers of Rinso,
                  invite you to sit back, relax and enjoy the story of
                  Amos 'n' Andy.
    MUSIC:        THEME UP AND END

    mc
```

A dramatic change from Bill Hay's understated nightly introduction of "Amos 'n' Andy, in person," the half-hour *Amos 'n' Andy Show* opened with a full ration of up-tempo Hollywood ballyhoo. Such full-throated announcers as Harlow Wilcox, Carlton KaDell and Art Gilmore sold Rinso each week with evangelical vigor.

and Elinor Harriot joined during the 1943–44 season by African American performers Ernest Whitman, Ruby Dandridge, Lillian Randolph, Jester Hairston, and James Baskett. The new show—and significantly it was now entitled *The Amos 'n' Andy Show*—was a rousing success, enduring for the next 12 years as one of the most popular weekly programs on the air.[5] But as popular as it was, as well remembered as it is, *The Amos 'n' Andy Show* is but a shadow of the series that preceded it.

Originally, the weekly programs tried to preserve the essential flavor of the original series. With Amos having settled down to married life with Ruby and his children—daughter Arbadella received a baby brother, Amos, Jr., in 1941—the story lines in the last years of the serial tended to focus primarily on Andy's romantic entanglements and on his business dealings with the Kingfish. The first few years of the half-hour series continued in this pattern, emphasizing plots that could be wrapped up with a surprise twist at the end. Under Gosden's close editorial supervision, the team of five writers under head writer Robert J. Ross consciously worked for a story structure inspired by the works of O. Henry.[6] And occasionally the half-hour episodes could display the same emotional impact and depth of characterization that had filled the serial.

A prime example of how attempts were made during the first season of the half-hour series to sustain the serial's mood can be found in the episode broadcast on Good Friday, 1944, a touching exploration of the often-troubled marriage of Sapphire Stevens and her husband, the Kingfish. Convinced through circumstantial evidence that her husband has been unfaithful, Sapphire confronts him and, in an emotionally wrenching scene, declares the marriage over.

> Sapphire--Don't talk to me George. Just let me get my stuff out o' dis house. An' here -- here's a weddin' ring dat ain't never been off my finger before. You can take this too. I don't consider myself married to you no longer.
>
> King---Oh, I don't want de weddin' ring --
>
> Sapphire--Well either take it or I'm goin' throw it away.
>
> King---All right, all right, give it to me---I'll put it in my pocket.

The Stevenses' argument is interrupted by a visit from the Reverend Johnson, played with quiet dignity by Ernest Whitman, who notices the piles of belongings in the middle of the living room and immediately sizes up the situation. But rather than confront the couple directly, the Reverend guides them on a very gentle recapitulation of their wedding vows, helping the battling spouses to realize that whatever misunderstandings or transgressions they might experience cannot break the bond of genuine love and commitment that keeps them together.

> Reverend--You remember, George? You held her ring in yo' hand like yo' have it now. An' first I said -- We are gathered here to unite this man and this woman in marriage --- which is an institution ordained of nature in the very laws of our being for the happiness and welfare of mankind.
>
> King---Yessah. Dat was many years ago, all right.

> Reverend--An' then I said, marriage is not meant for happiness alone, but for the discipline and development of character.
>
> Sapphire--Sometimes we forget that, I guess....
>
> Reverend--An' do you remember how you embraced each other after the ceremony?
>
> King---Yessah. I do, Reverend.
>
> Reverend--That's it. You held each other closely. Just like that.
>
> Sapphire--(whispering) George ---

Freeman Gosden and Ernestine Wade played this scene with a subtle sincerity—never exaggerating, never overemoting, and giving the Stevenses' reconciliation a feeling of real emotional impact. And even as the studio audience beheld the unaccustomed sight of a white actor playing a tender love scene opposite an African American woman, they responded to the power of the dialogue, applauding warmly as the curtain music played. Here, as in the serial days, *Amos 'n' Andy* proved itself able to transcend common stereotyped portrayals of African American life and depict its characters as genuine, fully rounded human beings.

But as the 1940s wore on, there was a gradual shift in the tone of the program. Sentimentality was out of fashion, as radio comedy during the war years grew louder and more aggressive—and *The Amos 'n' Andy Show* was forced to fall in line with that trend. There was an increasing tendency to play to the studio audience—measuring the success of the script by the loudness of the laughs. Where Correll and Gosden had refused to rehearse during the serial era, the sitcom now opened its doors to the public for a live-audience dress rehearsal two days before the actual broadcast.

By 1946, with the arrival of Joe Connelly and Bob Mosher, a writing team with a sharp comic style, the Kingfish had become the central character of the program, and it was he who drove the plots. As a result, the subtle mixture of self-importance, guilelessness and vulnerability that had characterized Andy was gradually replaced by a more generic sort of gullibility—and in order for the Kingfish's increasingly outlandish schemes to work, Andy had to be made not just gullible but more than a little stupid. And Amos receded even further into the background, his presence largely reduced to that of a brief walk-on, in which he would tip Andy off that once again the Kingfish had played him for a fool.

> King---Brother Andy, I got de greatest opportunity fo' you yo' done ever had in yo' life. It's chance a fo' you to leave Harlem ... I is done gone to all de trouble o' workin' out de deal. Me an' you split 50-50, you is goin' to homestead in Alaska. Dat's whut yo' goin' do.
>
> Andy---Homestead in Alaska?
>
> King---Yeh, de gov'ment will give yo' 160 acres wid oil on it, yo' live dere fo' three yeahs, sell it at a profit, an' we splits $40,000 in cold cash.
>
> Andy---Cold is right. Somebody told me it was so cold in Alaska dat de Eskimos go to Iceland fo' de winter.

> King---No, no, dat's where yo' wrong. De weather dere is mild. Yo' see, de Gulf Stream comes from de Suez Canal, goes through de Amazon River, mixes wid de hot backwash of de Mississippi, an' cuts through de Panama Canal, makes a beeline fo' Alaska which is 3,000 miles as de crow swims.
>
> Andy---You mean yo' gotta git out in de Gulf Stream up dere to keep warm?
>
> King---No, no, de hot air from de Gulf Stream billiards off of de Pacific Ocean, blows right in to Alaska, through de Aleutian-nation Islands. It's a kind of a cold. dat we call a warm cold [*Amos 'n' Andy Show,* Vol. 4, No 15, 1/7/47].

The O. Henry–style endings remained a constant feature of the scripts, however, with the Kingfish inevitably getting his comeuppance at the finish. But even as its creators insisted that the comedy grow out of recognizable, universal human traits, over the course of the late 1940s, the program and its characters became further removed from the everyday experiences Correll and Gosden had attempted to portray during the serial. Instead, the plots and characters took on a fanciful, stylized quality, as each week Andy and the Kingfish enacted a new variation on the ritual dance of the con man and mark. "The little airtight world of Amos 'n' Andy is a sort of Glocca Morra in blackface—infinitely desirable and totally unobtainable," wrote critic John Crosby in 1948. "Here the problems of birth and death, marriage and divorce, wealth and poverty, while no different from those of the outer world, somehow assume an air of gaiety and fantasy; human frailty is presented in softer, more endearing outlines, and all the perplexities of life are approached with the lilting innocence of childhood."[7]

Viewed strictly as situation comedy, the new series could often be extremely funny, in keeping with the exaggerated style of much postwar radio comedy—John Crosby went on to praise the series as "technically the most perfect comedy show" on the air, with the possible exception of Jack Benny's program[8], but it was no longer the gentle, philosophical, often-moving story it had been in its serial days. Where Correll and Gosden had pointedly avoided broadly played jokes and gags in their serial programs, the new series now embraced them. Writing in the *Saturday Review of Literature* in 1951, veteran radio scriptwriter Goodman Ace cut to the root of the reason for the program's change in tone. "After some years, the advertising agencies decided that chuckles were out of style," Ace observed. "'Let a belly laugh be your umbrella,' was the new song, and Correll and Gosden were pressured into doing a half-hour show with a studio audience. Now was the time for big laughs, and Correll and Gosden soon discovered that Amos could get no laughs, acting mostly as straight man to Andy and the Kingfish. The big jokes went to Andy and the Kingfish, with the Kingfish scoring the kingsize yaks."[9]

But the success of the weekly half-hour show came at a high cost. The Hollywoodization of the format took away what had been one of the key elements in the program's early success: the sense of a quiet daily visit with close friends. With Amos and Andy and the rest of the cast separated from listeners at home by the audible presence of a live studio audience, the illusion that the listener was actually there in the same room with them, overhearing their conversation, was shattered. Amos and Andy ceased to be real people and became simply characters in a show. At the same time, the characters began to interact more frequently with whites—both background characters and celebrity guest stars. Where Correll and Gosden had worked in the serial to minimize such interactions, thus ensuring that white listeners would identify with the black characters, the sitcom-era "integration" of Amos and Andy's all-black world by these white figures made it all too easy for white listeners who were so inclined to define the central characters as racial "others."

Bit by bit, the disciplines that had given the original *Amos 'n' Andy* its unique appeal were being eroded by the constant pressure to adapt the series to its brash new format and to ensure that the necessary belly laughs would be forthcoming. These changes were accelerated by the phasing out of key characters in Correll and Gosden's original serial-era supporting cast—notably Brother Crawford, who as a hard-working white-collar family man, had always offered an important counterbalance to the scheming of Andy and the Kingfish, and Gwindell, who by the early 1940s had evolved beyond his original antagonist role into another respectable white-collar type. Such characters had added depth and texture to the serial's world but weren't particularly *funny*. So it was that over the course of the 1940s they faded out of the sitcom—to be replaced by new, highly exaggerated characters like Lou Lubin's "Shorty the Barber," James Baskett's "Gabby Gibson," Eddie Green's "LaGuardia Stonewall," and Johnny Lee's "Algonquin J. Calhoun." These new characters got the belly laughs—and in the case of Baskett, Green, and Lee gave mainstream exposure to long-standing stars of the African American vaudeville stage. At the same time, however, these characterizations existed solely as vehicles for jokes and gags and lacked the central core of humanity that had distinguished their serial-era predecessors.

The humor of these characters did not depend intrinsically on the race of the characters or that of the performers, and *The Amos 'n' Andy Show* was far from unique in presenting such figures. Extreme anything-for-a-laugh characters were equally common on "white" programs in postwar radio—from the shiftless, scheming and irresponsible Frankie Remley character on *The Phil Harris–Alice Faye Show* to the oafish, stupid Clifton Finnegan of *Duffy's Tavern*; from Frank Nelson's overweening, acid-tongued floorwalker on *The Jack Benny Program* to the morbid graveyard humor of Digger O'Dell, The Friendly Undertaker, on *The Life of Riley*; from the Southern bombast of Senator Beauregard Claghorn of *The Fred Allen Show* to Joe Besser's wildly exaggerated "swish" characters on *The Abbott and Costello Show*. In such an era, the extreme characters portrayed in *The Amos 'n' Andy Show* were more likely to be taken by audiences as general comedy conventionalities than as specific racial caricatures and Correll and Gosden attempted to further offset the presence of such cartoonish characters by taking care to present well-spoken, nonstereotyped African Americans in background roles, with such black actors as Roy Glenn, Jester Hairston, and Dorothy and Vivian Dandridge often filling the parts. But social attitudes changed rapidly during the postwar years; with the increasing social and economic empowerment of a rising black middle class, *any* presentation of black characters in comic settings would come under increasing fire from activists. The stage was thus set for renewed controversy in the 1950s—focusing not on the *Amos 'n' Andy Show* radio series but on its ill-fated television offspring.

Correll and Gosden had pondered the coming of television and what it might mean to them since the early 1930s, but it was not until February 27, 1939, that they made their first appearance in the visual medium, in a special telecast from the grounds of the New York World's Fair. For this telecast, the performers appeared in street clothes and without any sort of makeup—riding up to the camera in the Fresh Air Taxicab and then proceeding on a tour of the grounds.[10] Television was still in its infancy and there was little reason at that early stage to give it serious thought.

However, by the mid–1940s after World War II, it became evident that television would emerge as a major force in popular entertainment—and Correll and Gosden were forced to give the medium serious consideration. From the outset, the

On a February afternoon in 1939, Correll and Gosden step before an iconoscope camera set up on the grounds of the New York World's Fair for their first encounter with the emerging medium of television. Here, the performers, bundled up against the cold, stand before the unfinished RCA Pavilion and gaze down the Avenue of Patriots toward the fair's towering Theme Center, the famous Trylon and Perisphere. The telecast, aired over RCA's New York station W2XBS, was meant primarily to test remote relay systems that would be used for Fair telecasts later in the year and was viewed by a handful of researchers and technicians in the New York area with experimental television receivers in their homes. (*Correll Family Collection*)

performers realized that presenting a straightforward adaptation of their radio series, featuring themselves in blackface, would be unacceptable and several options were considered. The first possibility to be explored found the performers experimenting with an unusual hybrid format—seeking not to literally visualize their characterizations but to present an almost impressionistic cross between radio and television. No blackface makeup would be used. Instead, the lighting trick the performers had first used on their Pantages vaudeville tour in 1929 would suggest dark skin. No attempt would be made to recast the multiple roles played by Correll and Gosden with individual actors. The performers would continue to play those roles as they had on radio, through changes of voice and manner and augmented by the wearing of different hats to designate each character. The idea would have subtly maintained the imagination-centered approach of the radio series by emphasizing the unreality of the visual images presented—but the concept never progressed beyond the initial tests.[11]

The next idea to be considered was equally innovative. Concerned that television viewers would not accept voices other than their own as those of Amos, Andy, and the Kingfish, Correll and Gosden decided to experiment with dubbing their own voices to silent film footage of African American actors performing in pantomime. However, the performers were not closed to the idea of ceding the performances entirely to a new cast. "If we can find actors with suitable voices," Gosden told an interviewer, "we'll let them do the talking."[12] The proposed use of film at this stage in network television's development was a major departure from accepted practice—and Correll and Gosden were discussing the idea nearly a year before the premiere of the first network series to be produced on film, NBC's *Fireside Theatre*. A filmed network television program offered interesting advantages—the quality would be uniform from station to station, an important consideration in an era when coast-to-coast network television circuits had not been completed, and many affiliates were forced to accept blurry kinescope footage instead of live telecasts. A filmed series would also offer the advantage of post-network exploitation: after the series network run had ended, the films could be syndicated to individual stations.

As these plans were taking shape in the summer of 1948, Correll and Gosden sold all rights to the series, in a $2.5 million deal, to the Columbia Broadcasting System[13]—ensuring lifetime financial security for themselves and their families but giving up creative control of the program in the process. Planning for the television series continued under the aegis of CBS and after unsuccessful experimentation with the audio dubbing idea, the decision was made to search for African-American actors who could closely duplicate the voice characterizations established by Correll and Gosden. The talent search that followed took nearly three years to complete and involved hundreds of individual auditions, but by 1950, the choices were made, with legitimate stage actor Alvin Childress as Amos, "race movie" director/star Spencer Williams, Jr., as Andy, and the unforgettable Tim Moore, a veteran of nearly 50 years in black vaudeville, as the Kingfish. African American performers already appearing in the radio series, including Ernestine Wade, Amanda Randolph, Johnny Lee, Jester Hairston, and Roy Glenn, would be retained in the television version.

Production on the television series got underway at the Hal Roach Studios in Hollywood in the fall of 1950, and the pilot episode, an adaptation of Connelly and Mosher's 1/16/49 radio script entitled "Rare Coin Show," was shot under the supervision of director Abby Berlin—best known for his work on the long series of "Blondie" features at Columbia Pictures—over three days in early October, as the first CBS situation comedy program to be filmed on the West Coast, preceding *I Love Lucy* by nearly a year.[14] As the series went into regular production at the Roach Studios in February 1951 Abby Berlin was unavailable to accept a permanent appointment as the series' director and was replaced by Charles Barton, a veteran of B-grade comedies at Universal Pictures.

Almost immediately, conflict erupted between Gosden, Barton, and producer James Fonda over the broad visual slapstick that came to dominate many of the episodes and over the quality of the work submitted by new members of the writing team. "There were serious disagreements on every script," recalls Freeman F. Gosden, Jr. "The new writers lost the sensitivity and perfection that had been key factors in *Amos 'n' Andy*'s success."[15] Further strife grew out of the network's insistence that the actors duplicate the vocal inflections of the radio versions of their characters as exactly as possible rather than attempt to interpret the characterizations for themselves. This created friction when Gosden attempted to coach the performers on the set. The NAACP's formal protest of the television program immediately following its broadcast premiere in June 1951 only served to amplify the tension, and Gosden's complaints to CBS President William Paley about Barton and Fonda failed to produce results. "Paley said he could not afford top talent," continues Freeman F. Gosden, Jr. "After a while, Dad gave up."[16]

Under the supervision of Fonda and Barton, the visual adaptation of *The Amos 'n' Andy Show* would take the characters even further down the broadly comic path that had been followed during the late years of the radio program—and, in doing so, completed the process of erasing the complex psychological underpinnings Correll and Gosden had attached to the characters 20 years earlier. Andrew H. Brown was no longer a conflicted, insecure man bluffing his way through life in an often-hostile world—he was now merely a likeable dolt. "Here was a difference between radio and television we had not foreseen," recalled William Paley in 1976. "Correll and Gosden had created a warm and funny fantasy world in the listeners' imagination on radio. When that world became visual, it also became concrete and literal. *Amos 'n' Andy* remained on radio in some form until 1960. But the television show, under attack by black leaders for its entire life, left the network after two seasons."[17]

Although the organized NAACP protest petered out by the end of 1951, unable to achieve a consensus among ordinary black Americans, the video version of *The Amos 'n' Andy Show* was canceled by its sponsor, the Blatz Brewing Company, at the end of its second season. CBS made an additional 13 episodes for first-run syndication in the fall of 1953, and episodes continued to air as reruns for the next 13 years before being withdrawn from distribution in early 1966. Protests and controversy have dogged the television program even after its disappearance from the rerun market,

11. The Later Years

```
                                          SHOW #1172
              "THE AMOS 'N' ANDY MUSIC HALL"
TAPED:   WEDNESDAY, MARCH 4, 1959       TC:  7:05-7:28:55 PM NYT
BDCST:   TUESDAY, MARCH 17, 1959        KNX: 7:05-7:28:55 PM PST

AMECHE:     It's the Amos 'n' Andy Music Hall.
THEME:      SNEAK SUSTAINED CHORD UNDER AMECHE:  HIT FULL HERE FADE FOR:
AMECHE:     Good evening, this is Jim Ameche inviting you to the Amos
            'n' Andy Music Hall, brought to you every Monday through
            Friday by Freeman Gosden and Charles Correll - Amos 'n'
            Andy - and starring George "Kingfish" Stevens as Master
            of Ceremonies.
MUSIC:      THEME UP AND OUT
COMMERCIALS
1.       Grove
2.       Fram Corporation
3.
4.       Nash
5.       Fram Corporation
CAST:    RUBY                           ELINOR HARRIOT
         MADAM QUEEN                    LILLIAN RANDOLPH
         MISS BLUE                      MADALINE LEE
RECORDS:
         THREE LITTLE WORDS             LES PAUL & MARY FORD
         YOU'RE GETTING TO BE A HABIT WITH ME   FRANK SINATRA
         SUPPOSIN'                      FRANKIE LAINE
         WHEN THE BLUE OF THE NIGHT     BING CROSBY
         YOU'RE MY EVERTYHING           JERRY VALE

    TB
```

The song list on the title page of this *Amos 'n' Andy Music Hall* script suggests the overall tone of Correll and Gosden's last radio effort—middlebrow entertainment geared to an older audience. Note also that even at the end of their careers, the performers remained intensely loyal to longtime supporting cast members, making room for them on the program wherever possible.

and although bootlegged copies have circulated widely on home video, CBS has so far refused to sanction any sort of official re-release.[18]

The radio version of *The Amos 'n' Andy Show* continued through the 1950s protests unscathed. But radio itself was then a dying medium, and when the weekly series finally ended in the spring of 1955, the performers had already moved into their next program—*The Amos 'n' Andy Music Hall*, a nightly feature of recorded music, sandwiched between pre-recorded bits of character dialogue. Coasting on the familiarity of the characters, this final series endured for nearly six years.

On November 25, 1960, CBS aired the final broadcast of *The Amos 'n' Andy Music Hall*, dropping the series with most of the other long-form dramatic and comedy offerings on the network schedule—casualties of a new era in broadcasting that had no place for the form of entertainment Correll and Gosden had pioneered. "I wrote to Correll and Gosden how I felt about it," recalled William Paley, acknowledging his own sadness that the curtain was falling not just on their program but on the Golden Age of Radio that they had helped create. "'I just wanted you to know what a depressing feeling it gives me to face up to this fact.'"[19]

The farewell was brief and subdued. After one last project—providing voices for the 1961–62 ABC-TV animated series *Calvin and the Colonel*, which reworked late-era *Amos 'n' Andy Show* plot ideas into funny animal stories—Correll and Gosden slipped quietly into retirement.[20] The performers rarely commented on the controversy that had clouded their final years, but in a 1961 interview Charles Correll acknowledged that the world of the 1960s had left their work behind. "As Amos and Andy, Freeman and I never did anything to demean Negroes—we never typed them," Correll told the *Los Angeles Herald Examiner*. "But a national sponsor would be a fool to risk putting it on a network today. Things have changed too much."[21]

Charles Correll remained active and gregarious in his later years, raising four children with his wife Alyce in a breathtaking home in Holmby Hills.[22] During his retirement he remained the friendly, accessible man he had always been—granting frequent interviews, responding readily to fan mail, and remaining close to such former *Amos 'n' Andy* colleagues as Elinor Harriot Nathan and organist Gaylord Carter. Correll often visited old friends in Chicago—making a point of staying at the Drake Hotel, where *Sam 'n' Henry* had begun 40 years before—and it was while making one of these visits that he suffered a fatal heart attack. On September 26, 1972, he passed away at the age of 82.[23] In commenting on his partner's death, Gosden acknowledged the deep and lasting friendship the two men had shared. "We were partners for 32 years and friends for 50. During all that time, we never exchanged an unkind word."[24]

Freeman Gosden never appeared before a microphone again after 1962. He enjoyed a quiet retirement with his wife, Jane, and his four children, dividing time between his home in Beverly Hills and his summer residence in Palm Desert where he had befriended his neighbor, former President Dwight D. Eisenhower. As the former president's favorite golfing partner, Gosden was the prime mover in securing Eisenhower's support for the construction of a state-of-the-art, nonprofit medical facility in Rancho Mirage—eventually named the Eisenhower Medical Center—and

Although Freeman Gosden seldom publicly discussed his radio work during the years of his retirement, to the end of his life he gladly signed autographs as "Amos." This 1940s arcade card is one of the last items signed by the performer before his death in 1982.

Gosden was appointed to serve as a charter member of its board of trustees in 1966. After five years of planning and fund-raising, the hospital was completed in 1971, with Gosden continuing to serve as a trustee until he was forced to curtail his activities following a heart attack that same year.[25] He had little contact with most of his former radio colleagues after Correll's death but he did remain close to two veterans of the *Amos 'n' Andy Show* cast—Ernestine Wade, who for 15 years had portrayed the Kingfish's no-nonsense wife Sapphire, and Jester Hairston, best known for his role as Sapphire's brother Leroy.[26] Although he responded to fan mail when he was able to, Gosden generally avoided the public eye during the last years of his life and usually declined interview requests—reluctant to discuss the controversy that had surrounded *Amos 'n' Andy* in its final years. A friend observed that "it bothered him to the end of his life that *Amos 'n' Andy* fell from public esteem."[27]

On August 19, 1981, Gosden delivered his final performance—speaking by telephone and offering a quick sampling of his familiar voice characterizations to an assembly of well-wishers in his hometown of Richmond, who had gathered to celebrate "Freeman F. Gosden Day," declared by the Richmond City Council as a tribute on the fifty-second anniversary of *Amos 'n' Andy*'s network premiere.[28] His health declined rapidly over the next year, and on December 10, 1982, Freeman Gosden passed away in a Los Angeles hospital at the age of 83.[29]

12. MAKING THE POINT

"Dey might git yo' nerve, dey might git yo' goat, dey might git yo' money, but don't fo'git dey ain't got you."

—Amos Jones

ANALYSTS HAVE LONG DEBATED the depiction of "blackness" in *Amos 'n' Andy* as well as the question of whether that depiction was in any way an "authentic" image—and this debate has tended to create the impression that race was the central theme of the program. But was it?

Academic Michele Hilmes sums up a common view of the program in her essay "Who We Are—Who We Are Not," arguing that *Amos 'n' Andy*'s primary message was one of cultural exclusion—a message that allowed whites of varying ethnic backgrounds to define their "whiteness" in contrast to the "blackness" of Amos and Andy Such a message therefore classified African Americans as permanent outsiders.

> *Amos 'n' Andy*'s wholly artificial discourse at once identified problems experienced by the outsider trying to assimilate and projected a representation of nonassimilation in its extreme form onto a small and easily identified minority—African Americans.[1]
>
> …White audiences were free to see themselves in the vast majority of representations on radio, to read out the dissimilarities between their own ethnic experience and that of the vast undifferentiated "America" constructed on the air, and to pose this identity in strict and stark contrast to those defined as "black." Black audiences found themselves forced out of this easy identification with the mainstream of radio, specifically assigned to another place by traits marked by the outset as the "not-me."[2]

Certainly the predominant image of black characters on radio fits Hilmes's description—the chuckling maids, the shuffling bellboys and porters, the wise-cracking Rochesters, all subordinate in their roles and their activities to those of whites. Was *Amos 'n' Andy* really any different? Could audiences—white or black—ever truly see themselves in the residents of Correll and Gosden's world?

In support of her argument, Hilmes cites *Amos 'n' Andy*'s use of wordplay routines as demonstrations of the "cultural incompetence" of the characters. "Indeed," she contends, "it is as a foil to problems of cultural assimilation that *Amos 'n' Andy* achieves some of its most typical humor." This is true enough—the theme of "strangers in a strange land" was a common one in the series during its early years, drawing humor out of Amos and Andy's mishaps in settling into their new lives in the North. However, Hilmes overlooks or ignores the fact that this type of humor appeared less and less in the series as it matured. As early as 1931 the heavy emphasis on wordplay and cultural-displacement humor had disappeared, consistent with the growth and development of the characters. While never becoming fully urbanized, neither did Amos and Andy remain perpetual "strangers" in their new surroundings. Hilmes goes on to contend that "its use of dialect reinforces the idea of a kind of permanent cultural 'accent,' emphasizing the unassimilability of African Americans as a group."[3] Here, as throughout her discussion of the program, Hilmes overlooks or ignores the significant elements of *Amos 'n' Andy* that sharply contradict her thesis. Contrary to her central assertion, the contrast between "white" and "black" in the original *Amos 'n' Andy* was often neither strict nor stark.

A careful examination of their work reveals that, in fact, Correll and Gosden were unique in the era in which they lived and worked for their presentation of African American characters who were essentially indistinguishable from the rest of Hilmes's "vast undifferentiated 'America.'" Without visual cues to establish their color, and without the aural cue of dialect, the educated middle- and upper-class blacks who occasionally interacted with Amos and Andy were, in fact, easily mistaken for whites and required specific contextual clues to establish their racial identity. The presence of these characters in the narrative clearly carried an assimilatory message by presenting blacks who displayed none of the "not-me" traits then assigned by popular culture to "blackness."

It is difficult to imagine, for example, a more completely assimilated African American character than William Taylor. Over the years, Correll and Gosden filled in a detailed backstory for Taylor—he came to Chicago in 1897 and began his career in business by opening a small lunchroom, which he soon built into a chain of lunchrooms, which he then sold in order to invest the proceeds in a clothing store, a garage, and a contracting firm. Although Taylor had come from the South, he was a college-educated man who spoke without a trace of dialect.[4] His voice, his personality, and his point of view all marked Taylor as an impeccably middle-class American—whose example his future son-in-law Amos might one day follow.

> Taylor---I suppose you realize Amos that Ruby is all that I have left in the world. She is very dear to me and she has made our home very pleasant. I knew the time would come when she would want to get married and I've made up my mind not to stand in her way --- although I WOULD like to know that she would be comfortable and have a few things that I believe she deserves.
>
> Andy---Dere you is Amos.
>
> Amos---Yessah, yessah, yo' see Mr. Taylor, I know I ain't got a lot o' money but I goin' try to give Ruby ev'vything I kin to make her happy.

12. Making the Point 155

Andy---He's in love wid her alright Mr. Taylor. I ain't neveh seed him like he is befo' --- an' I done knowed him all his life.

Taylor---Well Amos, you want to give her an engagement ring for Xmas? When do you plan on getting married?

Amos---Well, to tell yo' de truth Mr. Taylor, I thought I'd give her de 'gagement fo' Xmas, yo' see --- an' den some time next year --- soon as I make enough money -- if dat's alright wid yo', we'll git married.

Andy---Yo' see Mr. Taylor, we is in de taxicab bizness an' I is de president of de comp'ny an' next yeah I'se goin' put on a big drive fo' money an' cou'se I gives Amos part o' whut we take in so maybe next yeah he'll have mo' money dan he got now.

Taylor---Well Amos, if you two WOULD get married, where would you plan on living --- here at the house?

Amos---Nosah, Mr. Taylor, we'd count on gittin' a flat somewhere --- a little flat o' some kind.

Taylor---Well, it would be no bother to me. We have plenty of room here.

Amos---Nosah, thank yo' Mr. Taylor --- I thank yo' just de same but I b'lieve it be better if we git a little flat 'cause we done talked dat oveh. I feel better 'bout it.

Taylor---Oh yes. Well Amos, I'm going to tell you something.

Amos---Yessah, yessah.

Andy---Listen to Mr. Taylor now when he talks to yo'.

Taylor---Amos, I love Ruby as much as a father could love a daughter. She is a sweet girl. I don't know if Ruby has ever gone into details with you or not, but when Ruby was a little girl, her dear mother died. I have tried to raise Ruby and although somewhat handicapped, I'm proud to say that we have been very happy together and Ruby has proven to be a wonderful pal as well as a daughter to me. I have made up my mind never to stand in her way when the time came for her to get married. I know that she loves you Amos and if she thinks that you are the one to make her life happy, I am satisfied. I would like however to know that you are in a position to take care of her but that can be worked out later. So Amos, I'll say to you "God bless you." You have my permission. Shake hands [Episode 233, 12/22/28].

Amos's refusal to impose on Taylor's home after he and Ruby are married and his promise to wait until he is financially able to support a wife before going ahead with the marriage demonstrate his own aspiration to the same middle-class values. Throughout the series, Amos remains committed to these goals. Consider the following exchange, in which Andy gets on his partner's nerves by repeatedly attempting to correct his grammar.

Andy---If you say "is -- is" one mo' time, I goin' knock yo' head off.

Amos---Alright den, I'll just shut up Andy.

Andy---Now, lemme tell yo' whut "is" is. You know I is been to school. When I finished de day school I went to night school. I been to mornin', afternoon, an' night school.

Amos---I ain't arguin' 'bout dat. I a-mits dat. I ain't been to school much.

Andy---Dat's de trouble wid yo' now --- comin' 'round heah is-is'in --- yo' just ain't been to school.

Amos---I didn't git de CHANCE to go to school.

Andy---Well, dere you IS.

Amos---But if I ever have any chillen, I goin' send dem to school an' give dem more schoolin' dan I had a chance to git if I kin [Episode 727, 7/21/30].

Amos here expresses the classic assimilationist position—"my children will have the educational advantages that I didn't" Although in this scene Correll and Gosden are underlining the pompous Andy's tendency to pretend knowledge he does not possess—and by doing so they are pointedly mocking pseudointellectuals in general, the puncturing of pretentiousness being a common theme in *Amos 'n' Andy*—there is no suggestion in the context of the scene that Amos's position is anything but honestly and earnestly felt nor is there any aspect to the scene to suggest to the audience that his comments should be taken as anything but serious.

Amos is determined to succeed in life. He sets goals and he pursues them with a dogged determination that provides a steady theme for most of the series' first decade. Resolving in 1928 not to marry Ruby until he is financially able to support her, he worked and saved for a full seven years—weathering setbacks and disappointments and frustrations but never losing sight of his objective. And once that goal was finally achieved, he resolved to continue moving forward—epitomizing the American middle-class success model and inviting audiences of all races to identify with the universality of his experiences.

Amos---Sweetheart -- I is so happy I don't know whut to do.

Ruby---I am too, darlin'.

Amos---Look at dat baby. Ain't she sweet? Oh darlin', dat is de sweetest baby I ever seed in my life.

Ruby---She IS sweet. Look at her big brown eyes.

Amos---Dey pretty, ain't dey?

Ruby---I think our little baby looks like you, darlin'.

Amos---Tell yo' de truth, sweetheart, de baby's so little I can't tell WHO it's gonna look like. How you feel?

Ruby---I feel fine. I want you to stop worryin' though darlin' --- our little girl is here now --- everything's gonna be fine.

Amos---Yo' know sweetheart, I wanted to say dis to yo' before, but I ain't zackly had a chance. I don't know how to tell yo' dis but --- well --- dis little baby is OUR baby --- it belongs to us --- it's our own flesh an' blood --- dis little baby is brought me an' you closer together, an' I promise you honey, dat fo' de rest o' my life I'll work hard, so dat I kin always take care o' you an' our baby [Episode 2441, 10/22/36].

To compare the fumbling, naïve, and self-conscious Amos of 1928 with the Amos of 1936, a mature, responsible man with a wife and child, living in a comfortable apartment, and supporting himself and his family by the operation of a viable small business, is to be confronted with a textbook example of successful assimilation into the value system of mainstream 1930s America and a pointed repudiation of the minstrel stereotypes of laziness, shiftlessness, and dishonesty. With no white characters present with whom they could identify, white listeners found themselves compelled to identify with Amos—not as an unassimilable racial "other," but as an embodiment of their own aspirations. These elements of *Amos 'n' Andy* emphatically and explicitly contradict Michele Hilmes's classificaton of the program as part of "a discursive universe that assigned 'black' racial identity only to characterizations that fit with minstrel stereotypes."[5]

The theme of cultural marginalization in modern analyses of *Amos 'n' Andy* is a common one, with one of its earliest mainstream exponents being communications historian Erik Barnouw. Working largely from memory in his 1966 discussion of the program, Barnouw argued that much of the popularity of Correll and Gosden's program stemmed from the need of white listeners for reinforcement for their prejudices and perhaps for an anodyne for subconscious racial guilt.

> In retrospect it is easy—at the time it was less easy—to see ... "Amos 'n' Andy" as part of the ghetto system. All of it was more readily accepted and maintained if one could hold onto this: 'they' were lovely people, essentially happy people, ignorant and somewhat shiftless and lazy in a lovable quaint way, not fitting in with higher levels of enterprise, better off where they were [the Fresh Air Taxicab Company of America, Incorpulated], essentially happy, happy.... It could make South Side poverty somehow charming and fitting. The nation needed the fantasy.[6]

Barnouw's glib dismissal of the program has deeply influenced treatments of the series by subsequent broadcasting historians, but did Barnouw genuinely grasp the real appeal, the real message of *Amos 'n' Andy*? Were Correll and Gosden merely subtle apologists for the untenable racial system of early twentieth-century America? A careful review of the content of the program itself suggests another answer. Far from the shallow and stereotypical image of "essentially happy people" projected onto the program by Barnouw, the underlying mood of *Amos 'n' Andy* in its serial years was in fact one of melancholy restlessness, of a distinct unwillingness to placidly accept one's lot in life, and certainly not a Sambo-like happy-go-lucky inertia. Amos and Andy were no one's Sambos—and although their enterprises were often precarious, and although Andy's bombast often undermined Amos's progress, the partners nevertheless remained determined to build a self-sufficient future for themselves.

In this way, the characters embodied the restless determination of Depression-era America itself.

Considered from this perspective, it becomes quite evident that Correll and Gosden intended *Amos 'n' Andy* as something far more than a simplistic reiteration of comic stereotypes. Above and beyond its humorous elements, the original *Amos 'n' Andy* was an allegorical morality play constructed around the unending conflict between the practical values embodied by Amos and the impractical posturing represented by Andy. Both Amos and Andy are striving for the "American Dream" but differ sharply both on how they define that dream and on how they hope to achieve it. Andy expects assimilation—represented in his worldview by the symbols of respect and power that accompany economic success—to be handed to him, while Amos understands that he will accomplish nothing unless he takes control of his own destiny, focusing his aspirations on substance rather than symbols. Amos cares less about others viewing him as a success than he does about actually succeeding. Andy is constantly disappointed and frustrated by his failures and is easily discouraged by the slightest obstacles and is consequently doomed to forever remain an outsider. But Amos pushes forward in spite of all obstacles to make slow but steady progress, realizing that every step forward, no matter how small, brings him that much closer to his ultimate goal.

> It isn't comedy alone that gets "Amos 'n' Andy" over. Far from it. It's the philosophy they put in their nightly broadcast—the homely interpretation of human emotions. As a matter of fact, if you analyze their performance carefully, you'll find that there's quite a paucity of comedy. At least the slap-bang kind...
>
> Their contrasts are a masterpiece of stage management. Here we have on one side the lovable and hard working Amos, eager to get along, saving, generous, keen to sense the tricks of the parasitic Pat Pending and the high-sounding words of the likable, but not altogether trustworthy, Kingfish. And on the other side, the lazy, bumptious Andy, who will never learn how to say no to anything, who likes to think big and work little. Bring in the types represented by the other members of the cast, and you have the whole panorama of humanity. Put them through their conflicting paces, and you run head on into the problems which you and I encounter every day.[7]

Amos 'n' Andy was unique among radio programs of the 1920s and 1930s for the innovative nature of its format, the depth of its characterizations, and above all the dramatic and sociological complexity of its narrative. The result is a many-layered work that lends itself readily to multiple interpretations. But it is easy—especially given the tendency of modern academics to dwell exclusively on the program's racial implications—to miss the real point of the series, the real message that above all others it carried to its original audience. Beneath the dialect, behind the racial imagery, beyond the four-flushing of Andrew H. Brown and the machinations of the Kingfish, the thematic center of the original *Amos 'n' Andy* is surprisingly simple and straightforward: to succeed in business, to succeed in romance, to succeed in life, one must persist.

12. Making the Point

Amos---Andy! Andy, answer me, you ain't 'sleep.

Andy---I know I ain't.

Amos---Lift up yo' head. I wanna talk to yo'.

Andy---Whut yo' want?

Amos---How come you run away from de hotel?

Andy---Amos, it just got me, dat's all. I was workin' dere doin' de best I could, an' I just couldn't cut it, dat's all. An' I thought o' dis place here, made me think o' how happy I used to be when I was heah in de taxicab office, got to wishin' dat I was back heah, neveh stahted dat hotel bizness --- an' I felt like I wanted to come oveh heah an' sit down in heah by myself.

Amos---I know how yo' feel, but you ought not to run out on de hotel when yo' git busy like dat.

Andy---I know it Amos, but my brain just got tangled up --- ev'ybody was wantin' sumpin' at de same time, an' I just had to git out.

Amos---I know how yo' feel.

Andy---Look at dis office heah boy. Heah's where we worked, an' worked --- den we give it up, moved oveh to de hotel. Why can't we get back heah, git out o' dat hotel mess?

Amos---Dis ain't no time to feel like dat though Andy.

Andy---I feel like givin' up, dat's whut I feel like.

Amos---I know, Andy, but dis ain't de time to give up --- when things look tough like dis an' we ain't makin' money, dat's de fust thing yo' think about, but dis ain't no time to do it --- dat's when we gotta plug hardeh den we IS plugged befo' ---- if peoples gived up when dey got down, why dey'd NEVER git nowhere. I know how yo' feel --- yo' feel like you is licked ---- but you can't think dat way ---- ev'ything goin' come out alright --- ev'ybody in de world, no matter how much money you think dey got gits down in de dumps sometimes an' de rich an' de poor both sometimes feel like givin' up, but dey don't do it. Dey keeps on fightin' an' when dey fight enough dey comes back an' dey comes back strong --- it might take time to do dis but boy, don't give up. A coward is de one dat gives up, an' you ain't no coward --- now, I ain't goin' jump on yo' an' I ain't goin' let de Kingfish jump on yo' --- I just want yo' to tell me dat yo' ain't goin' give up an' you'll try to fight 'cause de real man fights when things look de toughest.

Andy---Alright Amos. I'll try again.

Amos---Dat's de stuff --- now come on ---- put yo' arms 'round me. Dey might git yo' nerve, dey might git yo' goat, dey might git yo' money, but don't fo'git dey ain't got you.

Andy---Yo' right son [Episode 1329, 6/24/32].

In the world of *Amos 'n' Andy,* no crisis is ever as deep as it seems at first glance and no problem is insurmountable. There is always hope that a better future lies

Their day's work done, Correll and Gosden leave Studio F following their broadcast of August 22, 1935. As the original caption for this NBC publicity photo states, the performers were on their way out of the studio before the end of their closing theme.

ahead but only for those who are determined to keep working for it, regardless of the obstacles.

In 1930, Correll and Gosden received what may have been their finest tribute, in a letter to the black-owned *Baltimore Afro-American*, in which the author concluded that "It [the program] has all the pathos, humor, vanity, glory, problems and solutions that beset ordinary mortals—and therein lies its universal appeal."[8]

The author of that statement? Journalist and future civil rights leader Roy Wilkins. In later years, Wilkins's views of the program would evolve, even as the program itself changed form. By the early 1950s, Wilkins helped lead the NAACP campaign against *The Amos 'n' Andy Show* television series—even as he continued to privately acknowledge the positive qualities in Correll and Gosden's work.[9]

Wilkins's conflicted, changing, and sometimes contradictory views on the program mirror those of society itself—cultures may progress, but their artifacts do not. The same qualities that made *Amos 'n' Andy* a progressive, innovative depiction of African American characters in the late 1920s were outdated by the early 1950s—and those innovations are often incomprehensible to observers more than three quarters of a century removed from the program's original social context. Today, *Amos 'n' Andy* is a complex relic of an often-confusing past, and modern commentators tend to see in the program what they have been conditioned to see—conditioning that may involve racial issues and political ideologies that have nothing to do with the content of a radio program. It is far simpler, far more comfortable, and far less challenging to their own assumptions for these modern analysts to criticize Freeman Gosden and Charles Correll for what they were not than to attempt to understand what they actually *were* to the three generations of radio listeners of all races and backgrounds who embraced their creation.

Multiple interpretations of *Amos 'n' Andy* abound—but a detailed examination of the work itself suggests that, more than any other factor, it was Correll and Gosden's nightly presentation of a sincere, enduring story of persistence in the face of adversity that set the performers apart from their legion of imitators and earned for them the title "Radio's All-Time Favorites." Other comedians may have been funnier, other dramatists may have been more profound, but Amos Jones and Andy Brown spoke to 1930s America in simple, direct language that went straight to the national heart. The 40 million listeners who followed the series at the peak of its success were not encouraged to view Amos and Andy as minstrel stereotypes or as representatives of an unassimilable underclass. In the never-say-die adventures of these two characters, millions of Americans of all backgrounds saw *themselves*.

APPENDIX: BY THE NUMBERS

IN THE BUSINESS OF broadcasting, success is invariably measured by the numbers. Since the early 1930s, program ratings have been used as a tool for calculating the popularity of any given program, but these statistics can be misleading if not examined closely. Broadcast executives have long known how to manipulate these figures for their own purposes, and broadcast historians must be wary of drawing flawed conclusions from an incorrect interpretation of the statistics.

This has often been the case with historical interpretation of the ratings popularity of *Amos 'n' Andy*. In particular, the program's sharp rise to popularity in the early 1930s—and its supposed sharp decline during the middle and latter portion of that decade—have been cause for much speculation. One popular theory goes so far as to suggest that a sharp drop in the audience of *Amos 'n' Andy* between 1931 and 1933 contributed to a substantial decline in overall radio listening—leading to a near-panic in the broadcasting industry—and to a rush to develop new forms of programming in an effort to halt that decline.[1] This interpretation has found its way into the folklore of broadcasting but it is an interpretation based on a faulty understanding of the actual data. While *Amos 'n' Andy* did in fact see a decline in the size of its audience over the course of the 1930s, the information to be presented in this appendix will prove conclusively that this decline was neither as sharp nor as significant as has been suggested, and that the fluctuation of the ratings during the 1930s can find more reasonable explanation by comparison with the flow of the series' story lines. A careful examination of this ratings information will also shed light on the decision by *Amos 'n' Andy* creators Freeman Gosden and Charles Correll to end their original series in early 1943 and to replace it with a modernized weekly half-hour situation comedy—a program that then surpassed the listenership of even the peak years of the original series and maintained a consistently high level of popularity well into the mid–1950s.

Amos 'n' Andy Serial Audience 1930-43

Season	1930-31	1931-32	1932-33	1933-34	1934-35	1935-36	1936-37	1937-38	1938-39	1939-40	1940-41	1941-42	1942-43
Amos 'n' Andy	29,904,	25,617,	23,993,	26,004,	20,673,	22,238,	19,519,	19,488,	16,531,	13,548,	14,137,	14,168,	12,032,
Strongest Competitor	0	0	19,749,	15,877,	15,093,	9,741,6	6,613,2	7,840,0	7,921,0	13,432,	11,523,	15,523,	14,848,
Season Leader	20,440,	19,431,	47,823,	43,083,	35,218,	44,476,	31,039,	44,128,	40,294,	40,412,	43,005,	43,366,	52,352,

Ratings information was first tabulated in 1930 by the Cooperative Analysis of Broadcasting, a nonprofit organization under the supervision of statistician Archibald Crossley. Ratings were calculated by means of telephone calls made four times daily to a random sampling of listeners in 33 urban markets. These callers would be asked to recall the programs they had heard the previous evening. While this system was far from foolproof, it provided the first hard evidence available to broadcasters on the size of their audiences. In 1934, the C.E. Hooper Company, a for-profit enterprise, offered its own ratings service in competition to that of the C.A.B. with a system based on concurrent telephone calls. Listeners were phoned at random and asked to name any radio program to which they were listening at that moment. The Hooperratings service soon became the industry leader and remained so until 1949, when the service was absorbed by a competitor, A.C. Nielsen, Incorporated.

It is important to note, however, that none of these rating systems factored in rural audiences—the surveys for both C.A.B. and Hooper were conducted only in metropolitan areas. The surveys also failed to include communal listening in public places—which for *Amos 'n' Andy* in the early 1930s is likely to have incorporated a sizable chunk of the audience. During 1930, many theaters interrupted their scheduled presentations to broadcast *Amos 'n' Andy* from the stage, and many stores and other public establishments presented the program over public-address systems for the convenience of shoppers. Ample anecdotal documentation survives of such public listening, and it must be concluded that the audience figures that can be assumed from the available ratings figures (at least during the "craze" years of 1930–31) are extremely conservative. Contemporary estimates of the *Amos 'n' Andy* audience during the early part of 1930 routinely ran from 40 to 50 million people.[2]

Table 1 offers a graphic display of ratings data showing the average popularity of *Amos 'n' Andy* between the start of the C.A.B. ratings service during the 1930–31 season and the end of the original 15-minute nightly serial version of the program in February 1943. The figures represent the percentage of "radio homes" tuning in to the program during the rating period in question.[3]

Alongside the ratings information for *Amos 'n' Andy*, the table also presents for comparison purposes the rating for the strongest competition program in the *Amos 'n' Andy* time slot, which was 7 P.M. Eastern time weeknights for the entire period under consideration. (A Saturday evening *Amos 'n' Andy* broadcast was also aired in the 7 P.M. time slot through November 8, 1932.) The competition programs rated for each season are as follows:

- 1930–31, 1931–32—No competing program registered a measurable rating.
- 1932–33 through 1935–36—*Myrt and Marge*, a dramatic serial of backstage life written by Myrtle Vail (CBS).
- 1936–37 through 1938–39—*Easy Aces,* an urbane comedy serial of middle-class married life, written by Goodman Ace (NBC-Blue).
- 1939–40 through 1941–43—*Chesterfield Time,* popular music presented by Fred Waring and His Pennsylvanians (NBC-Red).

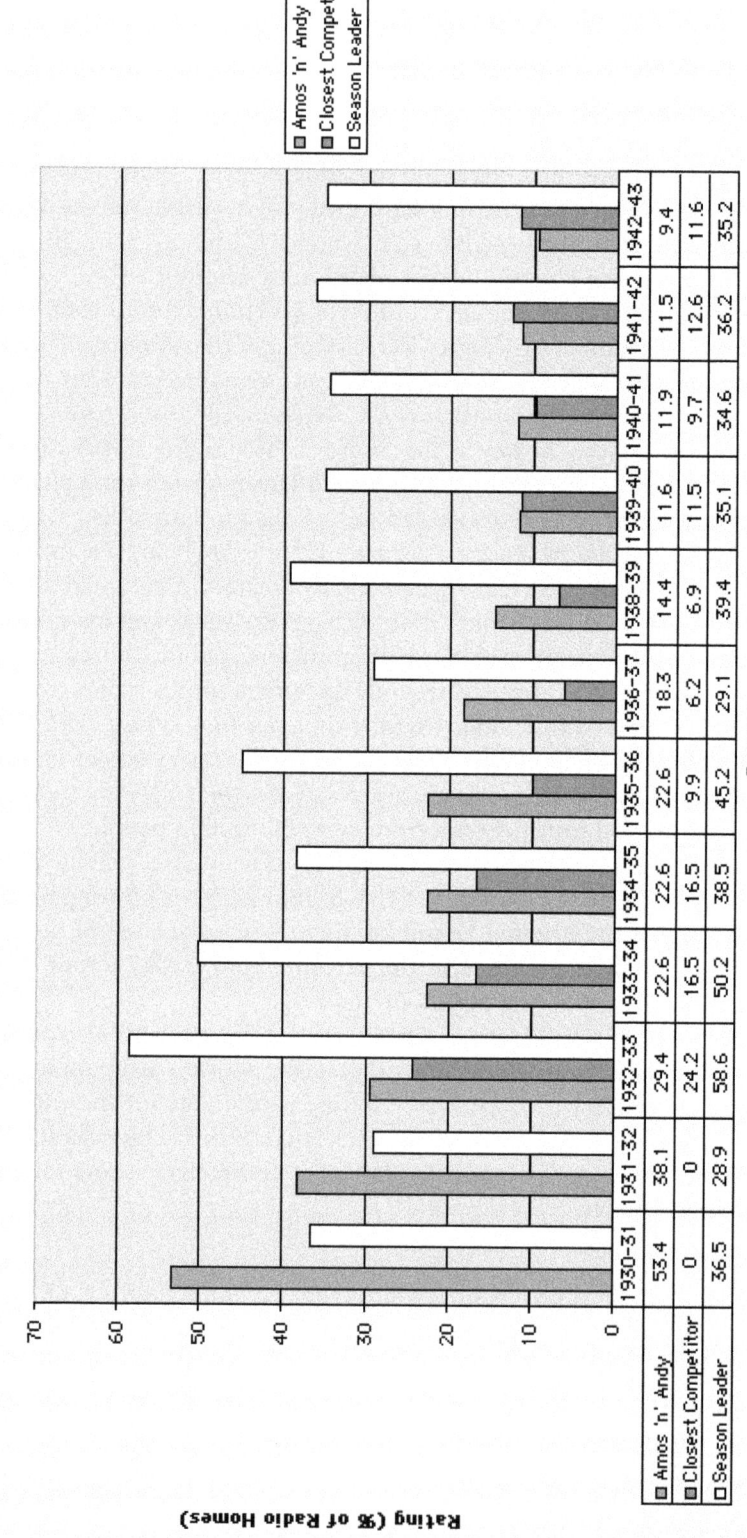

Also shown for comparison purposes is the rating for the most popular network program for each season. For seasons during which *Amos 'n' Andy* itself was the ratings leader, the program with the second-highest rating is shown. These season leaders are as follows:

- 1930–31: *Amos 'n' Andy* was season leader, second highest rating was *Fleischmann's Yeast Hour* (Rudy Vallee), NBC, 36.5.
- 1931–32: *Amos 'n' Andy* was season leader, second highest rating was *Chase & Sanborn Hour* (Eddie Cantor), NBC, 28.9.
- 1932–33: *Chase & Sanborn Hour* (Eddie Cantor), NBC, 58.6.
- 1933–34: *Chase & Sanborn Hour* (Eddie Cantor), NBC, 50.2.
- 1934–35: *Fleischmann's Yeast Hour* (Rudy Vallee), NBC, 38.5.
- 1935–36: *Major Bowes' Original Amateur Hour*, NBC, 45.2.
- 1936–37: *Texaco Town* (Eddie Cantor), CBS, 29.1.
- 1937–38: *Chase & Sanborn Hour* (Edgar Bergen), NBC, 39.4.
- 1938–39: *Chase & Sanborn Hour* (Edgar Bergen), NBC, 35.1.
- 1939–40: *Chase & Sanborn Program* (Edgar Bergen), NBC, 34.6.
- 1940–41: *Jell-O Program* (Jack Benny), NBC, 36.2.
- 1941–42: *Chase & Sanborn Program* (Edgar Bergen), NBC, 35.2.
- 1942–43: *Pepsodent Show* (Bob Hope), NBC, 40.9.

As can be seen, there was indeed a sharp decline in the percentage rating of *Amos 'n' Andy* between 1930 and 1931 and between 1932 and 1933. But does this decline in *rating* translate into an equally drastic loss of *audience*? A careful examination of these figures will reveal that it did not.

The key to a proper interpretation of these statistics is an understanding of the concept of "radio homes." This term means exactly what one would expect it to mean—the number of homes equipped with at least one radio receiver. Table 2 reveals the steady increase in the number of radio homes during *Amos 'n' Andy*'s era as a nightly serial program. While the increase in radio homes becomes less sharp after 1932–33, at no point during the period does the number decline.

Knowing the number of radio homes for each season allows us to calculate a reasonable estimate of the size of the overall audience for each season. The standard assumption in the broadcasting industry in the 1930s was that for every "radio home" an average of four people would be listening. To estimate the audience for a particular program becomes, then, a matter of multiplying the total number of radio homes by the percentage rating of the program in question—and then multiplying that result by four. By that method, the total audiences of *Amos 'n' Andy* and of its closest competitors in the 7 P.M. Eastern time slot are as follows in Table 3.

Here it may be seen that while the percentage rating of *Amos 'n' Andy* may have declined sharply between 1930 and 1931 and 1932 and 1933, this decline was offset

Radio Homes 1930-43

by a sharp increase in the number of radio homes. The resulting drop in the actual listening audience for *Amos 'n' Andy* was far less steep than the percentage rating would seem to indicate. As some listeners dropped away, they were replaced by newer listeners. This increase in radio homes can be directly attributed to the availability of cheap "midget" radio receivers, first on the market during 1931 and widely available at low prices, often on "easy credit terms." This trend allowed lower-income Americans ready access to radio for the first time, even in spite of the deepening Depression and these lower-income listeners showed a marked preference in C.A.B. surveys for serial fare like *Amos 'n' Andy*.

Nonetheless, a decline in overall radio listenership was noted in the C.A.B. report for 1931–32. The survey noted that 644 out of every 1,000 families surveyed reported using their sets at least once on an average weekday during the first four months of 1932, compared to 745 out of every 1,000 families during 1930—with listening having fallen off most sharply among upper-income set owners. In an analysis published in 1939, C.A.B. manager A. W. Lehman attributes the largest part of this decline to upper-income listeners having finally become "satiated with the novelty of radio." In a footnote, editor Edgar Gruenwald of the *Variety Radio Directory* speculates that a craze for mystery programs during the 1932–33 season may also have contributed to the decline in listenership by alienating female listeners, and it is he who first presented the suggestion that the decline of *Amos 'n' Andy* listenership from "previously astronomical" highs might have dealt a blow to overall listenership. Gruenwald is far less dogmatic on this last point than some latter-day authors, however, mentioning it only as one out of several contributing factors deserving further investigation.[4]

But was there, in fact, a decline in the total audience to which a decline in the popularity of *Amos 'n' Andy* could have contributed? If 64.4 percent of the 16,809,562 radio homes reported for 1932 were actually using their sets on a daily basis, this translates to a total active audience of 43,301,431 people. If 74.5 percent of the 14,000,000 radio homes reported in 1930–31 were using their sets on a daily basis, the total active audience would work out to 41,720,000—a net *gain* of nearly 1.6 million listeners overall. The "decline in the overall audience" commented on by the C.A.B. in 1932 and pondered in the decades since by broadcast historians is little more than a statistical myth. Although *Amos 'n' Andy* did lose approximately 20 percent of its audience between 1930 and 1932—approximately six million people—few of these lost listeners appear to have given up entirely on radio. But why did this decline occur?

A sharp increase in the audience of the leading program for each season will be noted beginning in 1932 to 1933. This development can be traced primarily to the craze for "personality" programming that began during the 1930–31 and 1931–32 seasons with the arrival first of Maurice Chevalier and then of Eddie Cantor on the Sunday night *Chase & Sanborn Hour*, which reached its height during 1932 and 1933 with Cantor's continued tenure on that program. During 1932 and 1933, a wave of Broadway and vaudeville performers, including Ed Wynn, Jack Pearl, Jack Benny, Fred Allen, and Fannie Brice followed Cantor's lead, entering radio as a hedge against the disastrous economic conditions then prevalent in the legitimate theater, and these big-name programs, produced under lavish budgets by advertising agencies, soon became the dominant program form. The rush of interest in these high-profile performers tended to divert public attention away from those performers already established in the medium. Thus, it may be suggested that rather than a decline in the popularity of *Amos 'n' Andy* helping to spur the creation of these new programs, the creation of these new programs *contributed* to the *Amos 'n' Andy* decline. Fads thrive on publicity, and it is a demonstrable fact that *Amos 'n' Andy* received far less publicity from 1932 to 1933 forward than it had received between 1929 and 1931, as more and more attention went to the newer radio stars—and it is likely that the publicists themselves had exhausted public interest in Correll and Gosden with the endless stream of material published about the performers during the height of the *Amos 'n' Andy* craze. Press clippings from 1930 to 1931 alone fill ten volumes in the collection of scrapbooks in the Correll-Gosden Collection stored at the University of Southern California while clippings from 1933 to 1937 are contained in a single scrapbook.

In addition to the overall trend to large-scale programming, there are two other factors that probably contributed to the gradual shrinkage of the *Amos 'n' Andy* audience: a leveling off in the content of the series and increased direct competition in the 7 P.M. time slot.

First, it is important to understand that the huge audience of 1930–31 was the by-product of a nationwide craze. Beginning in late 1929 and continuing through the end of 1931, *Amos 'n' Andy* was less a radio program than a national mania—and this mania was fed by several especially well-written and suspenseful serialized story lines presented on the program during this period. Beginning with the "Great Home Bank" story line of February/March 1930, followed by the "Van Porter Affair" through the summer months, and culminating with Andy's desperate attempts to escape from his planned marriage to Madam Queen during the fall and winter of 1930–31, Correll and Gosden managed to stir their audience to a fever pitch of excitement. The resulting enthusiasm for the program in the popular media undoubtedly helped to inflate the audience. The audience peaked between January and March of 1931 during Madam Queen's breach-of-promise suit against Andy, and while interest remained strong through the remainder of the year, there was bound to be something of a leveling off in the audience as the craze began to subside. Correll and Gosden understood that an audience could not be maintained at white-hot intensity for long, and they made a point of alternating heavier subject matter in their story lines with lighter fare. Many casual listeners who had been swept up by the publicity surrounding the series during the more dramatic sequences could be expected to fall away once the emphasis had shifted to other subject matter.

Following a short but potent story line in the spring in which Amos's fiancée Ruby Taylor contracted a near-fatal case of pneumonia, Correll and Gosden coasted through the middle of 1931, sending their characters on a vacation trip to a lakeside campground in upstate New York, where Andy enjoyed a summer fling with a local girl, and his dealings with her family continued into mid-autumn. While amusing and well written, this sequence lacked the high drama of the breach-of-promise story line. But the series regained its earlier intensity during the final months of the year with the "Jack Dixon Affair," a sequence in which Amos was accused of first-degree murder in the shooting death of a cheap criminal who had been cheating elderly women out of their savings. This story line came to an abrupt and shocking end just before Christmas, when it was revealed that the entire murder story was simply a bad dream. The story lines that followed were far less intense and not as involving: the Kingfish became interested in professional wrestling and promoted Andy in a match against a bruiser named "Bullneck Mooseface," following which Amos, Andy, and the Kingfish went into partnership with Madam Queen in the operation of a reducing spa. These low-key story lines were followed in the spring of 1932 by the leading characters' involvement in a new business venture, the Okey Hotel—and, while filled with interesting character development, this sequence lacked a suspenseful hook or a strong adversarial character likely to inspire word-of-mouth discussion of the program. Under these circumstances, it is easy to understand the decline in the audience.[5]

A second major factor is the advent on CBS of *Myrt and Marge*, the first rival program to offer any significant competition to *Amos 'n' Andy*. Sponsored by Wrigley's Chewing Gum in the 7 P.M. time slot, this program was a gritty story of theatrical life featuring former stage actress Myrtle Vail as a hard-boiled chorus girl, and her daughter Donna Damerel as her naïve young protégé. The often-spicy story lines displayed an edgier approach to serial drama when compared to the sentimental morality-play atmosphere of *Amos 'n' Andy*. The contrast between the two programs was sufficient to attract a substantial audience for the new program—and it is likely that a small percentage of *Amos 'n' Andy* listeners defected to the CBS offering during this period of creative doldrums for the older feature.

Myrt and Marge started strong but peaked early. The success of the competing program was met by a strong counterattack by Correll and Gosden, who presented a series of tense, dramatic story lines during the winter of 1932–33. In December, Amos was devastated by a request from Mr. Taylor, the father of his fiancée Ruby, that he consider stepping aside in favor of Taylor's new business partner, an up-and-coming young man who Taylor felt would be better able to provide for his daughter. No sooner had this story line ended with Amos exposing the new suitor as a fraud than a fresh crisis erupted: the Okey Hotel was placed under the control of abrasive efficiency expert Frederick Montgomery Gwindell, who proceeded to fire Amos, Andy, and the Kingfish from their own business and to antagonize Andy by his energetic pursuit of Madam Queen. Gwindell seized every opportunity to publicly humiliate his vanquished rival and planned to marry Madam Queen in the spring—only to have her turn away from him at the altar and fall sobbing into Andy's arms. Andy soon found himself being sued for alienation of affection, in a lengthy courtroom sequence that rivaled the earlier breach-of-promise sequence in its dramatic sophistication. These powerful story lines helped *Amos 'n' Andy* to regain some of its lost ground. Indeed, it is important to point out that even though the program's *rating* declined during this season the size of its audience *increased* compared to that of the previous year. This phenomenon demonstrates the danger of too literal an interpretation of ratings information and once again contradicts the "disastrous decline" theory.

The decline of the 1934–35 season may be attributed in part to Correll and Gosden's decision in mid-1934 to temporarily discontinue the program—going off the air for eight weeks in order to take their first vacation since 1928. This disruption of a long-time habit may have caused some listeners to explore other alternatives—although, as will be seen from *Myrt and Marge*'s decline over the same span, radio listening at the 7 P.M. hour in general was on the decline during this period. During much of this season, the locale of *Amos 'n' Andy* was shifted from Harlem to the small town of Weber City—and although this lengthy and complex story line offered some of the most sophisticated character development of the entire series, the plotting tended to meander during the winter months and may have caused some listeners to lose interest. The summer of 1935 offered a suspenseful and well-crafted murder mystery, in which Amos was accused of poisoning a woman who had become obsessed with him until his detective work proved the death to be an accidental suicide. While this sequence was an impressive venture into straight drama for Correll and Gosden, it may have proven jarring to listeners who enjoyed the more down-to-earth aspects of the series.

Amos 'n' Andy again regained ground during 1935 and 1936, a season in which Correll and Gosden introduced a number of fresh ideas to the series. The fall of 1935 found the lead characters opening a grocery store—and December was marked by preparations for Amos and Ruby's long-awaited wedding, a ceremony that aired on Christmas Night. Economic difficulties faced the newlyweds from the beginning, culminating in a foreclosure on the grocery store, and these melodramatic, drawn-from-real-life sequences helped to rekindle enthusiasm for the series for those listeners who might have been alienated by the grimness of the murder story. Also a likely contributing factor to the resurgence of the series during this season is the fact that in September 1935, the program shifted from the NBC Blue network to the more powerful NBC Red network.

During the summer of 1936, the Kingfish was assigned by the Harlem newspaper where he had worked as a gossip columnist to travel to Hollywood for a story on movie-studio life, and Amos, Andy and Lightning accompanied him on this trip—a sequence that for the first time brought name guest stars to the world of *Amos 'n' Andy*. When the travelers returned to Harlem, subtle hints were dropped that Ruby was pregnant; although none of the characters made explicit mention of this fact, careful listeners were able to pick up on the clues. The excitement surrounding the birth of the baby in late October and an accompanying "Name the Baby" contest conducted by the sponsor continued to build interest. Actress Elinor Harriot became a regular cast member during the fall of 1936, giving voice to Ruby, and during 1937 she portrayed several additional female characters, including Sapphire Stevens, the Kingfish's wife. Even as Amos and Ruby were adjusting to their new roles as parents, Andy found himself doing the same by taking in a homeless six-year-old orphan girl known only as "Pun'kin," portrayed by actress Terry Howard. For the first time, voices other than those of Correll and Gosden were regularly heard on the program, and in December, the performers further broke with precedent by devoting two Friday night broadcasts to tabloid minstrel shows, based on the idea that the Mystic Knights of the Sea were putting on the events as charity fund-raisers. These two programs, presented before live audiences, and with musical guest stars Frank Parker and Benny Fields, generated substantial publicity for the program at year's end.

Meanwhile, *Myrt and Marge* faded out of the 7 P.M. time slot, moving to the daytime soap-opera schedule, and CBS replaced the series with a nondescript musical feature. The only major competition for *Amos 'n' Andy* for the next three years was *Easy Aces*, a cleverly written comedy of manners that tended to appeal to an upscale audience. While there was a slight decline in the *Amos 'n' Andy* audience between 1936 and 1938, it appears to have been more of a part of the overall decline in 7 P.M. listening than anything that could be directly caused by the content of the series.

There was a dramatic drop in the audience, however, in 1938 and 1939—possibly due to a shift in the program's network during the spring of 1939. Campbell's Soup, the sponsor, brought the program to CBS as of April 1st, and while the shift brought the series to a greater number of stations than had carried it during the last years of its NBC run, these affiliates were often smaller and less powerful than competing NBC outlets. In some rural areas, listeners found CBS stations difficult to tune and it is likely that this shift caused Correll and Gosden to lose more listeners than it gained.

NBC sold the 7 P.M. time slot vacated by *Amos 'n' Andy* to Liggett and Myers Tobacco, which presented a quarter-hour musical program featuring Fred Waring and his Pennsylvanians. Waring had a strong appeal to middle-American listeners, and as overall 7 P.M. listenership continued to decline, the musical program offered brisk competition—especially when broadcast over NBC's stronger outlets. *Amos 'n' Andy* rebounded during 1940–41, generating interest through the addition to the cast of African American character actress Ernestine Wade, who gave voice to several characters during this period, most notably the sharp-voiced Sapphire Stevens, previously played by Elinor Harriot. Further interest was generated by the birth of Amos and Ruby's second child, Amos Junior. Guest stars occasionally appeared during this period as well, such as comedian Fred Allen, who appeared as himself on the May 8, 1941, episode in reciprocation for an appearance by Correll and Gosden on his program.

During 1941 and 1942, the United States entered the World War II—and for the first time since ratings had been kept, *Amos 'n' Andy* lost control of the 7 P.M. time slot. Several factors likely contributed to this change: shift workers in war plants were more inclined to listen to musical programs than dramatic features while on the assembly lines, and it is likely that fewer people were at home to follow a continuing serial program. Likewise, millions of American men were entering military service—greatly shrinking the overall radio audience since military listenership was never included in rating statistics. Finally, the popularity of the early-evening comedy-drama serial in general was in steep decline during the early 1940s—by 1942 only

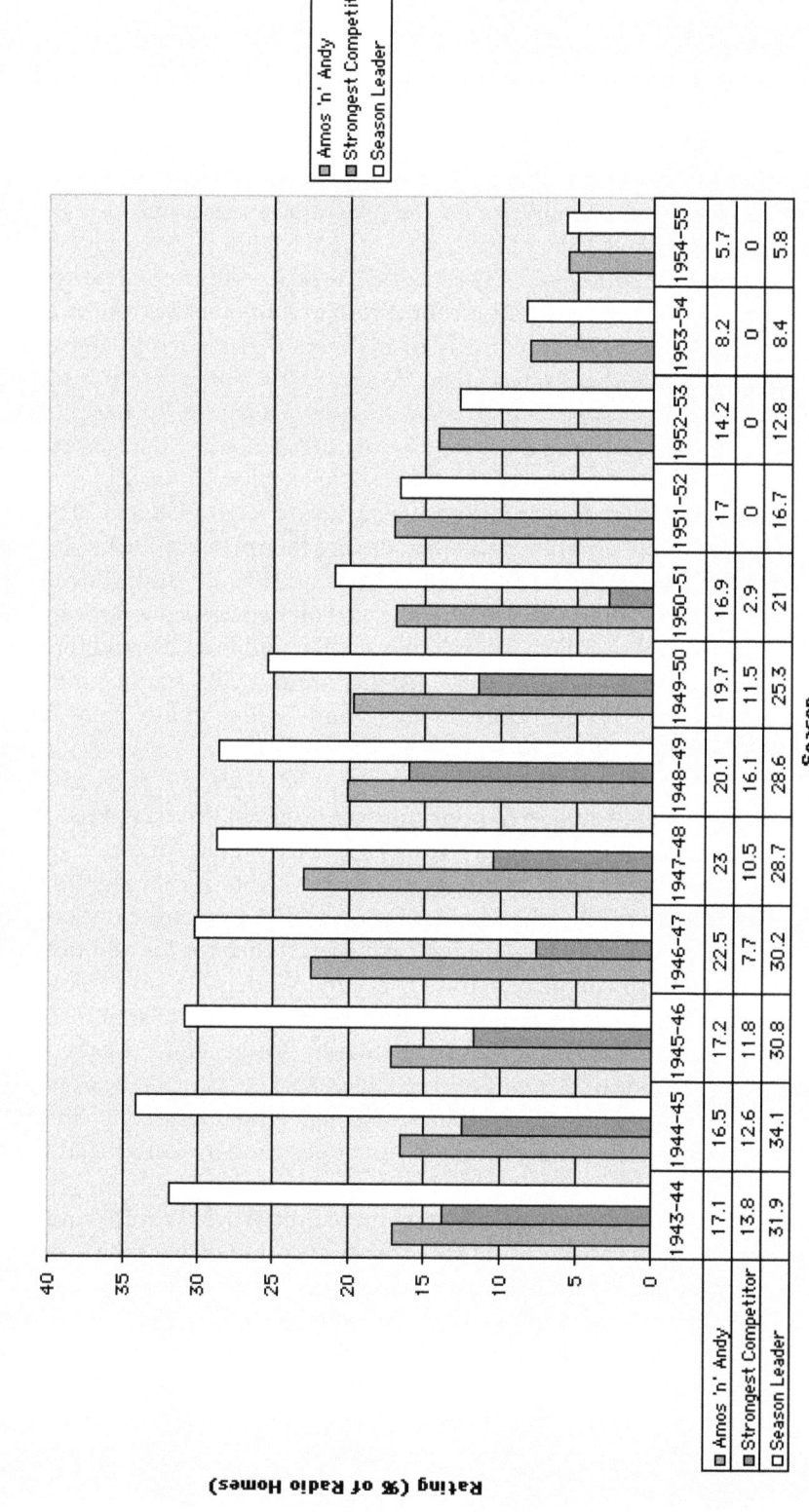

Amos 'n' Andy and *Lum and Abner* were still broadcasting in that format. These changes in the composition and the mood of the audience sealed the fate of *Amos 'n' Andy.*

Rumblings of a change in format for the venerable program began to be heard as early as 1940, but the earliest definite indication of a change in the works came on August 24, 1942, when Correll and Gosden appeared as guest artists on *Victory Theatre,* a half-hour program sponsored by the Treasury Department on behalf of war bonds. Their program took the form of a self-contained half-hour comedy-drama, in which Andy was devastated to learn that his new girlfriend was part of a burglary gang, and it is likely that the performers intended this broadcast as an on-air audition for a new format.

In early 1943 the Campbell Soup Company advised the performers that they would be unable to renew their contract upon its expiration in February. Metal rationing had cut into the company's supply of cans and as a result they were being forced to cut back on soup production for the civilian market. With this cutback, the company decided to temporarily discontinue all radio advertising. Rather than sign with a new sponsor in the middle of the season, Gosden and Correll decided to take the opportunity to restructure their series. *Amos 'n' Andy* left the air on February 19, 1943; in a brief talk at the conclusion of the program on that date, the performers assured their listeners that they would return.

When the program returned to the air in October, it was as a half-hour situation comedy, performed each Friday night for Lever Brothers' Rinso laundry soap before a live audience and then broadcast again over NBC. The new series got off to a strong start, against strong competition from the *Jimmy Durante–Garry Moore Program* on CBS—and this first season for the new series set the tone for those that would follow, as demonstrated by the ratings percentages displayed in Table 4.

Strongest competition for *The Amos 'n' Andy Show* during its situation comedy era was as follows:

- 1943–44 through 1944–45: *Jimmy Durante–Garry Moore Program*, a musical variety program (CBS).
- 1945–46: *Inner Sanctum Mysteries*, thriller drama (CBS).
- 1946–47: *Vox Pop*, audience participation (CBS).
- 1947–48: *We the People,* audience participation (CBS).
- 1948–49 through 1949–50: *Phil Harris–Alice Faye Show*, situation comedy (NBC).
- 1950–51: *Juvenile Jury,* children's panel discussion, (MBS).
- 1951–52 through 1954–55: No competing program registered a measurable rating.

Season leaders during the situation comedy era were as follows:

- 1943–44: *Fibber McGee & Molly* (NBC).
- 1944–45: *Bob Hope Show* (NBC).

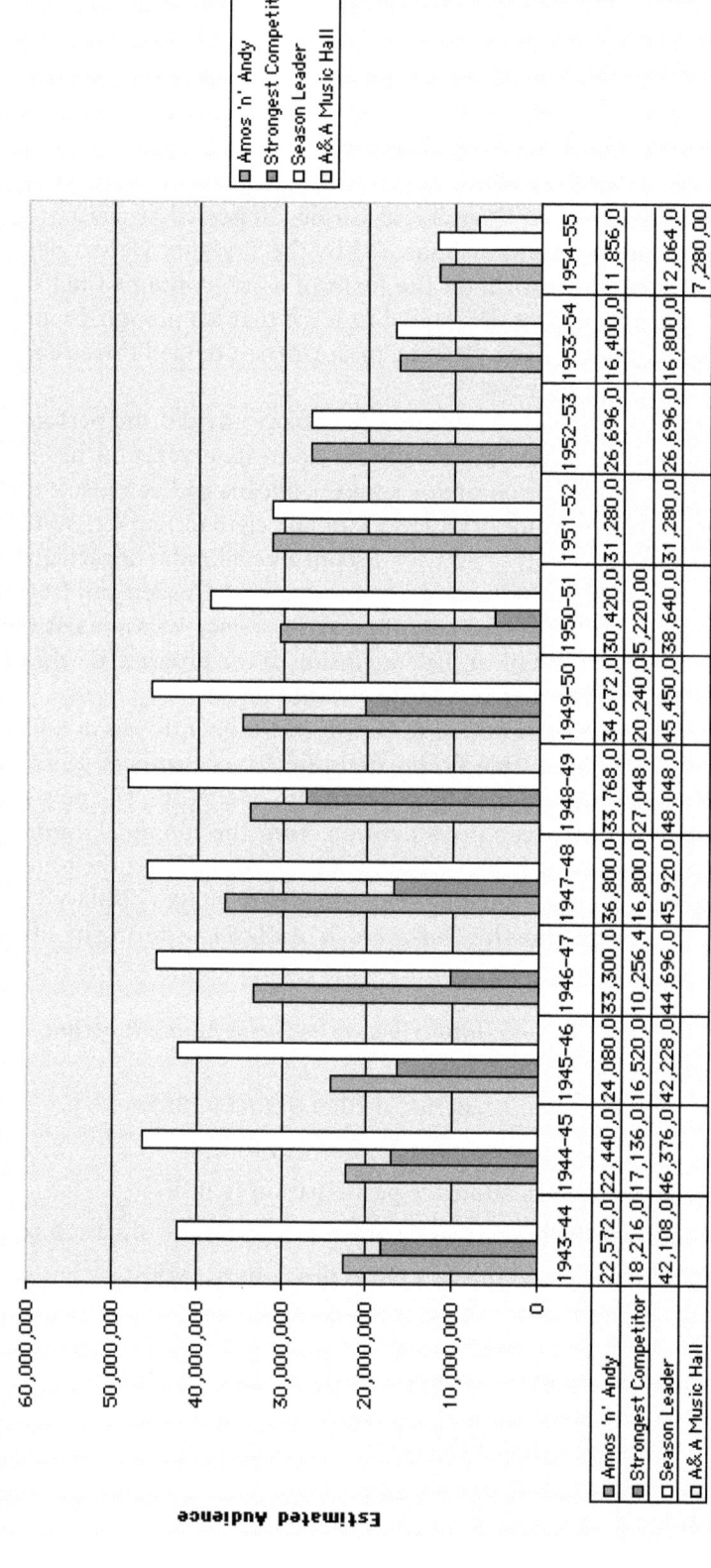

- 1945–46, 1946–47: *Fibber McGee & Molly* (NBC).
- 1947–48: *Fred Allen Show* (NBC).
- 1948–49: *Lux Radio Theatre* (CBS).
- 1949–50: *Jack Benny Program* (CBS).
- 1950–51: *Lux Radio Theatre* (CBS).
- 1951–52, 1952–53: *Amos 'n' Andy Show* (CBS).
- 1953–54: *People Are Funny* (NBC).
- 1954–55: *Jack Benny Program* (CBS).

The size of the listening audience may be estimated by the same formula used in calculating the serial-era audience figures, and the 1954–55 season will include statistics for the *Amos 'n' Andy Music Hall* series, a nightly program of recorded music and dialogue that began in September 1954. These figures are shown in Table 5.

The conversion of *Amos 'n' Andy* resulted in an immediate recovery of ground lost during the latter half of the 1930s, rebuilding the listening audience to the level it had reached during the middle of that decade. However, with the 1946–47 season, the series saw a dramatic increase, with two major factors most likely responsible.

In 1945–46, Lever Brothers moved the program from Friday night to Tuesday night, making it a portion of the strongest radio-comedy block then on the air. NBC's Tuesday night schedule was a dominant force in radio listening throughout the mid-1940s, with *Fibber McGee & Molly*, Bob Hope, and Red Skelton the star attractions. Moving into the schedule at 9 P.M., *Amos 'n' Andy* became the lead-in for this block. The following season, the popular *Inner Sanctum Mysteries* feature on CBS was dropped by its sponsor, Thomas J. Lipton Company, in favor of the audience participation series *Vox Pop*—a move that proved disastrous for both Lipton and CBS. The power of *Amos 'n' Andy* as lead-in to the NBC Tuesday night comedy block cut deeply into this weaker competition.

The second major factor was, of course, the end of World War II, and the demobilization of millions of servicemen who returned to the civilian world and civilian radio listening. Comedy programs had proven to be the most popular features distributed to servicemen abroad by the Armed Forces Radio Service—*Amos 'n' Andy* had been among the AFRS offerings since March 1944—and listening tastes developed while in the service were easily carried back into civilian life.

These factors combined to give *The Amos 'n' Andy Show* its largest audience ever between 1946–47 and 1947–48. While the listenership in terms of the percentage of total radio homes during the 1930–31 season remains the more impressive accomplishment, it is still notable that an estimated eight million more people heard Correll and Gosden in 1947–48 than when the program was at the height of its Depression-era craze.

In September 1948, in a tax-reducing deal, Freeman Gosden and Charles Correll incorporated themselves and then sold their newly formed corporation to the Columbia Broadcasting System, turning over control of the series and their own services as performers to the network in exchange for an estimated $2.5 million. As of October 10, 1948, *The Amos 'n' Andy Show* aired Sunday nights at 7:30 P.M. Eastern time over the CBS network. Like their earlier defection from NBC in 1939, this move resulted in a small drop in their listening audience, with their 1948–49 audience averaging about three million less than during their final season on NBC.

The increasing popularity of television cut slightly into the overall radio audience during the late 1940s and early 1950s—but for millions of Americans, the new medium did not become a local reality until the lifting of the Federal Communications Commission's 1948 freeze on the issuance of new television station licenses in 1952. *The Amos 'n' Andy Show* lost nearly ten million listeners between the 1952–53 and 1953–54 seasons, a drop most likely attributable to the increase in television viewing that accompanied the sudden wave of new television stations signing on the air following the termination of the freeze.

The television version of *The Amos 'n' Andy Show* aired over CBS-TV from June 1951 to June 1953, a period coinciding with the series' tenure at the top of the overall radio ratings. Heavy promotion of the radio series by sponsor Rexall Drugs during this period may have helped keep the radio version in the minds of listeners even as the television series was riding a wave of publicity. Not all the publicity received by the television program was positive—the National Association for the Advancement of Colored People began its campaign against the TV series the night of its premiere and continued its criticism through the remainder of 1951. The publicity created by this protest fizzled out by early 1952, however, and there is little indication of any crossover impact on the ratings popularity of the radio series, which remained remarkably high in comparison to the overall size of the radio audience until the weekly program left the air in the spring of 1955.[6] In the fall of 1954, Correll and Gosden began *The Amos 'n' Andy Music Hall,* a nightly recorded-music feature that ran through November 1960, and while this new series never approached the popularity of their previous programs it began with a respectable audience of more than seven million listeners at a time when the nighttime radio listening audience was rapidly evaporating.

Freeman Gosden and Charles Correll have long been considered radio's most enduring performers. Their career spanned the entire history of network radio as a major entertainment medium. And despite changes in format and despite latter-day controversies, their audience remained remarkably loyal over the entire course of that career.

CAST AND CREDITS

Serial Cast (1928–1943)

Amos Jones .... Freeman Gosden
Andrew H. Brown .... Charles Correll
George "Kingfish" Stevens .... Freeman Gosden
John Augustus "Brother" Crawford (Lunchroom partner, bookkeeper,
   brother-in-law of Madam Queen) .... Freeman Gosden
Willie "Lightning" Jefferson .... Freeman Gosden
Frederick Montgomery Gwindell (Efficiency expert, private investigator,
   newspaper reporter) .... Freeman Gosden
Prince Ali Bendo (Crystal gazer, sent to prison in 1937) .... Freeman Gosden
Flukey Harris (Boxer, handyman, inventor) .... Freeman Gosden
William Lewis Taylor (Ruby's father—general contractor, clothing
   store owner, garage owner) .... Freeman Gosden
Sylvester (Garage mechanic) .... Freeman Gosden
Robert "Pop" Johnson (Lodge trustee, owner of the Okey Hotel) .... Freeman Gosden
Roland Weber (Former coal miner, self-made oil millionaire and
   real estate investor, killed in 1934 car accident) ..... Freeman Gosden
Madam Queen (Beauty-shop owner) .... Freeman Gosden
Ed Hyams (Upstairs neighbor in Chicago) .... Freeman Gosden
Bill Harvey (Advance man for Honest Tom's All-Star Carnival) ...... Freeman Gosden
Spud Cook (Earl Dixon's henchman) .... Freeman Gosden
Dean Fitzer (Chicago rental agent) .... Freeman Gosden
"Big Boy" White (Andy's old friend from Georgia) .... Freeman Gosden
The Short Order Cook (Employed at Big 3 Lunchroom and Okey Hotel) .. Freeman Gosden
Johnny Cook (Smarmy fake lawyer who calls everyone "pal") .... Freeman Gosden
Bucky Read (Lodge brother who's behind in his dues) .... Freeman Gosden
Jack Rockwood (The Traveling Man, salesman for the Double
   Waterproof Raincoat Company) .... Freeman Gosden
Freeman Talbot (Shoe salesman) .... Freeman Gosden
Gram'pa Wilson (Hattie Wilson's grandfather) .... Freeman Gosden
Mr. Grimes (Pushy used car salesman who never takes "no" for
   an answer) .... Freeman Gosden
Ambrose Crawford (Brother Crawford's uncle) .... Freeman Gosden
Brother Summerset (Commercial photographer) .... Freeman Gosden
"Scrappy" (Andy's wrestling trainer) .... Freeman Gosden

H.M. Griffin (Wrestling promoter, manager of Bullneck Mooseface) ..... Freeman Gosden
"Poundcake" (Old friend from Atlanta who works as a carnival wild man under the name of "Wild Woofo") .... Freeman Gosden
Jerry Rockwood (Coach of the Wholesale Butchers and Packers Union football team) .... Freeman Gosden
Reverend Willis Johnson (Minister) .... Freeman Gosden
Phillip L. Wiggins (Automotive accessories salesman) .... Freeman Gosden
Lawyer Frank Gilbert (Defended Amos and Andy in the Chicago pawnshop robbery) .... Freeman Gosden
Lawyer Richard Rada (Prosecuted Andy in 1928 Widow Parker breach-of-promise case) .... Freeman Gosden
Lawyer O.D. Fisher (Associate of the Kingfish) .... Freeman Gosden
Lawyer M. Smith (Prosecuted Andy in 1931 Madam Queen breach-of-promise case) .... Freeman Gosden
Lawyer L. Sprague Jefferson (Represented F.M. Gwindell in 1933 alienation-of-affection case) .... Freeman Gosden
Ace Berry (Hack lawyer) .... Freeman Gosden
Roscoe Brownlee (Publicity agent for Weber City, exposed as criminal by Amos) .... Freeman Gosden
Pete Jenkins (Former grocer from Chattanooga, advises Amos and Andy at the A&A Grocery Store) .... Freeman Gosden
Henry Van Porter (Real estate/insurance agent) .... Charles Correll
Pat Pending (Inventor/stock promoter, associate of the Kingfish) .... Charles Correll
Mr. Hopkins (Farmer, Amos and Andy's employer in Georgia) .... Charles Correll
Charlie Johnston (Upstairs neighbor in Chicago) .... Charles Correll
Mr. Jarvis (Chicago used car dealer who sells Amos and Andy the Fresh Air Taxicab) .... Charles Correll
Honest Tom (Carnival promoter) .... Charles Correll
Stanley Hubbard (Lodge brother from St Paul, Minnesota) .... Charles Correll
Officer Albert Pierce (Chicago policeman) .... Charles Correll
Chester Back (Private detective known as "Operator 13") .... Charles Correll
Emmett Matthews (Widow Parker's father) .... Charles Correll
Mr. Hotchkiss (Harlem bank executive frequently consulted by Amos) ..... Charles Correll
John "The Whale" Miller (Lodge official in Harlem) .... Charles Correll
Harrison "The Mackerel" Holliway (Lodge official in Chicago) .... Charles Correll
Jasper Rogers (Ex-convict who Brother Crawford is trying to help go straight) .... Charles Correll
Honest Joe (Pawnbroker) .... Charles Correll
Fred Washington (Rooming-house operator on South Side of Chicago) ... Charles Correll
The Landlord (Rooming-house operator, East 134th Street, Harlem ..... Charles Correll
Lawyer Wilson Spielman (Represented Andy in 1928 Widow Parker breach-of-promise suit) .... Charles Correll
Lawyer Joseph Wagner (Represented Amos in 1929 grand larceny case) .... Charles Correll
Lawyer Jackson (of the firm of Jackson, Jackson, Jackson, and Jackson) .... Charles Correll
Lawyer Collins (Represented Andy in 1931 Madam Queen breach-of-promise suit) .... Charles Correll
Lawyer Brooks (Represented Amos in 1931 Jack Dixon murder case dream sequence) .... Charles Correll
Lawyer Henry Lucas (Represented Andy in 1933 alienation-of-affection case) .... Charles Correll
Lawyer Perkins (Advisor to Andy) .... Charles Correll
Snoop Washington (Associate of the Kingfish, an income-tax lawyer and private investigator) .... Charles Correll

Cast and Credits

Good Lookin' (No-account slick-haired drugstore Romeo, works as
    musician, also known as "George") .... Charles Correll
Mr. Pierson (Rental agent for the Big 3 Lunch Room) .... Charles Correll
Hastings Wilson (Hattie Wilson's uncle) .... Charles Correll
Sir Francis Jackson (Genealogy promoter) .... Charles Correll
Joe Parker (Advance man for Kaufman's Bigger and Better Colored
    Carnival) .... Charles Correll
Dr. Shipley (Physician) .... Charles Correll
Dr. Bent (Insurance examiner, friend of the Kingfish) .... Charles Correll
Dr. Joe Herring (Physician, friend of the Kingfish) .... Charles Correll
Dr. Porter (Physician, delivered Arbadella) .... Charles Correll
Willie Leland (Newsreel cameraman, friend of the Kingfish) .... Charles Correll
Louisiana Hercules (Champion shot-putter, contestant in the Harlem
    Colored Olympics) .... Charles Correll
Julian Nathan Kalinkowitz (Theatrical manager for Andy and
    Señorita Butterfly) .... Charles Correll
George Drinkwater (Caretaker in Weber City, Millie Drinkwater's
    grandfather) .... Charles Correll
Joshua H.B. Williams (Oil-stock swindler, revealed as black-sheep
    relative of Mrs. George Washington) .... Charles Correll
Audy Fox (Efficiency expert hired by Amos in 1929) .... Charles Correll
Jack Young (Criminal from New York who tried to rob the Taylor
    Garage, exposed by Amos and Sylvester) .... Charles Correll
Earl Dixon (Criminal who framed Amos for grand larceny in 1929,
    sent to prison for ten years) .... Charles Correll
Jack Dixon (Criminal who brutally beat Amos, later found murdered
    in dream sequence) .... Charles Correll
Arthur DeBelford (Ne'er-do-well brother of Mrs. Stevens from
    Portland, Maine, uses assumed name) .... Charles Correll
Mr. Greentree (Publicity agent hired to promote the Harlem Colored
    Olympics) .... Charles Correll
Henrietta Johnson (Amateur actress, revealed as the sister of Señorita
    Butterfly) .... Harriette Widmer
Ruby Taylor Jones (College student, medical office receptionist,
    practical nurse, married Amos 12/25/35) .... Elinor Harriot
Sapphire Stevens (Name revealed in 1933, also known as
    "Mrs. Kingfish") .... Elinor Harriot (1937-38),
                                                              Ernestine Wade (1939-43)
Clara Van Porter (Society matron, wife of Henry Van Porter) ... Elinor Harriot (1937–38),
                                                                        Ernestine Wade (1939–43)
Mrs. C.F. Van DeTweezer (Society matron, wife of Charles Francis
    Van DeTweezer) .... Elinor Harriot
Harriet Lily Crawford (Wife of Brother Crawford, sister of Madam
    Queen) .... Edith Davis
Pun'kin (Homeless orphan girl found by Andy, custody later shared
    by Amos and Ruby and Lightning and Dixie) .... Terry Howard (1936–37),
                                                                          Elinor Harriot (1937)
Arbadella Jones (born 10/20/36) .... Loretta Poynton (1936),
                         Elinor Harriot (1937–39), Barbara Jean Wong (1940–43)
Genevieve Blue (Andy's secretary, a former Texas beauty queen) .... Madaline Lee
Dorothy Blue (Genevieve's twin sister) .... Madaline Lee
Mrs. Adam Johnson (Woman from Marietta, Georgia, who claims
    Andy married her in 1928 under an assumed name) .... Elinor Harriot
Valada Green (Andy's 1939 fiancée, a.k.a. "Puddin' Face") .... Ernestine Wade

Sara Fletcher (Local gossip, nicknamed "Needlenose") .... Ernestine Wade
Widow Armbruster (Wealthy heiress, 1940–41) .... Lillian Randolph

Characters Spoken About but Never Portrayed

Mamie Henderson (Amos's former fiancée who broke his heart)
Geranium Washington (Young daughter of Fred the Landlord)
Mrs. Washington (Wife of Fred the Landlord, doesn't like Andy)
Ivan S. Peters (Slick New Yorker who married Mamie, only to abandon her after only a few weeks)
Rosie Waite (School friend of Ruby Taylor, infatuated with Andy)
Lulu Parker, a.k.a. Widow Parker (Fiancée of Andy in Chicago, married five times, sued Andy for breach of promise)
John Watkins (Businessman from Detroit, married Widow Parker in early 1929)
Tootsie Blake (Flapper, friend of Widow Parker, infatuated with Amos)
Mrs. Lillian Taylor, a.k.a. Aunt Lillian (Ruby Taylor's aunt, with whom she lives in New York, later revealed as Ruby's biological mother)
Flossie White Johnson (Young stenographer formerly employed by the Kingfish, eloped with elderly Pop Johnson)
Sadie Blake (Beautician, former employee of Madam Queen, infatuated with Andy)
Mrs. Blake (Sadie's mother, divorcée)
Sapphire Green (Operator of a rival beauty shop)
Mrs. Carnation James (Grandmother of Madam Queen and Mrs. Crawford)
Peaches Thompson (Friend of Madam Queen, infatuated with Amos)
Susie Porter (Shopgirl, infatuated with Andy)
Alphonso Crawford (Son of Brother and Mrs. Crawford; the Crawfords have a second child, whose name is never revealed)
T.N. Trueheart (Associate of the Kingfish, inventor)
Hattie Wilson (Resident of Lake Chiskabiskawiskachew, infatuated with Andy)
Gracie Mills (Friend of Madam Queen, infatuated with Amos)
Lefty from Philadelphia (Henchman of Jack Dixon)
Spike (Henchman of Jack Dixon, formerly his boss until Dixon turned the tables)
Willie (Operator of express wagon, assaulted by Jack Dixon)
"Owl" (Amos's Friend who knows everything that's happening on the streets)
The Seventh Avenue Gang (Street toughs who ran Jack Dixon out of town after his henchman assaulted one of them)
Lula May (Baby found abandoned in Fresh Air Taxicab, adopted by the Landlord and his wife)
Bullneck Mooseface (World's Colored Heavyweight Wrestling Champion, defeated Andy in a match)
Dixie Davis Jefferson (Friend of Sadie Blake's from Richmond, Virginia; married Lightning, 2/26/32; formerly infatuated with Andy)
Pearly (High diver with Kaufman's Bigger and Better Colored Carnival, infatuated with Andy)
G. Sampson Smith, Jr. (Professional promoter from Philadelphia, general manager of the 1932 Harlem Colored Olympics)
"Greenlight No Stop Henry" Vickers, Sam Gleason the Human Jackrabbit, Ralph McGonigal the Harlem Express, "Special Delivery Frank" White, "Springfoot Lee" Moore, "No Local Stops Harvey" Smith, Harry Peters, the Harlem Limited, Casey Jones Rutledge, "Third Alarm" Dawson, "One-Way Traffic Murray" Walker, Jerome Green the Human Skyrocket, "Fast-Freight Bob" Wilson, Horace Harley the Greased Pig, "Rubber Heels Ely" Holmes, "Here He Comes an' Dere He Goes Phil" Buckner, "Boomerang Ed" Winter, "Up-an'-Gone Hal" Dean, Fred Bailey the Human Whippet, and Ray Hamilton the Fireman's Choice (Athletes competing in the 1932 Harlem Colored Olympics)
Val Valentine (President of Valentine's National Colored Matrimonial Bureau)

Raymond (Madam Queen's husband, a merchant seaman; lost at sea in 1932)
Clifton Mills (Business partner of Mr. Taylor, infatuated with Ruby; involved in shady dealings, exposed by Amos)
Mr. and Mrs. Ira Whitestoner (Harlem society leaders)
Charles Francis Van DeTweezer (Stockbroker, Harlem society leader)
Mr. and Mrs. Van Dyke (Harlem society leaders, bridge partners of the Van Porters)
Mr. and Mrs. George Thomas Washington (Harlem society leaders)
Fifi (French maid briefly employed by Madam Queen)
Alice Barton (Widow, infatuated with Andy)
Arabella Barton (21-year-old daughter of Widow Barton, also infatuated with Andy)
Ferdinand, Ferdinand, Ferdinand and Ferdinand (Business consultants who employ F. M. Gwindell as one of their efficiency experts)
Luella Walker (College friend of Ruby Taylor)
Millie Carter (The Kingfish's mother-in-law)
Señorita Butterfly a.k.a. Annie Johnson Weber (Dancing instructor, theatrical partner of Andy, married Roland Weber, infatuated with Amos; died of accidental poisoning in 1935, which led to murder charge against Amos)
Eula Jimson (Daughter of tourist camp operator, infatuated with Andy)
Jack "Booboo" Jimson (Eula's oversized brother, a lumberjack)
H.L. Jimson (Eula's father, operator of tourist camp, who moves to New York at Andy's suggestion)
Millie Drinkwater (Resident of Weber City, infatuated with Andy)
Miss Elizabeth F. Sanders (Bank examiner, classical violinist, infatuated with Amos)
Dr. W.L. Dickinson (Ruby's employer, later appointed head of a colored hospital in Richmond, Virginia)
Fred Speed (The Australian Whip Cracker)
Magnolia Jenkins (Infatuated with Andy, daughter of Pete Jenkins)
Philip (Teenage boy tricked into committing robberies by Prince Ali Bendo)
Anna-Bell Williams (Swindler, daughter of Joshua H.B. Williams)
Ed and Bob Sparrow (Credit jewelers)
The Cherry Brothers (Doctors, operators of a clinic in Harlem)
Slim Jackson (Shoeshine attendant at the barbershop, "the meanest man in the world")
Rosa Lee Smith (Slim Jackson's fiancée)
Shorty (Jazz musician with whom Andy briefly shares a room after Amos's marriage)
The Alley Lawyer (So-called because he advises prisoners from the alley behind the jail)
Flora Matthews (Schoolteacher, infatuated with Andy)
Violet Garden (Chorus girl and aspiring actress, infatuated with Andy)
Elizabeth Rockford (Widow, infatuated with Andy)
Pauline Gibson (Head of a counterfeiting ring in Portland, Maine, infatuated with Andy)
Mrs. DeBelford (The Kingfish's sister-in-law, wife of Arthur DeBelford)
Sam Blackwood (Boxer, opposed Flukey Harris in a 1938 bout)
Mlle. Henrietta DeWitt (Manager of the Bluebird School of Singing, Andy's voice teacher)
The Wow Girl (West Indian dancer, managed by the Kingfish in 1941)
Amos Jones, Jr. (Amos and Ruby's second child, born 1941)

(Many character names in the series were derived from real-life friends and acquaintances of Correll and Gosden.)

Announcer .... Bill Hay (1928–42), Carlton KaDell (Pepsodent commercials, 1937), Ken Niles (Campbell's hitchhike commercials, 1938–43), Del Sharbutt (1942–43)
Substitute Announcers .... Wallace Butterworth (1930), Olan Soule (1936), Carlton KaDell (1936), Joe Parker (1937–38), Ernest Chappell (1940)
Orchestra .... Joseph Gallicchio (1929–32, 1936–37)

Organist .... Dean Fossler (1932–37), Gaylord Carter (1937–43)
Vocal Quartet (for the two Mystic Knights of the Sea Friday Night
    Minstrel Shows, 12/4/36, 12/11/36) .... The Four Vagabonds
              (John Jordan, Norval Taborn, Robert O'Neil, Ray Grant, Jr.)
Written by .... Freeman Gosden and Charles Correll
Creative Producer .... Freeman Gosden
Agency Producer .... For Lord & Thomas: Henry Selinger (1929–34),
        Basil Loughrane (1934–37), for Ward Wheelock Inc.: Diana Bourbon (1938–43)

Sitcom Cast (1943–1955)

Amos Jones .... Freeman Gosden
Andrew H. Brown .... Charles Correll
George "Kingfish" Stevens .... Freeman Gosden
John Augustus "Brother" Crawford .... Freeman Gosden
Willie "Lightning" Jefferson .... Freeman Gosden (1943–51, 1952–55),
                                      Horace "Nick" Stewart (1951)
Frederick Montgomery Gwindell .... Freeman Gosden
Flukey Harris .... Freeman Gosden
Henry Van Porter .... Charles Correll
Sapphire Stevens .... Ernestine Wade
Clara Van Porter .... Ernestine Wade (1943–44)
Sara Fletcher .... Ernestine Wade (1943–44)
Shorty Simpson .... Lou Lubin (1944–50)
Gabby Gibson .... James Baskett (1944–48)
Reverend Johnson .... Ernest Whitman (1944–45)
George Washington .... Ernest Whitman (1944)
Sadie Simpson .... Hattie McDaniel (1945–47)
LaGuardia Stonewall .... Eddie Green (1947–49)
Algonquin J. Calhoun .... Johnny Lee (1949–54)
Leroy Smith (a.k.a. Leroy Hancock) .... Jester Hairston (1944–55)
Ruby Taylor Jones .... Elinor Harriot
Sadie Blake .... Ruby Dandridge
Harriet Lily Crawford .... Ruby Dandridge
Arbadella Jones .... Barbara Jean Wong
Genevieve Blue .... Madaline Lee
Madam Queen .... Lillian Randolph
Ramona "Mama" Smith .... Amanda Randolph (1951–54)
Supporting roles .... Ernest Whitman, Joseph Kearns, Ken Christy,
    Roy Glenn, Ruby Dandridge, Dorothy Dandridge, Vivian Dandridge, Jester Hairston,
    "Wonderful" Smith, Lasses White, Willard Waterman, Sara Berner, Elvia Allman, Jean
    Vander Pyl, Shirley Mitchell, Millie Bruce, Will Wright, Leo Cleary, Corny Anderson,
                    Vince Townsend, Amos Reece, Herbert Rawlinson
Musical Performers .... The Mystic Knights of the Sea Quartet (1944–45),
        The Delta Rhythm Boys: Carl Jones, Kelsey Pharr, Lee Gaines, and Traverse
      Crawford (1945–47), The Jubilaires: Ted Brooks, John Jennings, J. Caleb Ginyard
          and George McFadden (1947–49), The Jeff Alexander Chorus (1947–49)
Orchestra .... Lud Gluskin (1943–47, 1954–55), Jeff Alexander (1947–54)
Announcer .... Harlow Wilcox (1943–45, 1951–55), Carleton KaDell
      (1945–47), Art Gilmore and John Lake (1947–48), Ken Carpenter (1949–50),
      Ken Niles (1950–51), Griff Barnett (Rexall commercial spokesman, 1951–54)
Script Supervision .... Freeman Gosden and Charles Correll
Head Writer .... Robert J. Ross
Writing Staff .... Joe Connelly and Bob Mosher, Artie Fisher, Bob Fisher,

Paul Franklin, Harvey Helm, Shirley Illo, Dave Schwartz, Hal Kanter et al. From 1946 forward, the writing staff was usually maintained at five members including Ross, Connelly, Mosher, and two secondary contributors at any one time. Three complete scripts were produced each week, from which elements would be combined to assemble the final program.

Creative Producer .... Freeman Gosden
Agency/Network Producer .... For Ruthrauff & Ryan: Glenn Middleton (1943–48), for CBS: James Fonda (1948–55)

CHAPTER NOTES

Unless otherwise noted, all primary source documents cited are from the author's collection.

Preface

1. William Manchester, *The Glory and the Dream: A Narrative History of America 1932–1972* (Boston: Little, Brown, 1972), p. 7.
2. Perhaps the most overt recent attempt at obliterating the memory of *Amos 'n' Andy* can be found in Don West, "Broadcasting and Cable's Men of the Century," *Broadcasting and Cable,* 12/20/99. Correll and Gosden are resolutely ignored by the publication long regarded as the unofficial "voice of the industry" in this discussion of "100 individuals who made signal contributions to the Fifth Estate during the 20th century," an omission that reveals either a pronounced lack of historic understanding on West's part or an attempt by the editors of the magazine to avoid controversy by deliberately denying Correll and Gosden due recognition for their accomplishments. In West's article another man—1940s entrepreneur Frederick W. Ziv—is given credit for "pioneering syndication," nearly 20 years after Correll and Gosden pioneered the concept of the "chainless chain" and inspired the syndication boom of the early 1930s.
3. Orrin E. Dunlap. "The Saga of Amos 'n' Andy," *New York Times,* 7/8/34.

Chapter 1

1. For full-length discussions of the history and development of blackface minstrelsy and its influence on American popular entertainment, see Dailey Paskman and Sigmund Spaeth, "*Gentlemen, Be Seated!*": *A Parade of the Old-Time Minstrels* (Garden City, NY: Doubleday, 1928); Carl Frederick Wittke, *Tambo and Bones: A History of the American Minstrel Stage* (Durham, NC: Duke University Press, 1930); Robert Toll, *Blacking Up: The Minstrel Show in Nineteenth-Century America* (New York: Oxford University Press, 1974); and W. T. Lhamon, *Raising Cain: Blackface Performance from Jim Crow to Hip Hop* (Cambridge, MA: Harvard University Press, 1998).

2. Biographical notes on Gosden from Nicholas A. Sharp, "Freeman F. Gosden," in *The Scribner Encyclopedia of American Lives: Volume I 1981–1985* (New York: Scribner, 1998). See also Melvin P. Ely, *The Adventures of Amos 'n' Andy: A Social History of an American Phenomenon* (New York: Free Press, 1991), pp. 14, 21–23. Notes on the Gosden family's Baltimore roots from *1850 U. S. Census,* Baltimore City, MD, Ward Six, enumeration district 306, visit 304, National Archives. On the foreclosure, see *Chancery Court Papers,* Chancery Record 169, p. 192: 9/24/1845: 5591—*American Life Insurance and Trust Co. vs. Joseph Barling et al.*, Maryland State Archives.
3. Notes on Walter Gosden's Civil War service from Civil War Muster Rolls, via Ancestry.com, box/extraction/record 823 and box/extraction/record 2062. Also compare enumeration district 0111, visit 0036, *Virginia 1910 Census Miracode Index,* via Ancestry.com. Walter Gosden's employment listed in *Richmond City Directory, 1889–90,* compare Ely, p. 14. Walter Gosden's participation in the Rangers' final skirmish is described in detail by J. L. Milne, "First Complete Life Story of Amos 'n' Andy," *Detroit Free Press,* 4/7/30.
4. Freeman Gosden quoted in *Richmond Times Herald,* 10/27/90.
5. For descriptions of Jackson Ward, see Federal Writers Project, Works Progress Administration, *The Negro in Virginia* (New York: Hastings House, 1940), and Robert Winthrop, *The Jackson Ward Historic District* (Richmond: City of Richmond, 1970).
6. See Milne.
7. Ibid. Also W.T. Christian, "Boyhood Days of Amos 'n' Andy," *Radio Digest,* June 1930, pp. 14–15. William B. Gosden's suicide is described in the *Richmond Dispatch,* 3/11/1902, which includes a detailed account of the circumstances leading up to the death. For a description of the accident that claimed the life of Emma L. Gosden and her daughter Minnie Bowles, see *Richmond Times-Dispatch,* 9/12/17, 9/13/17, and

9/14/17. Mrs. Gosden and her daughter, Mrs. T. Knight Bowles, were passengers in an open touring car struck by a speeding sedan driven by J.P. Schmitz of Richmond at the intersection of Lombardy Street and Grove Avenue. Both women were thrown from the car and sustained severe head injuries. Emma Gosden died about an hour after the accident at a nearby hospital, while Minnie Bowles died about nine hours later. A coroner's jury found Schmitz liable for the deaths due to his reckless operation of a motor vehicle, and he was charged with involuntary manslaughter. The driver of the car in which Mrs. Gosden and Mrs. Bowles were riding, J. T. Regensberg of Barnesville, Virginia—a relative of Emma Gosden—was initially charged as well, but was not found liable in the inquest.

8. Ibid.

9. Notes on Garrett "Snowball" Brown from F. J. McDermott, "Hometown Stories of Amos 'n' Andy," *The New Movie Magazine,* September 1930, pp. 26, 106, 111. McDermott, a reporter for the *Richmond Times-Dispatch,* bases much of this article on an interview with Brown himself—the only such interview known to exist. Additional information on Brown appears in Ely, pp. 23–25. Arthur Frank Wertheim, *Radio Comedy* (New York: Oxford University Press, 1979), p. 24; and Ann Webb, "The Making of Amos' Philosophy," *Winston-Salem* (NC) *Journal and Sentinel,* 5/4/30. The only listing for a Garrett Brown in the 1910 Virginia Census is found in enumeration district 0082, visit 0406, *Virginia 1910 Census Miracode Index,* via Ancestry.com, and it identifies Garrett Brown, age fourteen, as the son of Camila Brown, age forty. Given that Garrett "Snowball" Brown is described as an orphan in all other accounts of his background, it is possible that the census listing is not the Brown who lived in the Gosden home. References to baseball-card collecting in the 1909–11 era later found their way into several *Amos 'n' Andy* scripts. See, for example, Episode 1326, 6/21/32, in which Amos reminisces about collecting these cards during his own boyhood. The specific source of Brown's nickname is unknown—it was often a generic term applied to black children in the turn-of-the-century South—but it may have derived from John Fox's popular 1903 novel *The Little Shepherd of Kingdom Come,* which features a young black character called "Snowball."

10. Christian, pp. 14–15, and McDermott, p. 106.

11. Garrett Brown also served in World War I, enlisting in the U.S. Army in the spring of 1917 and serving for 18 months. After his discharge, Brown returned to Richmond, where he worked at a variety of jobs. Interviewed by McDermott in 1930, Brown was revealed as an avid fan of *Amos 'n' Andy* and as still in regular contact with Freeman Gosden. Freeman F. Gosden, Jr., recalled that his father spoke of Brown often and had frequently related stories of their childhood experiences. F. F. Gosden, Jr., correspondence with the author, 11/25/00.

12. Christian, pp. 14–15. Gosden's wartime introduction to the technical side of radio led to his involvement in the late 1930s in amateur radio, as licensed ham operator W6QUT.

13. Ann Steward, "Amos 'n' Andy Join the Show," *Radio Digest,* July 1930, pp. 10–13. This article contains the only known interview with Joe Bren, in which he discusses his work with Correll and Gosden. See also Ely, pp. 26–46, much of which is drawn from Bren-era clippings in the Correll Family Collection.

14. Steward, pp. 10–13.

15. Charles Correll interviewed on tape by Richard Correll, "Same Time Same Station," KRLA, Pasadena, CA, broadcast on 1/14/73. See also Charles J. Correll and Freeman F. Gosden, *All About Amos 'n' Andy and Their Creators, Correll and Gosden* (New York: Rand, McNally, 1929), p. 23; and Jack Gaver and Dave Stanley, *There's Laughter in the Air* (New York: Greenberg, 1945), p. 138, which offers a specific date—August 12, 1919—for Correll and Gosden's first meeting, although no citation is offered for the source of this date. Ely, p. 34, extrapolating from Correll scrapbook evidence, dates the first meeting of Correll and Gosden to September 1920, but Correll himself, in the 1973 KRLA interview, used the 1919 date, which in turn matches the citation in *All About Amos 'n' Andy.*

16. Biographical notes on Correll from Nicholas A. Sharp, "Charles J. Correll" in *The Scribner Encyclopedia of American Lives: Volume I 1981–1985* (New York: Scribner, 1998). See also Ely, pp. 11–14. Data on Joseph Correll's employment from *Peoria City Directory, 1890,* via Ancestry.com.

17. Robert R. Goldenstien, "Boyhood Days of Amos 'n' Andy," *Radio Digest,* June 1930, pp. 15, 104; and Robert R. Goldenstien, "Hometown Stories of Amos 'n' Andy," *The New Movie Magazine,* September 1930, pp. 25, 110–11.

18. Ibid. See also Ely, p. 13.

19. Charles Correll quoted in *Peoria Journal-Star,* 5/20/2002, reprinted from issue of 5/22/49.

20. Goldenstien, "Boyhood Days," p. 104. Compare with Correll quoted in *Peoria Journal-Star,* 5/20/2002.

21. Steward, pp. 10–11; also Goldenstien, "Boyhood Days," p. 104; and Milne; Ely, p. 36. Details on Correll's employment history in the 1910–17 era from *Peoria Journal,* 1/26/35, and *Peoria Journal-Star,* 5/20/2002.

22. Jack Pardidon quoted in *Detroit Free Press,* 4/4/30.

Chapter 2

1. Correll and Gosden interviewed by Paul De Lott, "Hol' De Phone Please, We Is Bein' In-Tro-View'd," *The Poultry Item,* January 1933, p. 27.

2. *New York Times,* 8/27/33.

3. Freeman F. Gosden, Jr., correspondence with the author, 4/29/2003.

4. Correll interview, 1/14/73. See also Freeman F. Gosden, "Amos Looks at Andy," *Radio Life,* 10/10/43, p. 23.

5. Ely, pp. 37–41, culled from miscellaneous clippings in Correll scrapbooks.

6. Ibid.

7. Steward, p. 12.

8. Correll interview, 1/14/73. Also the following Victor records in author's collection: 19886: All I Want To Do/Let's Talk About My Sweetie (mxs 34578-5/34579-5), recorded 3/2/26 (Correll—piano,

Gosden—tiple); 20088: Roundabout Way To Heaven/That's Why I Love You (mxs 35056-3/35057-3) and 20107: Georgianna (35059-3), all recorded 5/26/26 (Delos Owen—piano); 20286: Meadow Lark/Kiss Your Little Baby Good Night (36406-4/36435-3) and 20255: Elsie Schultz-en-Heim/I Just Want to Be Known as Susie's Feller (mxs 36433-3/36434-3), all recorded 9/29/26 (Delos Owen—piano).

9. Steward, p. 13, and Correll interview, 1/14/73. Although Correll recalled the Calumet Baking Powder Company station in Chicago as WQGA, examination of Department of Commerce station licensing records reveals that no such station existed in 1925, instead identifying WQJ as the Calumet station. WQJ was eventually purchased by the *Chicago Daily News* and consolidated into WMAQ.

10. Louise Summa, interviewed by Ruth Geri in "The Woman Behind Amos 'n' Andy," *Radio Mirror*, February 1935.

11. WEBH program listings as published in *Radio Digest* during the summer of 1925.

12. Summa, interviewed by Geri.

13. Correll interview, 1/14/73. See also James R. Crowell, "Amos 'n' Andy Tell Their Own Story in Their Own Way," *American Magazine,* April 1930, p. 26; and Correll and Gosden, pp. 31–32.

14. Correll and Gosden, *All About Amos 'n' Andy*, pp. 31–32, and Ely, p. 52. The mind-reader characterization would prove to be an enduring bit for Correll and Gosden, turning up in *Sam 'n' Henry* before it finally inspired the creation of the Prince Ali Bendo character in *Amos 'n' Andy*. See Victor 20093, "Sam and Henry at the Fortune Teller's" and *Amos 'n' Andy,* Episodes 535 through 537, 12/9–11/29.

Chapter 3

1. Correll and Gosden, *All About Amos 'n' Andy*, pp.31–32, and Ely, p. 52.

2. Program listings for WGN-WLIB as published in various 1926–27 issues of *Radio Digest*. Bill Hay's reminiscence from Mark Quest, "Amos 'n' Andy Backstage at WMAQ," *Radio Digest,* March 1930, p. 13.

3. Brian A.L. Rust, *Victor Master Book: Vol. 2, 1925–36* (Stanhope NJ: Walter C. Allen, 1970). The two rejected sides are matrix numbers 34058-2 ("Blinky Moon Bay") and 34059-2 ("Kinky Kids Parade"). Both sides still exist in the vaults of BMG, successor to Victor, but have never been released. "Kinky Kids Parade" had already been recorded for Victor during 1925 by Paul Whiteman and his Orchestra (Victor 19753 mx 33305-3, recorded 8/12/25). Another released version of the selection would be recorded for Victor by the prominent vaudeville comediennes Rosetta and Vivian Duncan (Victor 19987, mx 33667-5, recorded 2/12/26).

4. Wertheim, pp. 23–24; see also Orrin R. Dunlap, Jr., "Amos 'n' Andy: The Air's First Comic Strip," *Literary Digest,* 4/19/30, p. 42. Henry Selinger subsequently left WGN to take a position with the Lord and Thomas advertising agency, and after *Amos 'n' Andy* moved to NBC under Pepsodent sponsorship in 1929, he served for several years as agency supervisor for the series. While at Lord and Thomas he used *Amos 'n' Andy* as a model when assisting Arkansas dialect performers Chet Lauck and Norris Goff in the development of a network format for their *Lum and Abner* series.

5. Herb Galewitz, ed., *Great Comics: Syndicated by the Daily News/Chicago Tribune* (New York: Crown Publishers, 1972), reprinting a lengthy excerpt from *The Gumps* 1922–23 "Widow Zander" story line. This sequence eventually led to a breach-of-promise suit filed by the Widow against the haplessly naïve Uncle Bim, with both the story line and the extraordinary public response to it prefiguring later developments in *Amos 'n' Andy*.

6. "Freeman Gosden—Amos of *Amos 'n' Andy*," New York: Columbia Biographical Service, Columbia Broadcasting System, 9/15/39. Gosden's marriage to Leta Schreiber, a Tribune Company secretary, took place five months after the marriage of Correll to Iowa native Marie Janes. The Corrells were divorced in 1937, and Charles remarried later that year to M. Alyce McLaughlin, a former dancer, and the couple remained together until Charles Correll's death in 1972. The Gosdens divorced in 1940, and Freeman remarried in 1944 to Jane Elizabeth Stoneham—daughter of the late owner of the New York Giants baseball team—and the marriage would endure until Freeman Gosden's death in 1982.

7. Correll quoted in *Charleston* (WV) *Daily Mail,* 3/8/31.

8. Correll interview, 1/14/73. See also Correll quoted by John C. West, *Chicago Today,* 2/6/72. Gosden quoted by Jerry Lazarus, *Richmond Times-Dispatch,* 8/20/81.

9. Bert Williams quoted in James Clyde Sellman, "Minstrelsy," *Microsoft Encarta Africana* (Redmond, WA: Microsoft, 1999). For a full-length discussion of the "liberating" aspects of blackface as an underclass cultural ritual, see Lhamon, Jr.

10. Charles Correll interviewed by Richard Lamparski, "Whatever Became of Amos 'n' Andy," recorded 6/30/69, and Correll interview, 1/14/73.

11. Correll interview, 1/14/73, compare Summa interviewed by Geri, and Hay interviewed by Quest, "Amos 'n' Andy Backstage." The characterizations of Sam and Henry bore little resemblance to the actual speaking voices of Correll and Gosden—both of whom spoke with pleasant, midrange baritones. The idea of contrasting the bulky Henry with the smaller Sam was specifically inspired by the contrast in size between the comic strip characters Mutt and Jeff.

12. For an excellent narrative discussion of the rise of continuity strips in the early 1920s see chapter VII, "Every Man's Art," in Colton Waugh, *The Comics* (New York: Macmillan, 1947), which devotes specific attention to the *Chicago Tribune–New York Daily News* family of strips, including *The Gumps*. See also Maurice Horn, editor, *100 Years of American Newspaper Comics* (New York: Gramercy Books, 1996), for specific discussion of the individual strips cited.

Chapter 4

1. Correll quoted in *Charleston* (WV) *Daily Mail,* 3/8/31.

2. Gosden quoted in *Charleston* (WV) *Daily Mail,* 3/8/31.

3. Representative scripts of *Sam 'n' Henry* from January and February of 1926 are available in Charles J. Correll and Freeman F. Gosden, *Sam 'n' Henry* (Chicago: Shrewsbury Publishing Co., 1926).

4. Victor records by *Sam 'n' Henry* include 20032: Sam Phonin' His Sweetheart 'Liza/Sam & Henry at the Dentist's (mxs 35328-3/35329-2, recorded 4/20/26); 20093: Sam's Speech at the Colored Lodge/Sam & Henry at the Fortune Teller's (mxs.35066-2 recorded 5/27/26 and 35073-3 recorded 5/28/26); 20375: Sam & Henry Rollin' the Bones/Sam & Henry Buying Insurance (mxs. 35067-2/35068-3, recorded 5/27/26); and 20788: Sam's Big Night/The Morning After (mxs. 39092-2/39093-2, recorded 7/7/27). Several additional skits were recorded but not released. In addition, a brief interpolation by Sam and Henry appears on Correll and Gosden's recording of "Let's Talk About My Sweetie" on Victor 19886.

5. Correll interviewed by Lamparski, 6/30/69. The first publicity to officially reveal the true identities of Sam and Henry appears to have been the announcement of Victor 19886, which featured the performers as Sam and Henry and as themselves in late March 1926. See Ely, p. 279, n. 29. Bill Hay's reminiscence from Quest, "Amos 'n' Andy Backstage."

6. Undated review from *American Appraisal News* reprinted on the dust jacket of the Shrewsbury *Sam 'n' Henry* compilation book.

7. Helena W. Freeland, *Radio Digest*, 11/15/26.

8. Maurice Wetzel, "What Innovations Portend in our Radio of Tomorrow," *Radio Digest,* Spring 1928. None of Wetzel's experimental recordings from 1927 to 1928 are known to have survived.

9. Correll interview, 1/14/73; Correll interviewed by Lamparski, 6/30/69. See also Abel Green and Joe Laurie Jr., *Show Biz from Vaude to Video* (New York: Henry Holt, 1951), p. 241. Correll and Gosden played the Balaban & Katz theatres again in 1928, and their salary swelled to $5,000 per week. The *Sam 'n' Henry* candy bar, appearing on the market in early 1927, was a product of the Shotwell Manufacturing Company of Chicago, and the *Sam 'n' Henry* express wagon toy, with a retail price of $1, was produced by the C & S Specialty Company of Chicago.

10. 1926 Radio Industries Banquet: see "Imposing Array of Celebrities at N.Y. Dinner," *The Broadcast Listener,* October 1926, which refers to Sam and Henry as "WGN's inimitable colored boys." 1927 Banquet: see *Chicago Tribune*, 9/18/27 and "Mammoth Banquet Will Open Season," *Radio Digest,* September 1927, which describes the hookup of stations to cover the banquet but which went to press too early to include mention of Correll and Gosden's performance.

11. Michael J. Biel, chapter VI-2 : "The First Recorded Program Series—Amos 'n' Andy, 1928–29," in *The Making and Use of Recordings in Broadcasting Before 1936*, Ph.D. dissertation, Northwestern University, 1977. See also Correll and Gosden, *All About Amos 'n' Andy,* pp. 39–40, 110–11 and Correll interview, 1/14/73. WMAQ negotiations: see unpublished interview of Judith Waller by Dr. Michael Banks, 1971.

12. Correll and Gosden, *All About Amos 'n' Andy,* pp. 39–40, 110–11. Handwritten stalling dialogue is visible in the originals of the first 438 episodes of *Amos 'n' Andy*. Many scripts during this period also bear handwritten notations of the matrix numbers for each side recorded, along with precise timings for each side.

13. The *Amos 'n' Andy* comic strip ran from 3/19/28 until the spring of 1929, when Correll and Gosden left Chicago on an extended personal appearance tour and were no longer able to work with Mueller on the preparation of the strip. The strip was drawn in an odd combination of styles, depicting Amos, Andy, and the Kingfish as minstrel-style caricatures and depicting middle-class characters like the Taylor family in a noncaricatured, semirealistic manner.

14. By mid–1928, entrepreneur Raymond Soat had formed National Radio Advertising, the first company to sell recorded programming to individual advertisers, for distribution complete with recorded commercial continuity. The first series to be distributed by National Radio Advertising was on behalf of the Maytag Manufacturing Company of Newton, Iowa, and was released in November 1928. See Biel, pp. 419–34. By 1930, dozens of firms were involved in the business of recorded syndication, and the industry remains a major factor in both radio and television up to the present day.

15. Gilles working under Gosden: see Milne. Background on Moeller and Gilles: Betty McGee, "Broadcasting from the Great Midwest," *Radio Digest*, May 1931.

16. Amos 'n' Andy, episodes 1 through 4, 3/19–20, 22–23/28, with original names scratched out and "Amos" and "Andy" interpolated in Gosden's handwriting. The script for Episode 1 in the collection of the Library of Congress Manuscript Division is apparently a retyped version produced from the original, without the handwritten interpolations. An original copy of Episode 1 exists in the Correll-Gosden Collection, USC, and a photographic reproduction of the original page 1 of Episode 1 appears in Harry Steele, "Amos 'n' Andy: Here they Are," *Radio Guide,* week ending 4/6/35, p. 9. See also Steele, p. 27, for discussion of the source of the names, an account that is not incompatible with the version given in Correll and Gosden, *All About Amos 'n' Andy*, p. 52.

It should also be noted that the names of the Two Black Crows, a popular blackface team played in vaudeville and on phonograph records by George Moran and Charles E. Mack were "Willie" and "Amos," and the name "Amos" is in fact used for Mack's character on "Two Black Crows," parts 1 and 2, Columbia 935-D (mxs 143602/143603), recorded 3/14/27. No contemporary sources suggest that Correll and Gosden were influenced by this recording in their use of the name "Amos," but given the extreme popularity of this recording and its several sequels, it is unlikely that they were not aware of it. The "Willie and Amos Crow" characters were subsequently featured in Charles E. Mack's novel *Two Black Crows in the A. E. F.* (New York: Bobbs, Merrill and Co., 1928), and this novel, in turn, formed the basis for Moran and Mack's series of radio appearances on the Columbia Broadcasting System's "Majestic Theatre of the Air," sponsored by Grigsby-Grunow Company during the spring of 1928. The series received poor reviews, and the Crows were dropped from the program before the end of the year.

The common legend that Correll and Gosden thought of the names on the night of the first broadcast after encountering two men known as "Famous Amos" and "Handy Andy" is totally fictitious and is easily disproven by the fact that the names had been announced by the *Chicago Daily News* on 2/25/28—three weeks before the first broadcast of the new series. See Charles F. Caton, *Radio Station WMAQ: A History of its Independent Years (1922–1931)*, unpublished Ph.D. dissertation, Northwestern University, 1951, pp. 309–10.

17. Promotional announcement: Biel, pp. 403–4.

18. All *Amos 'n' Andy* script excerpts from Charles J. Correll and Freeman F. Gosden, *Amos 'n' Andy Radio Scripts*, MSS. 14,305, Manuscript Division, Library of Congress. Microfilm copies in possession of the author.

19. *Amos 'n' Andy*, episodes 1 through 4, 3/19–20, 22–23/28. See also thumbnail descriptions of the characters as they were seen by their creators ca. 1928 in Correll and Gosden, *All About Amos 'n' Andy*, pp. 43–44.

20. Description of Sylvester in Correll and Gosden, *All About Amos 'n' Andy*, pp. 47–48. See also *Amos 'n' Andy*, episodes 11 through 14, 4/2–3, 5–6/28 in which Amos and Andy meet Sylvester, Ruby, and Mr. Taylor for the first time. Mr. Taylor's full name is not revealed until episode 411, 7/17/29.

21. Shell-shaped "Fresh Air Taxi Co." logo stickers promoting the airing of the show on KFRC were given away by Shell dealers in California during early 1929 as a tie-in with the introduction of Shell-400 "Dry" Gasoline. Example in author's collection. See also Mark Quest, "Additional Facts in the Private Life of Amos 'n' Andy," *Radio Digest*, April 1930, p. 15, for a discussion of the 1929 tour and for photos taken in San Francisco of the performers riding in a "Fresh Air Taxicab" festooned with these Shell/KFRC stickers. Other known sponsors during the "chainless chain" period include Surebest Bread, which carried the series over KRLD, Dallas; the Crown Drug Company, which sponsored the broadcasts over WDAF in Kansas City; Pevely Dairy, sponsors of the program over KMOX in St. Louis; and Standard Oil Company of Kentucky, sponsors of the broadcasts over WSB in Atlanta. It is likely that there were others.

22. Quest, "Additional Facts," p. 15. A description of the Correll-Gosden stage show performed on this tour can be found in Ely, pp. 59–63, with particular emphasis on the unique special lighting effects that allowed the performers to transform instantaneously from the black Amos and Andy to the white Correll and Gosden. See also Mark Quest, "Private Life of Amos 'n' Andy," *Radio Digest*, February 1930, p. 114, for Gosden's own account of the warm enthusiasm with which a predominantly black audience at Chicago's Regal Theatre responded to this act.

23. Gosden interviewed by James R. Crowell, "Amos 'n' Andy—Their Philosophy," *Psychology*, August 1930.

24. "An Appreciation," fan letter from F.M. Hander and family, Oakland, CA, 8/19/29. Letter in Correll-Gosden Scrapbooks, USC.

25. Wertheim, p. 36; compare Harlow P. Roberts, "A Key to One Sponsor's Success in Radio," *Broadcasting*, 4/15/32, p. 13. Although Wertheim states that Benton and Lasker first discussed the program in May 1929, Roberts's comments make it evident that the initial discussion could not have occurred later than the end of 1928.

26. Roberts, p. 13.

27. Ibid.

28. Steele, "Amos 'n' Andy: Here They Are," p. 27. Correll and Gosden played the Pantages Theatre in Kansas City from 6/14 through 6/20/29. See *Kansas City Star*, 6/16/29, which indicates that they were playing four shows daily (and five on Sunday) in addition to performing their nightly broadcast live from the WDAF studio. The Wednesday night of their stay in Kansas City—ordinarily their night off from broadcasting—was taken up by an appearance in a special WDAF minstrel show. Given this schedule, it is likely that their conversation with Kaney would have been rather brief.

29. Ruth Adams Knight, *Stand By for the Ladies: The Distaff Side of Broadcasting* (New York: Coward-McCann, 1939), pp. 42–43.

30. Correll interview, 1/14/73.

31. Ibid.

32. Steele, "Amos 'n' Andy: Here They Are," p. 8.

33. Caton, p. 310. Although the announcement of the contract first appeared in the *Chicago Daily News* for 7/27/29, it is likely that the agreement was signed at the time of Correll and Gosden's visit to New York earlier in the month. During their time in New York, the performers spent several days touring Harlem, familiarizing themselves with the geography of the area and pinpointing locations between East 134th and East 137th Streets for the taxicab office, the lodge hall, and Amos and Andy's rooming house. See Albert R. Williamson, "Amos 'n' Andy in Harlem," *Radio Digest*, June 1930, pp. 10–13.

34. "Theme Songs That Click: Amos 'n' Andy's Tag Melody," *Radio Guide*, 5/12/34, p. 4.

Chapter 5

1. "Amos and Andy in Person Take the Air Every Night for a Year," National Broadcasting Company Press Release, 7/27/29.

2. Kay Trenholm, "Last Night on WJZ," *New York Sun*, 8/20/29.

3. Gosden quoted by Ben Gross, *I Looked and I Listened: Informal Recollections of Radio and TV* (New York: Random House, 1954), p. 154.

4. Roberts, p. 13.

5. Ibid.

6. Telegram to the Pepsodent Company from Charles M. Armstrong, Secretary of State, State of Colorado. Clyde B. Davis, "Secretary of State Sends Telegram Objecting to 5 PM Broadcast of Feature," *Rocky Mountain News*, 11/15/29, in Correll-Gosden Scrapbooks, USC, quoted in Wertheim, p. 52.

7. Roberts, p. 13. See also "Across the Desk," editorial, *Radio Digest*, January 1930, p. 6, for a contemporary assessment of the protest.

8. "*Amos 'n' Andy*," *Time*, 3/3/30.

9. A.S. (Arthur H. Samuels), "On the Air," *The New Yorker*, 3/22/30.

10. Crowell, "Amos 'n' Andy Tell Their Own Story."

11. Hubert Foss in *Radio Times*, quoted in Charleston (WV) *Daily Mail*, 10/5/30.
12. Roberts.
13. Gosden interviewed by Crowell, *Psychology*, August 1930.
14. O. O. McIntyre, "Amos 'n' Andy," *Cosmopolitan*, May 1930.
15. Examples of *Amos 'n' Andy* merchandise in author's collection.
16. Mordaunt Hall, "Amos 'n' Andy Open Mayfair Theatre," *New York Times*, 10/25/30. An audience of approximately 2,300 people packed the house for the opening performance.
17. Mordaunt Hall, *New York Times*, 10/29/30.
18. "The Shadow Stage," *Photoplay*, December 1930.
19. In 1956, *Check and Double Check* was released to television as part of a package of RKO-Radio feature films leased by RKO General, Inc., to a firm called C&C Television, Inc. Low-contrast 16mm dupes were prepared from the original 35mm materials, with the opening credits reedited to replace the RKO logos with a generic "C&C Movietime" logo. The film was available for television syndication well into the 1960s, and in 1958 fell into the public domain when RKO failed to renew its copyright. The film has since circulated widely in poorly duped 16mm copies, and in 1978 it was part of the first generation of public-domain features to appear on home video. The picture and sound quality of these public-domain copies is usually dismal and make modern-day viewings of the film an even more trying experience. While the original negative appears to be lost, the original 35mm master positive print and soundtrack of *Check and Double Check* are preserved by the Library of Congress, and a well-preserved 35mm print with original RKO titles was used as the basis for an official video release of the film by Turner Home Entertainment in 1991 (RKO Collection No. 6213). This same print has occasionally been shown by the Turner Classic Movies cable channel. The Library of Congress also holds the negative for the foreign release of the film, assembled from alternate takes. What little reputation the film currently enjoys is due primarily to the appearance by Ellington and his band, and there is suggestion that Ellington developed a friendship with Correll and Gosden as a result of his work on the picture. See Ely, pp. 167–68. Ellington himself was a fan of the *Amos 'n' Andy* program in the early 1930s—the title of his 1932 composition "Ducky Wucky" was inspired by Madam Queen's nickname for Andy.
20. Freeman F. Gosden, Jr., correspondence with the author, 11/25/2000. Correll quoted by Charles Denton, "Voices of Experience," *TV Weekly, Los Angeles Herald Examiner*, October 10–15 1961, p. 5.
21. Richard B. Jewell, "RKO Film Grosses, 1929–1951: The C. J. Telvin Ledger," *Historical Journal of Film, Radio, and Television*, vol. 14, no. 1, 1994, p. 43.
22. Bart Andrews and Arghus Julliard, *Holy Mackerel!: The Amos 'n' Andy Story* (New York: E.P. Dutton, 1986), p. 44. Six years after *Check and Double Check*, Correll and Gosden would be enticed into making a brief appearance in *The Big Broadcast of 1936* for Paramount, but this would be their final film performance. In 1933, the performers agreed to provide voices for a series of animated shorts to be produced by Van Beuren Productions of New York and to be distributed by RKO. Correll and Gosden traveled to New York in March 1933 to record the voice tracks for the first two films in the series—"The Rasslin' Match" (released 1/5/34), which was loosely based on a story line from early 1932 in which the Kingfish promoted a match between Andy and wrestler Bullneck Mooseface, and "The Lion Tamer" (released 2/2/34). The animation was produced for the films after the voice tracks were recorded, and Correll and Gosden appear to have had little control over this aspect of the production. Dissatisfaction with the quality of the films led Correll and Gosden to walk out on the project, and the performers were subsequently sued by Van Beuren for breach of contract. Correll and Gosden followed with a countersuit, but the matter apparently fell by the wayside when Van Beuren went out of business in 1936. See *New York Times*, 3/19/35.
23. "Honeyboy and Pal Off to Lost Diamond Mine," *Radio Digest*, April 1930, pp. 72–23. See also Wertheim, p. 28. NBC run: see Jay Hickerson, *The Ultimate History of Network Radio Programs and Guide to Circulating Shows* (Hamden CT: Self-published, 1992), p. 184.
24. *Pittsburgh Courier*, 1/18/30.
25. *Chicago Defender*, 1/25/30.
26. *Who's Who on the Air* (New York: Ludwig Bauman and Sons, 1932). See also Ely, pp. 166–67. Miller and Lyles, childhood friends from Columbia, Tennessee, formed their partnership while attending Fisk University together shortly after the turn of the century, and they began their professional stage careers in 1907, performing in a flamboyant comic style and invariably appearing in full blackface makeup. Making their Broadway debuts in the pioneering all-black revue "Darkydom" 1915), the team went on to score a string of successful shows, including "Shuffle Along" (1921), "Runnin' Wild" (1923), and "Rang Tang" (1927). However, their 1928 production, "Keep Shufflin'," proved a critical and commercial failure, and the team dissolved after the show closed, reuniting briefly for one final stage collaboration, "Sugar Hill," in 1931. Miller and Lyles also made a number of comic dialogue records for the OKeh and Banner labels, occasionally under the billing of "The Charcoal Twins."

Their routines contained comic elements that resembled certain elements in the later work of Correll and Gosden, particularly wordplay references to "routinin'" letters (see *Amos 'n' Andy* episode 12, 4/3/28) and a mathematical routine about "mulsifyin'" a column of figures (*Amos 'n' Andy* episode 3, 3/22/28). Although the material aired only once in the context of the radio program, Correll and Gosden performed variations on these themes in their Pantages theatrical tour in 1929 and their Publix tour in early 1930. In April 1930, Flournoy Miller—then preparing the book for "Lew Leslie's Blackbirds of 1930," which would run for only 57 performances that fall—threatened legal action against NBC, contending that Correll and Gosden's use of such material had led to confusion between the two acts. (See Walter Winchell," On Broadway," *New York Daily*

Mirror, 4/29/30.) Further information on the case can be found in the *Pittsburgh Courier,* 5/10/30, where it is stated that while Miller and Lyles claimed a "patent" on the comic material in question, they did not claim actual authorship—indicating only that a "colored writer" had originally created the routines for another, unnamed comedy team.

Given the fast-and-loose exchange of comedy material among performers and writers prevalent during the vaudeville era—and the fact that Miller and Lyles themselves were by their own admission not the originators of the material in question—it is unlikely that any suit over the provenance of the "routinin'" or "mulsifyin' an' revidin'" routines would have held up in court. There is no evidence that any legal action was ever actually filed over the matter, and Miller's threat may well have been a show-business publicity stunt—coming as it did at a time when his own reputation was in eclipse, and any mention of *Amos 'n' Andy* was likely to secure newspaper space. Indeed, a similar publicity thrust was mounted during early 1930 by the veteran white blackface team of James McIntyre and Thomas Heath—fixtures in stage minstrelsy since the 1870s—who ran advertisements in theatrical journals condemning Correll and Gosden as "imitators" of *their* act.

Late in life, Miller claimed that Correll and Gosden had appropriated two specific catchphrases from Miller and Lyles—"I'se regusted" and "It all depends on de sitch-ation yo' is in." (See handwritten autobiographical notes by F.E. Miller, in Flournoy Miller Personal and Professional Papers, Helen Armstead–Johnson Theater Collection, African American Theatre Arts Collection Project, Schomburg Center for Research in Black Culture, New York Public Library, New York.) However, it must be noted that there is no record in any of the *Amos 'n' Andy* scripts of Correll and Gosden ever using the "It all depends" phrase—nor has any evidence surfaced documenting the use of "I'se regusted" by Miller and Lyles prior to its use by Correll and Gosden. Given the prominence of Miller and Lyles on Broadway throughout the 1920s, it would seem reasonable to expect critics to have noticed and commented on the appropriation by Correll and Gosden of such a prominent catchphrase, but no such comments have been located.

However, it *can* be confirmed that Miller and Lyles preceded Correll and Gosden in the use of "re-" prefixes in the fancified reconstruction of elided unstressed initial syllables. See, for example, the use of "rescerned" for "concerned" by Miller and Lyles on their recording of "Can't Do It" (OKeh 4727-B, mx S-72006-B), recorded in October 1922, and "retelligence" for "intelligence" on "Sam and Steve" (OKeh 40186-A, mx. S-72732-A), recorded in August 1924. While it is possible that Correll and Gosden may have been influenced by Miller and Lyles in their use of this particular linguistic quirk, its documented presence in certain genuine African American dialects of the era (see note 7, for the "Speaking the Language" chapter of this work) indicates that Correll and Gosden could also have picked up the trait independently. There is no evidence available to conclusively prove either possibility.

It should also be noted that for several years prior to *Sam 'n' Henry,* Miller and Lyles had used the names of "Sam" and "Steve" for the characters they portrayed on their phonograph records—see, for example, the 1924 "Sam and Steve" recording cited above. However, "Sam" was a name used almost generically for blackface characters dating back to the nineteenth century, probably as a contraction of "Sambo," so Correll and Gosden's use of this name is probably a coincidence. The personalities and voices of "Sam and Steve," as portrayed on recordings by Miller and Lyles or as portrayed in the plot scenes of "Shuffle Along," in no way resemble those of *Sam 'n' Henry* as portrayed on radio by Correll and Gosden. In "Shuffle Along," Sam Peck and Steve Johnson are rival candidates for the mayoralty in the all-black Southern community of "Jimtown," and their continuous corruption of the political process for personal gain is the focus of the show's comic plot.

"Leading male duos in black Broadway musicals had typically been partners in crime in the plot. In "Shuffle Along," Steve and Sam collaborate only provisionally; the majority of their relationship consists of their repeated betrayals of each other and of Jimtown. They betray their original partnership as co-owners of a grocery store, first by running against each other in the election, next by stealing from the store to buy votes, and finally by hiring an investigator when they become suspicious of each other. The two men also betray the town by forming a secret political alliance, promising that the winner will make the loser Chief of Police. As soon as Steve wins the campaign, he betrays all those he made promises to, including, initially, Sam. In short, the plot demonstrates that there is no honor among thieves—or black male collaborators" [Rachel A. Rosenberg, "Looking for Zora's Mule Bone: The Battle for Artistic Authority in the Hurston-Hughes Collaboration," *Modernism/Modernity* 6.2 (1999), p. 86].

As can be seen, the caricatured relationship of Sam and Steve in "Shuffle Along" in no way foreshadows the deep, sincere friendship of Sam and Henry or Amos and Andy—rather it is more in line with the conventionalized relationships of secondary comedians in white musical comedy.

It is also important to note that Miller and Lyles performed conventional setup-punchline blackface comedy routines, either as standalone vaudeville material on stage or on recordings, or as interpolations in a loosely plotted revue—unlike the melodramatic serialized story lines and deeply textured characterizations that formed the basis of Correll and Gosden's radio work. Sam and Steve were merely comedy relief in "Shuffle Along," while other characters carried forward the serious, romantic elements of the plot. In *Amos 'n' Andy,* the title characters themselves carried both the serious and comic aspects of the story.

All these factors being so, it must be concluded that there is no justification for modern-day allegations that Correll and Gosden owed their success to material "purloined" from Miller and Lyles, or that Miller and Lyles were the "true creators" of *Amos 'n' Andy.*

27. *Radio Digest,* May 1931, p. 69. Finally acknowledging their error in denying Correll and Gosden the

privilege of syndicating their feature, the *Tribune* Company began syndication of *Louie's Hungry Five* in October 1930, and by the spring of 1931 the feature was being heard on approximately forty stations.

28. A collection of scripts converted to short-story form from the first year of *The Goldbergs* can be found in Gertrude Berg, *The Rise of the Goldbergs* (New York: Barse & Co, 1931). In 1931, the Pepsodent Company began sponsoring *The Goldbergs* as well as *Amos 'n' Andy*, and the two programs shared the services of announcer Bill Hay. Pepsodent continued with the series until 1934, and when the company discontinued its sponsorship the series went off the air for nearly two years, with the exception of a brief run on the Mutual network for Colgate in the spring of 1936. When it returned under the sponsorship of Procter and Gamble in the fall of 1937, it was in the form of a daytime soap opera, which took the Goldberg family out of the Bronx and deemphasized their ethnicity by relocating them on a farm in a rural Connecticut town. The series ran in this form until 1944, and it later returned to its Bronx roots for a half-hour family situation comedy version in the late 1940s, which had an even more successful run on television.

29. Dr. Ralph L. Power, "Cecil and Sally," *Radio Digest*, December 1930. *Cecil and Sally* began in 1929 over station KYA in San Francisco and was briefly heard over the West Coast American Broadcasting Company network (no relation to the later ABC) before moving to KPO and recorded syndication. By the end of 1930, the feature was being heard on 53 stations. In 1932, the Pepsodent Company—*Amos 'n' Andy*'s sponsor—bought the foreign rights to the program for distribution in Australia and New Zealand. *Cecil and Sally* proved one of the most durable recorded serials of the era, with over 1,100 episodes produced, and was still in distribution as late as 1937. Series creator Johnny Patrick went on to a prolific career as a playwright and Hollywood screenwriter, with his credits including *Teahouse of the August Moon* (1953, winner of the Pulitzer Prize for drama in 1954), *Three Coins in the Fountain* (1954), *Love Is a Many Splendored Thing* (1955), *High Society* (1956), *The World of Suzie Wong* (1960) and *Shoes of the Fisherman* (1968).

30. Hickerson, pp. 378, 414. Scripts for *The Stebbins Boys* are available in the Library of American Broadcasting, College Park, MD.

31. "The Laughs and Lives of Lum and Abner," *Radio Guide*, 9/25/37. Lauck and Goff had first planned a blackface act but were put off by the number of *Amos 'n' Andy* imitators already in the field. *Lum and Abner* ran until 1953, and in 1968 it returned to the air in the form of syndicated rebroadcasts. It remains in distribution to the present day and maintains a strong following among old-time-radio enthusiasts.

32. Summa quoted by Geri.
33. Correll interview, 1/14/73.
34. Gosden quoted in Quest. "Amos 'n' Andy Backstage."
35. Mary Jane Higby, *Tune in Tomorrow* (New York, Ace Books, 1968), pp. 35–36.
36. For a discussion of the earliest major experiments in U.S. radio drama see C.H. Huntley, "Tricks Used in Staging Invisible Shows," *Radio Broadcast*, November 1923, describing the programs of the WGY Players at WGY, Schenectady, NY. This anthology program represents the first known regularly scheduled dramatic series in American radio.

37. McIntyre.
38. Gilbert Seldes, *The Public Arts* (New York: Simon & Schuster, 1956), pp. 63–64.
39. Maynard Shipley, "Amos 'n' Andy—Why the Fresh Air Taxicab Has Beaten the Traffic," *The Debunker*, April 1931. *The Debunker* was founded and edited by crusading Socialist publisher Emmanuel Haldeman-Julius, an outspoken white supporter of African American civil rights in the 1920s and 1930s. The magazine's April 1931 issue, containing Maynard Shipley's article praising *Amos 'n' Andy*, also contains a blistering indictment of religious involvement in the Ku Klux Klan—under the title "The Klan Adopts Khrist"—and a graphic condemnation of a January 1931 lynching in the town of Maryville, Missouri.

40. Ibid.
41. Williamson, p. 11.
42. Orrin E. Dunlap, Jr., "Listening-In," *New York Times*, 5/10/31.
43. *Amos 'n' Andy*, episodes 242 to 251, 1/1/29 through 1/12/29.
44. *Amos 'n' Andy*, episodes 862 to 927, 12/27/30 through 3/13/31.

Chapter 6

1. Correll interviewed by Lamparski, 6/30/69. "Restoration comedy": see Richard Barrios, *A Song in the Dark* (New York: Oxford University Press, 1995), p. 268.

2. The first on-mike appearance by Madam Queen, in episode 913, 2/25/31, created enough of a stir that it warranted mention as a news item. See *New York Times*, 2/26/31, which stresses that "Amos" had played the role and that "no third person has been added to the cast." Although no recording of this broadcast is known to exist, an idea of what the voice might have sounded like can be found on Correll and Gosden's recording of "Who Is Your Who?" Victor 20826 (39087-3, recorded 7/6/27), in which Correll and Gosden interpolate a brief and comedic telephone conversation between a lover (Correll) and his sweetheart (Gosden, who in an adenoidal falsetto dismisses Correll as "you big cheese").

3. Howard Wilcox, "And Now it's Amos 'n' Andy 'n' Henrietta," *Radio Guide*, 6/15/35, pp. 11, 25.

4. In addition to Elinor Harriot's participation, actress/dialectician Edith Davis was also heard in the wedding episode, speaking a single line as Mrs. Crawford. Prior to the ceremony, the Dixie Melody Masters, a black Chicago-based concert quartet, performed "I Love You Truly." Copies of the script for this episode were made available as a premium by the Pepsodent Company in early 1936.

5. Andrews and Julliard, pp. 68–70. Before her death in 1983, Wade had become the subject of a rather bizarre urban myth—that she was the mother of 1970s rock star Billy Preston. "If I gave birth to Billy Preston," she is said to have laughed, "I wasn't there

at the time." Whether she actually offered this response or not, the denial is correct. Wade was in Hollywood at the time of Preston's birth in Texas in 1946.

6. "Barbara Jean Wong, Asian-American Media Trailblazer and Community Activist Passes Away," *Newsletter of the Museum of Chinese-American History,* Fall/Winter 1999, which includes a photo of the grown-up Wong with Correll and Gosden circa 1951. During the later years of *The Amos 'n' Andy Show,* Correll and Gosden were careful to introduce Wong to the live studio audience during the preshow warmup, so there would be no exclamations of surprise at the sight of a Chinese-American woman speaking the lines of a young African American girl. See also Correll interviewed by Lamparski, 6/30/69.

7. Bill Hay as told to Roger Cameron, "Here They Are!" *Radio Stars,* April 1935.

8. Gosden interviewed by George D. Mooney, *New York Times,* 12/1/40.

9. Bill Hay interviewed on "Same Time Same Station," KRLA, Pasadena, CA, broadcast 1/14/73.

Chapter 7

1. J.L. Dillard, "Black English and the American Establishment." In *Black English: Its History and Usage in the United States* (New York: Random House, 1972), p. 13.

2. A typical unsupported assertion of "bastardization" appears in Susan Douglas, *Listening In: Radio and the American Imagination from Amos 'n' Andy to Edward R. Murrow to Wolfman Jack and Howard Stern* (New York: Times Books, 1999), p. 108, although Douglas—basing much of her discussion of the point on that of Melvin Ely—also acknowledges the presence of authentic elements in the dialect. For an example of early debate on this issue, see "Amos 'n' Andy's Dialect, Is It Real?" *Radio Digest,* July 1930. Letters to the magazine were often critical of Correll's delivery and of Andy's habit of substituting "re-" for the unstressed initial syllables of certain words. According to the article, Gosden's delivery seemed more authentic to Southern readers than that of his partner, although some readers were critical of both. Interestingly, the article makes a considerable effort to differentiate between "minstrel" dialect and genuine "Negro speech" and presents a brief, nontechnical discussion of the different varieties of black dialect—while making no attempt to offer a definitive answer to the question posed in the title of the article.

3. See Dillard for a readable, accessible introduction to both the historic roots and the grammatical structure of African American Vernacular English. Much more technical in nature, but still the definitive work in the field, is William Labov, *Language in the Inner City: Studies in the Black English Vernacular* (Philadelphia: University of Pennsylvania Press, 1972). Labov's research marked the beginning of modern scholarship into the origins and structure of African American Vernacular English.

4. Walter M. Brasch, *Black English and the Mass Media* (Amherst: University of Massachusetts Press, 1981), p. xxv.

5. The phenomenon of bidialectism is defined and explored in Brasch, pp. 259, 267–69, 272, 287–88. See also Dillard, chapter 5, "The Negro Dialect and Southern Dialect," pp. 186–228, for a discussion of the influence African American Vernacular English has had on the speech of white Southerners; also especially see pp. 198–99 for a discussion of the phenomenon of bidialectism in white children.

6. Brasch, p. 223, offers a brief linguistic analysis of *Amos 'n' Andy,* noting both genuine African American language traits and the use of minstrel-derived humorous elements, a likely reference to the use of malapropism humor, but he fails to examine the specific structure of the *Amos 'n' Andy* dialect in detail. It is likely that Brasch based his analysis on examination of surviving recordings of post–1943 situation-comedy broadcasts rather than on a careful examination of original serial-era scripts. It is impossible to be certain—unfortunately, no sources for the analysis are cited in his notes for this chapter.

7. William Labov cited by Steven A. Holmes, *New York Times,* 12/30/96.

8. Correll interviewed by Lamparski, 6/30/69.

9. Brasch, pp. 223–24. See also Dillard, pp. 245–57, for a detailed examination of "fancy talk" and its relation to hypercorrected and malapropial speech.

10. Dillard, pp. 26–27, discusses the elision and fancified reconstruction of unstressed initial syllables and cites Charles S. Johnson, *The Shadow of the Plantation* (Chicago: University of Chicago Press, 1934) as having documented the form "revorce" for "divorce." Dillard discusses such forms further on p. 249, noting also the form "remorial" for "memorial," the latter being a form sometimes noted in *Amos 'n' Andy.* Occasionally, this habit could be used for intentionally satirical effect—as in the use of "repression" for "depression." While an apt commentary by Correll and Gosden on the economic conditions of the 1930s, "repression" is also used for "depression" by former Alabama slave Billy Abraham Longslaughter in a 1937 interview by a representative of the Works Progress Administration's Federal Writers Project. See F.L. Diard and J. Morgan Smith, "He Caned a Chair for President Buchanan," in *Alabama Slave Narratives,* volume 1, p. 261, Manuscript Division, Library of Congress.

11. "Amos 'n' Andy's Dialect, Is It Real?" p. 13.

12. Ely, pp. 23–24.

13. Brasch, p. 224, discussing the general use of "Afro-American idiomatic expressions" in the series. The absence of "jive" was noted by Alamena Davis, *Los Angeles Tribune,* 3/22/42, cited by Ely, p. 202. Davis was a black journalist who interviewed Correll and Gosden in early 1942 and who mildly criticized their failure to keep their slang up-to-date.

14. Taylor's voice as performed by Gosden survives in several syndication recordings of *Amos 'n' Andy,* among them episode 393, for broadcast 6/26/29, included in the boxed CD set *The Amos 'n' Andy Chronicles* (New Rochelle, NY: Great American Audio, Inc., 2000). The episode is misdated 6/28/29 in the set.

15. Compare Amos's speech in the 1929 recording cited above with his speech in the 4/3/39 broadcast of *Amos 'n' Andy,* as released on Radiola MR-1134, *The Rarest Amos 'n' Andy* (Sandy Hook, CT: The Radiola Company, 1981).

Chapter 8

1. Gosden quoted by Quest, "Private Life of Amos 'n' Andy," p. 114.
2. Ibid.
3. Ibid.
4. The first indication of Taylor's financial problems occurred as the bull market of 1928–29 was hitting its peak. In episode 451, 9/2/29, Amos received a letter from Ruby indicating that her father had lost a significant amount in a real estate deal and that it might affect plans for her to return to New York to resume school in the fall. The market hit its 1920s peak the day after this episode was aired and then began a precipitous skid that led ultimately to the crash in late October. Amos learned that Taylor had fallen victim to this pre-crash decline in episode 478, 10/3/29; Taylor had to sell most of his business holdings to cover his losses. Taylor's health began to decline in the wake of these losses, and in episode 589, 2/10/30, Amos learned that Ruby would have to go back to Chicago to take care of her father. The following day, in episode 590, 2/11/30, the Kingfish mentioned that he had heard that the Taylor Garage was destroyed in a fire, adding to Mr. Taylor's financial woes. By 1932, however, Taylor began a new business, going into partnership with a young Chicago man named Clifton Mills in the operation of a clothing store.
5. Telegram from Correll and Gosden to President Roosevelt, 3/5/33, and reply from Stephen Early, 3/6/33, Personal File 3795, Franklin D. Roosevelt Presidential Library, Hyde Park, NY.
6. Wertheim, p. 39.
7. Digest of Hearings, FCC Broadcast Division, Under Section 307(c) of *Communications Act of 1934*, October 1–20, November 7–12, 1934, pp. 123, 130.
8. George Frazier, "Amos 'n' Andy: Two Angels in Blackface," *Coronet*, March 1948, p. 92. A partial precedent for Amos's ordeal can be found in the chainless chain–era story line dealing with Earl Dixon and the Easy-Riding Taxicab Company, episodes 359 through 419, aired from 5/18/29 through 7/27/29. The characters of Earl Dixon and Jack Dixon are very similar and were probably played with identical voice characterizations by Charles Correll. However, while Amos was jailed in the earlier story line for a crime he did not commit, his interrogation was not depicted in the 1929 sequence nor is there any scene in the earlier story line to parallel the on-mike violence of Jack Dixon's assault on Amos in the 1931 sequence. Despite the similarity of the names, there is nothing in the 1931 sequence to indicate that Earl and Jack Dixon are related nor is any reference made to the events of 1929 in the 1931 story line. Correll and Gosden no doubt realized that most of their 1931 audience had not heard the earlier story.

The use of the "dream" device to conclude the Jack Dixon story line also had a precedent in an earlier script: episode 200, for broadcast on 11/13/28, concluded a brief three-episode sequence dealing with Andy's authorship of a "business encyclopedia" by revealing that the volume became a runaway success with thousands of copies sold. As Andy relished his triumph, the alarm clock rang, bringing an end to both his dream and the story line.

9. Correll and Gosden quoted by Frazier, p. 92.
10. Freeman F. Gosden, Jr., correspondence with the author 1/4/98 and 1/13/00. Gosden's original script for the Lord's Prayer sequence was deliberately ecumenical—although the Gosden family was Presbyterian, the script was submitted to a minister, a Catholic priest, and a Jewish rabbi for review before its initial broadcast, and Gosden took particular pride in the fact that none of the clergymen consulted suggested any changes. The 1940 sequence was not the first Christmas broadcast to revolve around a religious theme. In 1936, Gosden turned several minutes of the Christmas Eve program over to Dr. Preston Bradley, pastor of the nondenominational—and racially liberal—People's Church of Chicago for a sermon on the meaning of the holiday season, fitting Dr. Bradley's remarks into the program by having Amos and Andy tune him in on Amos's new radio. In 1937 Christmas Eve was marked by Amos's reading of the Nativity story from the second chapter of Luke, to the accompaniment of a soft rendering of "Silent Night" by the Paul Taylor Chorus, as Ruby, the baby Arbadella, Ruby's mother Lillian, the orphaned Pun'kin, and Andy gathered around the tree to listen. Christmas Eve fell on a weekend in 1938 and 1939, and no special broadcast was aired.
11. *Amos 'n' Andy* broadcast of 12/24/41, included on *The Rarest Amos 'n' Andy*. Gosden's dialect as Amos in this scene is extremely subtle.

Chapter 9

1. Cohen's long series of short stories, published throughout the 1910s and 1920s in *The Saturday Evening Post,* revolved around the activities of one Florian Slappey, a sharp-dressing, fancy-talking, self-satisfied hustler, and his interactions with the various fictitious residents of Birmingham, Alabama's "Dark town" section. Slipper's associates included such extravagant personalities as Julius Caesar Clump, Edwin Biscoe Fizz, Forceps Swain, Orifice Lattice, Callous Ditch, Lawyer Evans Chew, and Professor Aleck Champagne. Cohen's humor was generally as broadly played as the names of his characters, and those characters never approached the emotional development apparent in Correll and Gosden's characters. His use of dialect, however, is praised as "quite good" by Dillard (p. 250) and by Brasch (p. 153) as "better than that of most of his contemporaries." Several collections of Cohen's "Darktown" stories were published, including *Polished Ebony* (New York: Dodd, Mead, 1919), *Highly Colored* (New York: Dodd, Mead, 1921), *Dark Days and Black Knights* (New York: Dodd, Mead, 1923), *Bigger and Blacker* (New York: Dodd, Mead, 1925), and *Black and Blue* (New York: Dodd Mead, 1926). Cohen wrote a play, *Come Seven,* around the "Darktown" characters, which ran briefly on Broadway in 1921, and he contributed scripts to a series of all-talking "Darktown Comedy" shorts produced by Al Christie for Paramount from 1929 to 1930. Spencer Williams, Jr., later Andy in the television version of *The Amos 'n' Andy Show,* appeared in this series, cowrote several of the scripts, and received screen credit as a "dialogue consultant.") Cohen was also well known as a

skilled author of detective stories and of stories set in the world of smalltime professional boxing. In an odd irony, Cohen served as a contributing writer for the half-hour situation comedy version of *The Amos 'n' Andy Show* in the fall of 1945—but was unable to turn out satisfactory material and quit after six weeks.

2. Honeyboy and Sassafrass are discussed in note 23 of chapter 5, and Miller and Lyles in note 26 of chapter 5. Pick Malone and Pat Padgett were vaudevillians who attained their first network success as "Molasses 'n' January" on the *Maxwell House Show Boat* program in 1932 and remained on that series through 1937. As "Pick and Pat," the performers were featured on several different variety programs from 1933 forward, always featuring straightforward minstrel-style comic material. Katherine Tift-Jones was a Georgia heiress who dabbled in radio as a hobby, creating the character of "Calliope" as a tribute to her childhood nursemaid. *Miss Katherine and Calliope* was broadcast sporadically from 1929 into the mid-1930s, at both the network and local levels. Tess Gardella had played the character of Aunt Jemima on stage during the 1920s, and played the role on CBS from 1931to 1933. Harriette Widmer and Amanda Randolph played the role in unrelated series heard in the 1940s and 1950s. Ernest Whitman and Eddie Green, billed as "network radio's only colored comedians," were featured members of the cast for *The Gibson Family,* a "musical-comedy-drama" series heard over NBC during 1934 and 1935, and Green would team with actress Gee Gee Pearson on Louis Armstrong's *Fleischmann Harlem Revue* over NBC during 1936 and 1937. Eddie Anderson joined the cast of Jack Benny's weekly series in the spring of 1937, becoming well known as the wisecracking valet "Rochester." Clarence Muse, a distinguished stage and film actor, was active in local Los Angeles radio during the early 1930s and was featured, along with the Hall Johnson Choir, on Irvin S. Cobb's *Paducah Plantation* series in 1936–37. *John Henry—Black River Giant* was based on the writings of the white folklorist Roark Bradford and was enacted by an "all-Negro" cast headed by the Puerto Rican–born stage actor Juano Hernandez, who also cowrote the scripts.

3. *Eveready Hour,* broadcast of 5/15/28, air check of station WEAF, New York, Edison Diamond Disc experimental recording EXP 159-B. The author thanks Jerry Fabris of the Edison National Historic Site for providing access to this uncirculated recording, from which the dialogue cited was transcribed.

4. A hint of the retrogressive racial attitudes prevalent at the top levels of NBC during the 1930s may be found in a 5/1/35 memo from the network's Vice President in Charge of Programs John F. Royal to Continuity Acceptance Editor Janet MacRorie prohibiting the use of the word "nigger" over the NBC networks. In promulgating the ban, Royal complains "these darkies put a lot of pressure on us and they are sometimes too exacting" [Folder 245, Topical Folders 1922-1986, NBC History Files, Library of Congress].

5. Correll and Gosden depicted a third-degree police interrogation of both Amos and Andy as suspects in a pawnshop robbery in Episodes 75 through 77, 6/21 through 23/28, but the scenes are less intense than those in the 1931 sequence. The criticism of the interrogation by Hugh D. Harper of the National Association of Chiefs of Police is covered in the *Los Angeles Times,* 12/11/31, and it apparently made a significant impact on Correll and Gosden, who were careful to present law enforcement officers in a positive manner from that point forward.

6. Ely, p. 63.

7. Correll interview, 1/14/73.

Chapter 10

1. According to the 1930 U.S. Census, of the 2,803,756 black families tallied, only 209,779 reported owning a radio (7.5 percent of the total). This amounts to a conservative estimate of a total African American home audience of less than 840,000. It must be noted, however, that this estimate, does not take into account the phenomenon of communal listening in public places. See "Analyzing the Radio Audience—Its Size and Makeup," *Broadcasting,* 11/1/32.

2. Freeman Gosden interviewed by Quest, "Private Lives of Amos 'n' Andy."

3. Ely, pp. 152–53.

4. Gosden interviewed by Quest, "Private Lives of Amos 'n' Andy."

5. "In a Class by Themselves: Amos 'n' Andy," *Christian Science Monitor,* 2/20/29.

6. A. Wellington Clarke, "If Amos and Andy Were Negroes: What Numerous Negroes in Various Walks of Life Think of the Boys," *Radio Digest,* August 1930.

7. Ibid.

8. Ibid.

9. Ibid.

10. Ibid.

11. Ibid.

12. Ibid.

13. Ibid.

14. Ibid.

15. Bishop W.J. Walls, "What About Amos 'n' Andy?" *Abbott's Monthly,* December 1930.

16. Editorial, *Pittsburgh Courier,* 4/25/31.

17. Dr. Patrick Washburn, interviewed for *The Black Press: Soldiers Without Swords,* a film by Stanley Nelson (San Francisco: California Newsreel, 1998). For a booklength examination of Vann's career, see Andrew Buni, *Robert L. Vann of the Pittsburgh Courier* (Pittsburgh: University of Pittsburgh Press, 1974).

18. Buni, pp. 146–60, 222–26.

19. Ely, p. 175.

20. *Pittsburgh Courier,* 9/12/31.

21. *Pittsburgh Courier,* 10/31/31.

22. Editorial, *Louisville News,* reprinted in *Kansas City Call,* 8/28/31.

23. "The Campaign Against *Amos 'n' Andy,*" *Northwest Enterprise,* 11/5/31.

24. Ibid.

25. Jessie M. Vann, letter to Walter White of the NAACP, 7/17/51, quoted in Ely, p. 183. The final significant mentions of the *Amos 'n' Andy* campaign in the *Courier* occurred in the issue of 10/31/31, in the front-page report on "National Protest Day" and in the issue of 12/19/31, when an editorial notes the criticism received by the National Association of

Chiefs of Police about a sequence in which Amos was brutally interrogated by detectives.

26. Ely, p. 181 and fn. 46, p. 288. The national office of the NAACP did criticize a specific aspect of the series in the summer of 1933, questioning a story line in which Correll and Gosden had their characters drive from New York to Chicago to attend the World's Fair and had them spend several nights along the way in a "colored tourist camp." The NAACP criticized the implication that formal segregation of accommodations existed in the North, and while Correll and Gosden did not comment on the protest, they acknowledged it by avoiding any further discussion of "colored" accommodations in their scripts. See Ely, p. 201, and compare *Amos 'n' Andy* episode 1656, 8/17/33, containing the final reference to the "colored tourist camp" with episode 1668, 9/4/33, in which the "tourist camp" is discussed with no further reference to it being a "colored" facility. Also compare episode 2405, 9/2/36, in which the announcer's introductory remarks again refer to a "colored tourist camp," but "colored" is struck out in the script.

27. See scrapbooks, Correll-Gosden Collection, USC, for clippings gathered from the *Courier* at the height of the protest. See *Pittsburgh Courier,* 6/13/31, for the paper's specific indictment of the bigamy story line. The final mention of the bigamy charge against Madam Queen appears in episode 927, 3/13/31, in which Brother Crawford mentions that the Madam and Lawyer Smith are trying to resolve the issue. Although the context of this episode and those episodes of the previous two days suggests that there will be further development of the story, the bigamy angle abruptly disappears and is never mentioned again in the series. No documentation exists to definitively explain this sudden change, but, given the performers' sensitivity to criticism, it is likely that private protests were heard almost immediately. Suggestion of such criticism can be found in *Radio Digest,* May 1931, p. 87, in which columnist George Lottman questions whether the "Breach of Promise" story line was appropriate subject matter for a program with a large audience of children. This item appeared in print at roughly the same time as Vann's first criticisms of the series in the *Courier*.

In mid–1932, Correll and Gosden attempted to clean up the continuity problems created by this sudden change in story line by having the Madam go to Reno to seek a divorce—without ever directly mentioning the bigamy issue—only to receive the news that her husband Raymond had been lost at sea. Later re-creations of the breach-of-promise story line drew elements from this later sequence to create a new version of the story, in which the Madam believed her husband to be lost at sea at the time of her engagement to Andy—only to faint when she saw him seated in the rear of the courtroom. See "Amos 'n' Andy Show," Vol. X, No. 8, taped 10/31/52 for broadcast 11/16/52. Wertheim, p. 53, bases his discussion of the breach-of-promise story line on this spurious "revised" version and not on the actual 1931 scripts, despite the fact that the original materials were available to him.

28. "Why the Amos 'n' Andy TV Show Should Be Taken Off the Air," *NAACP Bulletin,* 8/15/51, conspicuously fails to mention the radio series, which during the 1950–51 season still attracted an audience of more than 30 million listeners as a Sunday night feature on CBS. The radio program was on summer hiatus when the TV protest began in June 1951 but resumed in October—to an even larger audience than that of the previous season. See also W. Richard Bruner, "Amos 'n' Andy Hassle Won't Stop TV Show," *Printers' Ink,* 6/20/51, p. 30, for a detailed comment from NAACP director Walter White in which he avoids any mention of the radio program. For Billy Rowe's favorable review of the television series, see *Pittsburgh Courier,* 7/7/51.

Chapter 11

1. Fred Allen, letter to H. Allen Smith, 5/3/41, in *Fred Allen's Letters* (Garden City, NY: Doubleday, 1965).

2. Freeman F. Gosden, Jr., correspondence with the author, 11/25/2000, and "Blackout," *Time,* 1/25/43, p. 51.

3. John K. Hutchins, "No Tears," *New York Times,* 2/28/43.

4. Correll and Gosden made their first broadcasts before a live audience on 12/4/36 and 12/11/36, in two special "Mystic Knights of the Sea Friday Night Minstrel Show" broadcasts, in which Amos, Andy, the Kingfish, and others were portrayed as taking part in entertainment programs put on by the lodge as fundraising events. Bill Hay interacted on air with the characters for the first time during these broadcasts, acting in the role of Interlocutor. Correll and Gosden first experimented with the half-hour format on 2/27/39, in a special episode that found Amos and Andy touring the grounds of the New York World's Fair in the company of Fair president Grover Whalen. There were no further deviations from the standard 15-minute, no-audience format in the regular series for the rest of the Campbell Soup run. However, on 8/24/42, Correll and Gosden appeared before a live audience with their first-ever complete-in-one-episode half-hour story as their contribution to the U.S. Treasury Department's *Victory Theatre* program, a performance likely intended as an on-air audition for a half-hour series. (The script for this program was rebroadcast, with minor revisions, on 1/5/45.) The regular half-hour series began on NBC for Lever Brothers Company on 10/8/43.

5. The half-hour series scored a "typical rating" of 17.1 during the 1943–44 season, up from 9.4 in the final year of the serial, and it never dipped below 16.5 until 1951. However, even in those years of declining overall radio listening, *The Amos 'n' Andy Show* remained a strong performer and was the top-rated radio program on the air between 1951 and 1953. Ratings are discussed in detail in the appendix of this work.

6. Freeman F. Gosden, Jr., correspondence with the author, 11/25/2000.

7. John Crosby, "Amos 'n' Andy—Ain't Dat Sumpin'," *Collier's,* 10/16/48.

8. Ibid.

9. Goodman Ace, *Saturday Review of Literature,* 7/21/51.

10. *New York Times,* 2/28/39, p. 3.
11. Freeman F. Gosden, Jr., correspondence with the author, 11/25/2000.
12. Freeman Gosden quoted by Florabel Muir, *Redbook,* March 1948, cited in Ely, p. 204. See also Frazier, p. 98. The idea may have been inspired by talk of a film version of the radio series *One Man's Family* in the late 1930s—a project scuttled by the insistence by series creator Carlton E. Morse that his radio cast be used to dub the soundtrack.
13. Crosby, p. 34. See also William S. Paley, *As It Happened* (New York: Doubleday, 1976), p. 193. The *Amos 'n' Andy* deal sparked a series of moves of NBC performers to CBS, a trend commonly but incorrectly referred to as "the Paley Talent Raids." Paley himself credits Lew Wasserman of the Music Corporation of America for initiating the Correll–Gosden move and the most important subsequent move, that of Jack Benny. Freeman F. Gosden, Jr., states that the idea to incorporate the program and sell it to CBS actually originated with his father and that Wasserman simply served as a go-between in facilitating the deal.
14. Andrews and Julliard, pp. 54–55.
15. Freeman F. Gosden, Jr., correspondence with the author, 11/25/2000. See also Correll interviewed by Lamparski, 6/30/69, for Correll's impression of the discomfort the TV actors felt when the series creators were on the set; and Edward T. Clayton, "The Tragedy of Amos 'n' Andy," *Ebony,* October 1961, pp. 66–73 for Spencer Williams's recollections of the on-set friction with Gosden. Barton hired as director: see Andrews and Julliard, p. 57. Prior to joining the *Amos 'n' Andy Show* television series, Barton's best-known work had been ten Abbott and Costello features at Universal.
16. Freeman F. Gosden, Jr., correspondence with the author, 11/25/2000.
17. Paley, p. 232. For a detailed examination and analysis of the NAACP protest, see Thomas Cripps, "Amos 'n' Andy and the Debate over American Racial Integration," in *American History, American Television: Interpreting the Video Past,* edited by John E. O'Connor (New York: Frederick Ungar, 1983).
18. CBS's copyrights on the *Amos 'n' Andy Show* television episodes and on the radio episodes aired from October 1948 to the end of the series were reaffirmed in *Silverman v. CBS, 870 F. 2d 40; 1989,* but radio episodes aired prior to October 1948 were ruled to be in the public domain, as CBS had failed to renew the original copyrights for these episodes on their expiration. CBS also lost its claim to the *Amos 'n' Andy* trademark in this case, with non-use for a period of 22 years having been ruled evidence of abandonment.
19. Paley, p. 228. Other long-running radio programs discontinued by CBS on the same day as the *Amos 'n' Andy Music Hall* were the soap operas *Ma Perkins, Young Dr. Malone, The Right to Happiness,* and *The Second Mrs. Burton.*
20. *Calvin and the Colonel* was created by former *Amos 'n' Andy Show* writers Joe Connelly and Bob Mosher, and the show told the story of Colonel Montgomery T. Klaxton, a Kingfish-like fox, and his usual patsy Calvin Burnside, an Andy-like bear. It aired for a single season over ABC-TV from October 1961 to September 1962. In what must have seemed a nostalgic coincidence to old-time *Amos 'n' Andy* listeners, the program was sponsored in part by Pepsodent. In interviews promoting the new series, Correll and Gosden made an effort to avoid any potential racial controversies by stressing that they were performing in "Southern" dialect. See Ben Gross, "Correll and Gosden Are Still Voices," *New York Sunday News,* 7/22/62.
21. Charles Correll interviewed by Charles Denton, "Experience Talks," *Los Angeles Herald Examiner TV Weekly,* 10/15–21/61.
22. The Corrells had twice suffered unexpected family tragedies. Their first child, a daughter, was stillborn in January 1939, and their second son, John Joseph Correll, died of a kidney ailment in July 1954 at the age of eight.
23. *New York Times,* 9/27/72.
24. *Boston Globe,* 12/11/82.
25. Ibid.
26. Freeman F. Gosden, Jr., correspondence with the author, 11/25/2000.
27. Andrews and Julliard, p. 103.
28. Ely, pp. 252–53.
29. *Boston Globe,* 12/11/82.

Chapter 12

1. Michele Hilmes, *Radio Voices: American Broadcasting, 1922–1952,* Minneapolis: University of Minnesota Press, p. 91.
2. Ibid., p. 90.
3. Ibid., pp. 91–92.
4. See *Amos 'n' Andy* episode 13, 4/5/28, for the series' first description of Mr. Taylor's business holdings; episode 411, 7/17/29, in which Taylor indicates that he has been in Chicago for 32 years; episode 789, 10/3/30, for a description of Taylor's background in the lunchroom business; and episode 2359, 6/30/36, for a detailed discussion of the Southern roots of the Taylor family.
5. Hilmes, pp. 93–94. The only citation offered by Hilmes for the scripts references "Scripts, Book 1, USC" (fn. 39, p. 304), but there is no indication if this reference is to *Sam 'n' Henry* or *Amos 'n' Andy.* Book 1 of the latter series would cover only a portion of 1928. The only lines of dialogue directly quoted by Hilmes are taken from the first episode of *Sam 'n' Henry* and from a tape dub that she identifies as "Democrats and Republicans." Hilmes is apparently unaware that this recording is not actually from an *Amos 'n' Andy* broadcast. It is actually an improperly attributed copy of a commercial phonograph record (Victor 21608, "The Presidential Election"). Such records were made for appreciation without the need for reference to the continuing serial story line of the radio series and were generically comic in a style that sharply differed from the radio series. The characterizations of Amos and Andy as heard on the Victor records are often inconsistent with the characterizations of the radio series, especially in the case of Amos.
6. Erik Barnouw, *The Golden Web: A History of Broadcasting in the United States, Volume 1— to 1933* (New York: Oxford University Press, 1966), p. 230.

The scanty annotation of sources in Barnouw's work makes it difficult to determine exactly how much research was done in writing the section on *Amos 'n' Andy,* but the only primary source consulted seems to have been the 1929 *All About Amos 'n' Andy* book. The original scripts for the series were not available for scholarly research until the early 1970s, making it impossible for Barnouw to have consulted them in the course of preparing his analysis.

7. James R. Crowell, "Amos 'n' Andy—Their Philosophy."

8. Roy Wilkins, Baltimore *Afro-American,* 3/22/30.

9. See Ely, pp. 170–71 and 191 for an analysis of other comments made by Wilkins about the series in 1930. See Ely, pp. 215–16 for an analysis of Wilkins's shift in position and mention of his comments regarding the characterization of Amos. Wilkins's interest in *Amos 'n' Andy* led him, around 1939, to visit Correll and Gosden at their Beverly Hills office for a private discussion of the series and its content, in which Gosden provided Wilkins with Crossley ratings figures documenting the program's significant popularity among black listeners. See F. F. Gosden, Jr., correspondence with the author, 12/13/99, and letter to the *Los Angeles Times* by members of the Correll and Gosden families, 3/17/97.

Appendix

1. This conjecture finds its most complete latter-day presentation in J. Fred MacDonald, *Don't Touch That Dial: Radio Listening in American Life 1920–1960* (Chicago: Nelson-Hall, 1979), pp. 28–29. No documentation is offered by MacDonald in support of his theory save for raw C.A.B. figures.

2. See, for example, *Amos 'n' Andy, Time,* 3/3/30, and "On the Air," *The New Yorker,* 3/22/30, for contemporary mentions of communal listening in theaters, and Valdo Freeman, *Hartford Courant,* 4/6/30, for a vivid description of communal listening to *Amos 'n' Andy* in the barbershops, poolrooms, and radio stores of Harlem. For contemporary audience estimates, see Mark Quest, "Lost, Strayed or Stolen: Amos 'n' Andy," *Radio Digest,* January 1930.

3. Ratings information is taken from the tables contained in Harrison B. Summers, editor, *A Thirty-Year History of Radio Programs in the United States, 1926–56,* Dept. of Speech, Ohio State University, 1958, and this is representative data offered as an average for each season.

4. Edgar A. Gruenwald, editor, *Variety Radio Directory 1939–40* (New York: Variety, 1939), p. 44 fn. Looking back from a vantage point seven years after the fact, Gruenwald suggests that the "decline in overall listenership" noted in 1932 will go down in history as one of "the strangest of its kind." However, it is interesting to note that this trend received no comment whatsoever in the pages of *Broadcasting* magazine, the industry's leading trade journal, during 1932. The decline in popularity of *Amos 'n' Andy* was examined in "These Falling Stars," *Radio Guide,* week of 10/30–11/5/32, p. 5. Surveys independently conducted by the magazine in Chicago and in New York revealed a definite leveling off in the program's audience—but that audience remained large. In Chicago, 53 percent of radio listeners surveyed tuned in *Amos 'n' Andy* at least occasionally but only 24 percent listened regularly. Many of the occasional listeners admitted they had ceased to listen regularly due to the "uninteresting" nature of the story lines over the previous year.

5. All story line summaries based on Freeman F. Gosden and Charles J. Correll, *Amos 'n' Andy Radio Scripts.* Microfilm copies in the possession of the author.

6. A detailed analysis of the NAACP protest of the *Amos 'n' Andy Show* television series may be found in Cripps. Note that the association conspicuously failed to mention the radio series at any point during the 1951 protest campaign.

BIBLIOGRAPHY

For Further Reading

A proper understanding of Correll and Gosden and their work begins with an examination of their actual writings. Freeman Gosden's personal copies of the original scripts of *Sam 'n' Henry* and *Amos 'n' Andy* are available to scholars in the Gosden-Correll Collection at the Annenberg Center of the University of Southern California. The Gosden-Correll Collection also includes the team's personal scrapbooks documenting press reaction to the series over its entire run.

Microfilm copies of scripts from 1928 through 1937 are available in the Manuscript Division of the Library of Congress.

Selected scripts from the first eight weeks of the show were published in book form by Long and Smith of New York in 1931, under the title *Here They Are: Amos 'n' Andy*.

Surviving Recordings

Few recordings are known to exist from the classic serial years of *Amos 'n' Andy*. Syndication recordings are accessible to researchers for the following "chainless chain" era episodes: 1/14/29, 1/15/29, 1/17/29, 4/21/29, 4/22/29, 4/23/29, 4/25/29, 4/26/29, 4/27/29, 5/19/29, 5/20/29, 5/21/29, 5/23/29, 6/8/29, 6/9/29, 6/10/29, 6/11/29, 6/13/29, 6/14/29, 6/16/29, 6/17/29 (second side only), 6/18/29, 6/20/29, 6/21/29, 6/22/29, 6/23/29, 6/24/29, 6/25/29, 6/27/29, 6/28/29, 6/29/29, 7/2/29, 7/5/29, 7/23/29, 7/25/29, 7/28/29, 7/29/29, 7/30/29.

Numerous other examples of discs from the syndication period are known to survive in private collections, but due to the monetary value of the discs researchers are generally denied access to the content.

The following network episodes survive in fragmentary form: 11/20/30 (apx. 2½ mins.), 12/5/30 (apx. 1½ mins.), 2/17/31 (apx. 2½ mins.), 1/9/33 (apx. 6 mins.), 2/15/33 (apx. 2 mins.), 2/22/33 (apx. 7 mins.), 8/9/37 (excerpts totaling apx. 40 seconds), 9/9/38 (apx. 4 mins.), 11/8/38 (apx. 4 mins), 2/1/39 (apx. 5 mins.), 2/21/39 (apx. 4 mins.), 10/9/42 (apx. 2 mins.), 2/19/43 (apx. 5 mins.)

The following complete (or reasonably complete) network episodes survive: 3/24/32 (poor-quality home recording), 8/19/36, 12/4/36 (both Eastern and Western versions), 2/27/39 (special 25-minute New York World's Fair broadcast), 4/3/39, 6/30/39, 9/21/39, 11/12/40, 12/24/41, 12/24/42.

Evidence exists indicating that daily recordings of *Amos 'n' Andy* were extension-spotted for Campbell's Soup by Ward Wheelock, Inc., on a number of non–CBS-affiliated stations in Canada from January 1940 into at least the summer of 1942. These recordings were likely made off the live CBS line in Montreal and processed and pressed into finished 16" vinyl transcriptions by the Compo Company of Lachine, Quebec, for broadcast approximately two weeks behind the live broadcast as heard in the United States. Each disc contained only the body of each episode, from Bill Hay's introductory comments to the fadeout. Theme music and commercials were contained on separate discs. While it is likely that at least some of these recordings do survive, none have surfaced with the possible exception of the 11/12/40 episode listed above, which may have come from a Canadian pressing.

Works of Special Note

Bart Andrews and Arghus Julliard, *Holy Mackerel! The Amos 'n' Andy Story* (New York: E. P. Dutton, 1986).

An odd book combining a pop-oriented history of the series with social analysis, this effort suffers from its bifurcated point of view and from its lack of footnoting. Although the book's discussion of the radio series is little more than a prologue, and it contains many factual errors, the volume does offer a solid, basic history of the *Amos 'n' Andy Show* television program, and presents useful background information on the members of its cast.

Joseph Boskin, *Sambo: The Rise and Demise of an American Jester* (New York: Oxford University Press, 1986).

An ambitious work that traces the long life of the Sambo stereotype in American popular culture, this book offers a valuable understanding of the historic context against which the content of *Amos 'n' Andy* may be assessed. The many manifestations of Sambo and his relatives on the stage, in popular literature, in merchandising, and in film are explored in detail. Unfortunately, Boskin's discussion of *Amos 'n' Andy* itself, in a section outlining how the threads of the stereotype began to unravel during the 1930s, is marred by sloppy and superficial research. Boskin's assertion that the various *Amos 'n' Andy* characters never had full names (a common trait of minstrel characters) is demonstrably false, he vastly overstates the importance of "rejoinders and quips in a rhythmical repartee" to the original series, and he falls into the common fallacy of presenting situations and quotations from the later situation comedy series as being representative of the serial. This fallacy, in turn, leads Boskin into a significant error: in discussing the nature of the Kingfish's role in the series, the author (on p. 170) attempts to support a point by offering a quote that is falsely attributed (fn. 11) to page 1 of the 5/22/28 script. This script, in fact, has no connection whatever to the point under discussion and contains none of the quoted dialogue. The lines cited were actually written 24 years later, for the "10,000th Broadcast" of 11/16/52 and cannot legitimately be used to support an argument relating to the content of the original series. However, it must be noted that despite questionable research, Boskin is aware of and acknowledges both the complexity and the more progressive aspects of the series—crediting *Amos 'n' Andy* as a step toward Sambo's ultimate demise.

Charles J. Correll and Freeman F. Gosden, *All About Amos 'n' Andy and Their Creators, Correll and Gosden* (New York: Rand McNally, 1929).

The only "official" biographical work on Correll and Gosden was in fact prepared by the publicity department of the *Chicago Daily News* in early 1929 to take advantage of the early popularity of the "chainless chain" series (and it was revised slightly for a second edition in 1930). While the book is very brief and admittedly superficial, it offers a useful window into how the performers wanted to be seen by the audiences of their time. Despite its shortcomings, it also offers valuable insights into the performers' working methods.

Thomas Cripps, "*Amos 'n' Andy* and the Debate over American Racial Integration," in *American History, American Television: Interpreting the Video Past*, edited by John E. O'Connor (New York: Frederick Ungar, 1983).

A carefully researched discussion of the 1951 NAACP protest of the *Amos 'n' Andy Show* television series, with a particular emphasis on the class-consciousness that drove it. The article has little relevance to the radio version of the program, other than to make it clear that the protest did not involve the radio series, and the chapter commits occasional errors of fact in discussing it (claiming for example that the radio cast was not racially integrated until 1948—when in fact the first black cast member joined the program in 1939). Nevertheless, the article offers valuable documentation for an important part of the program's history, one that has been heavily and inaccurately mythologized over the past 50 years.

Melvin P. Ely, *The Adventures of Amos 'n' Andy: A Social History of an American Phenomenon* (New York: Free Press, 1991).

As the title indicates, Ely's work is frankly a work of social history, not a performance biography, and views the program not simply as a radio program but as a window into mid-twentieth century American racial attitudes. Analysis of the program's content focuses on that perspective to the exclusion of all others, and detailed examination of the original scripts is confined primarily to the first two years of *Amos 'n' Andy*. Ely therefore fails to examine in any detail the evolution of the characters and their relationships beyond 1929—and this is perhaps the book's greatest flaw, given that the characterizations and the dramatic sophistication of the program evolved considerably between 1929 and the mid–1930s.

Ely's exclusive focus on the racial issues in the series also leads him to occasional false interpretations of what he did read—compare his discussion of the "Honest Tom's All-Star Carnival" story line from 1928 as an example of "white cupidity feeding on black stupidity" with the actual scripts, in which it is made evident through contextual clues that the carnival men who swindle the Mystic Knights of the Sea are themselves intended to be perceived as black, despite the absence of dialect in their speech. Compare Ely, pp. 89–90, with *Amos 'n' Andy* episodes 151 through 168, 9/17/28 through 10/7/28, especially episodes 163 through 165, 10/1/28 through 10/4/28.

While certain conclusions, assumptions, and interpretations are debatable—especially when compared against a detailed reading of the original scripts—in general Ely's account is balanced and thoughtful in its consideration of the pros and cons of the program in all of its incarnations, and his detailed examination of the black response to the program presents the definitive study of this aspect of the series. Ely also deserves praise for avoiding the self-indulgent deconstructionist jargon that tends to dominate current academic studies of popular culture. His book is a rare example of an academic work that is both scholarly and extremely well written.

Dale Howard Ross, *The Amos 'n' Andy Radio Program, 1928–1937—Its History, Content, and Social Significance.* Unpublished doctoral dissertation, University of Iowa, 1974.

Ross's examination of the first decade of the program presents a comprehensive discussion of the first three years of the series, followed by a less-detailed overview of the next seven years. Ross makes occasional interpretive errors similar to those of Ely—particularly a discussion of the 1928 "Pawn Shop Robbery" story line that is severely garbled and that fails to correspond with much of what is found in the actual scripts. Ross uses this discussion to draw a significant racial conclusion—claiming that Amos's use of a white attorney demonstrates that in the characters' world "the forces of law and order are white, the forces of crime and misrule are black." In the actual scripts, it is made clear through contextual clues that the attorney is in fact black. (Compare Ross, pp. 125–131, with *Amos 'n' Andy* episodes 74 through 89, 6/19/28 through 7/7/28—with special attention to page 128 as compared to episode 81, 6/28/28. See also Ely, p. 90, where the lawyer's race is correctly interpreted.)

Generally, however, Ross's discussion of the series is both perceptive and true to the original content, and his work offers a valuable resource for researchers looking for an easy-to-digest overview of the program in its prime years.

Arthur Frank Wertheim, *Radio Comedy* (New York: Oxford University Press, 1979).

Two chapters of this landmark study of radio comedy are devoted to the work of Correll and Gosden. One focuses on their background leading up to the creation of *Sam 'n' Henry*, and the other is devoted to *Amos 'n' Andy*, tracing the progress of the program from 1928 to early 1933. Wertheim offers substantial quotes from original scripts and was the only serious researcher ever to succeed in interviewing Freeman Gosden. Wertheim focuses on the popularity of *Amos 'n' Andy* through the Depression years, but he arguably overemphasizes the Depression as a factor in the program's success.

Books

Fred Allen, *Fred Allen's Letters*, edited by Joe McCarthy. Garden City: Doubleday, 1965.
Bart Andrews and Arghus Julliard, *Holy Mackerel! The Amos 'n' Andy Story*. New York: E. P. Dutton, 1986.
Erik Barnouw, *The Golden Web: A History of Broadcasting in the United States, Volume 1— to 1933*. New York: Oxford University Press, 1966.
Richard Barrios, *A Song in the Dark*. New York: Oxford University Press, 1995.
Joseph Boskin, *Sambo: The Rise and Demise of an American Jester*. New York: Oxford University Press, 1986.
Walter M. Brasch, *Black English and the Mass Media*. Amherst: University of Massachusetts Press, 1981.
Andrew Buni, *Robert L. Vann of the Pittsburgh Courier*. Pittsburgh: University of Pittsburgh Press, 1974.
Charles J. Correll and Freeman F. Gosden, *All About Amos 'n' Andy and Their Creators, Correll and Gosden*. New York: Rand, McNally, 1929.
_____. *Sam 'n' Henry*. Chicago: Shrewsbury Publishing, 1926.
Thomas Cripps, "*Amos 'n' Andy* and the Debate over American Racial Integration," in *American History, American Television: Interpreting the Video Past*, edited by John E. O'Connor. New York: Frederick Ungar, 1983.
J.L. Dillard, *Black English: Its History and Usage in the United States*. New York: Random House, 1972.
Susan Douglas, *Listening In: Radio and the American Imagination from Amos 'n' Andy to Edward R. Murrow to Wolfman Jack and Howard Stern*. New York: Times Books, 1999.
Melvin P. Ely, *The Adventures of Amos 'n' Andy: A Social History of an American Phenomenon*. New York: Free Press, 1991.
Federal Writers Project, Works Progress Administration, *The Negro in Virginia*. New York: Hastings House, 1940.
Herb Galewitz, editor, *Great Comics: Syndicated by the Daily News/Chicago Tribune*. New York: Crown, 1972.

Jack Gaver and Dave Stanley, *There's Laughter in the Air.* New York: Greenberg, 1945.
Abel Green and Joe Laurie, Jr., *Show Biz from Vaude to Video.* New York: Henry Holt, 1951.
Michele Hilmes, *Radio Voices: American Broadcasting, 1922–1952.* Minneapolis: University of Minnesota Press, 1998.
Maurice Horn, editor, *100 Years of American Newspaper Comics.* New York: Gramercy Books, 1996.
Charles S. Johnson, *The Shadow of the Plantation.* Chicago: University of Chicago Press, 1934.
Ruth Adams Knight, *Stand By for the Ladies: The Distaff Side of Broadcasting.* New York: Coward-McCann, 1939.
W. T. Lhamon, Jr., *Raising Cain: Blackface Performance from Jim Crow to Hip Hop.* Cambridge: Harvard University Press, 1998.
William Manchester, *The Glory and the Dream: A Narrative History of America 1932–1972.* Boston: Little, Brown, 1972.
Brian A. L. Rust, *Victor Master Book: Vol. 2, 1925–36.* Stanhope, NJ: Walter C. Allen, 1970.
Gilbert Seldes, *The Public Arts.* New York: Simon & Schuster, 1956.
James Clyde Sellman, "Minstrelsy," *Microsoft Encarta Africana.* Redmond, WA: Microsoft, 1999.
Nicholas A. Sharp, "Freeman F. Gosden," in *The Scribner Encyclopedia of American Lives: Volume I 1981–1985.* New York: Scribner, 1998.
_____. "Charles J. Correll," in *The Scribner Encyclopedia of American Lives: Volume I 1981–1985.* New York: Scribner, 1998.
Harrison Summers, *A Thirty-Year History of Radio Programs in the United States, 1926–1956.* Department of Speech: Ohio State University, 1958.
Colton Waugh, *The Comics.* New York: Macmillan, 1947.
Arthur Frank Wertheim, *Radio Comedy.* New York: Oxford University Press, 1979
Who's Who on the Air, New York: Ludwig Bauman and Sons, 1932.
Robert Winthrop, *The Jackson Ward Historic District.* Richmond, VA: City of Richmond, c.1970.

Periodicals

"Across the Desk," editorial, *Radio Digest*, January 1930.
Amsterdam News, 7/22/31.
"Amos 'n' Andy," *Time*, 3/3/30.
"Amos 'n' Andy's Dialect, Is It Real?" *Radio Digest*, July 1930.
"Analyzing the Radio Audience—Its Size and Makeup," *Broadcasting*, 11/1/32.
Baltimore Afro-American, 3/22/30.
"Blackout," *Time*, 1/25/43.
Boston Globe, 12/11/82.
Richard Bruner, "Amos 'n' Andy Hassle Won't Stop TV Show," *Printers' Ink*, 6/20/51.
Charleston (WV) *Daily Mail*, 10/5/30, 3/8/31.
Chicago Daily News, 2/25/28, 7/27/29.
Chicago Defender, 1/25/30, 8/22/31.
Chicago Tribune, 9/18/27.
W. T. Christian, "Boyhood Days of Amos 'n' Andy," *Radio Digest*, June 1930.
A. Wellington Clarke, "If Amos and Andy Were Negroes: What Numerous Negroes in Various Walks of Life Think of the Boys," *Radio Digest*, August 1930.
Edward T. Clayton, "The Tragedy of Amos 'n' Andy," *Ebony*, October 1961.
John Crosby, "Amos 'n' Andy—Ain't Dat Sumpin'," *Collier's*, 10/16/48.
James R. Crowell, "Amos 'n' Andy Tell Their Own Story in Their Own Way," *American Magazine*, April 1930.
_____. "Amos 'n' Andy," *Psychology*, August 1930.
Philip Curtiss, "Amos 'n' Andy 'n' Art," *Harper's Monthly*, April 1931.
Orrin E. Dunlap, Jr., "Amos 'n' Andy: The Air's First Comic Strip," *Literary Digest*, 4/19/30.
Ruth Geri, "The Woman Behind Amos 'n' Andy," *Radio Mirror*, February 1935.
Robert R. Goldenstien, "Boyhood Days of Amos 'n' Andy," *Radio Digest*, June 1930.
_____. "Hometown Stories of Amos 'n' Andy," *The New Movie Magazine*, September 1930.
Bill Hay as told to Roger Cameron, "Here They Are!" *Radio Stars*, April 1935.
C.H. Huntley, "Tricks Used in Staging Invisible Shows," *Radio Broadcast*, November 1923.
Richard B. Jewell, "RKO Film Grosses, 1929–1951: The C. J. Telvin Ledger," *Historical Journal of Film, Radio, and Television*, vol. 14, no. 1, 1994.
Kansas City Call, 8/28/31.
Kansas City Star, 6/16/29.
Los Angeles Times, 3/17/97.

"Mammoth Banquet Will Open Season," *Radio Digest*, September 1927.
F.J. McDermott, "Hometown Stories of Amos 'n' Andy," *The New Movie Magazine*, September 1930.
O. O. McIntyre, "*Amos 'n' Andy*," *Cosmopolitan*, May 1930.
New York Times, 10/25/30, 10/29/30, 5/10/31, 2/28/43, 9/27/72.
Northwest Enterprise, 11/5/31.
Mark Quest, "Private Life of Amos 'n' Andy," *Radio Digest*, February 1930.
_____. "Amos 'n' Andy Backstage at WMAQ," *Radio Digest*, March 1930.
_____. "Additional Facts in the Private Life of Amos 'n' Andy," *Radio Digest*, April 1930.
Peoria Journal, 1/26/35.
Peoria Journal-Star, 5/20/2002.
Pittsburgh Courier, 1/18/30, 4/25/31, 5/16/31, 6/13/31, 8/29/31, 9/12/31, 10/31/31, 12/19/31, 7/7/51.
Richmond Dispatch, 3/11/1902.
Richmond Times-Dispatch, 9/12/17, 9/13/17, 9/14/17, 8/20/81, 10/27/90.
Harlow P. Roberts, "A Key to One Sponsor's Success in Radio," *Broadcasting*, 4/15/32.
Rocky Mountain News, 11/15/29.
A.S. (Arthur H. Samuels), "On the Air," *The New Yorker*, 3/22/30.
"The Shadow Stage," *Photoplay*, December 1930.
Maynard Shipley, "Amos 'n' Andy—Why the Fresh Air Taxicab Has Beaten the Traffic," *The Debunker*, April 1931.
Harry Steele, "Amos 'n' Andy: Here They Are," *Radio Guide*, week ending 4/6/35.
_____. "Amos 'n' Andy: Here They Are," *Radio Guide*, week ending 4/13/35.
Ann Steward, "Amos 'n' Andy Join the Show," *Radio Digest*, July 1930.
"Theme Songs That Click: Amos 'n' Andy's Tag Melody," *Radio Guide*, 5/12/34.
Bishop W. J. Walls, "What About Amos 'n' Andy?" *Abbott's Monthly*, December 1930.
"Why the *Amos 'n' Andy* TV Show Should Be Taken off the Air," *NAACP Bulletin*, 8/15/51.
Albert R. Williamson, "Amos 'n' Andy in Harlem," *Radio Digest*, June 1930.
Winston-Salem Journal and Sentinel, 5/4/30.

Unpublished Works

Michael J. Biel, *The Making and Use of Recordings in Broadcasting Before 1936*, doctoral dissertation, Northwestern University, 1977.
C. F. Caton, *Radio Station WMAQ: A History of Its Independent Years (1922–1931)*, doctoral dissertation, Northwestern University, 1951.
Charles J. Correll and Freeman F. Gosden, *Amos 'n' Andy Radio Scripts*, MSS. 14,305, Manuscript Division, Library of Congress.
Dale Howard Ross, *The Amos 'n' Andy Radio Program, 1928–1937—Its History, Content, and Social Significance*, doctoral dissertation, University of Iowa, 1974.

Motion Pictures

The Black Press: Soldiers Without Swords, a documentary by Stanley Nelson. San Francisco: California Newsreel, 1998.
Check and Double Check, directed by Melville Brown. RKO Radio Pictures, 1930. Video version: RKO Collection No. 6213 (Atlanta: Turner Home Entertainment, 1991).

Sound Recordings

Song Recordings by Correll and Gosden, Recorded and Released by the Victo\r Talking Machine Company

Victor 19886: All I Want to Do/Let's Talk About My Sweetie (mxs 34578-5/34579-5), recorded 3/2/26 (Correll, piano; Gosden, tiple).
Victor 20088: Roundabout Way To Heaven/That's Why I Love You (mxs 35056-3/35057-3), recorded 5/26/26 (Delos Owen, piano).
Victor 20107: Georgianna (mx 35059-3), recorded 5/26/26 (Delos Owen, piano).
Victor 20286: Meadow Lark/Kiss Your Little Baby Good Night (mxs 36406-4/36435-3), recorded 9/29/26 (Delos Owen, piano).
Victor 20255: Elsie Schultz-en-Heim/I Just Want to Be Known as Susie's Feller (mxs 36433-3/36434-3), recorded 9/29/26 (Delos Owen, piano).

Victor 20826: Gorgeous/Who Is Your Who? (mxs 39084-3 /39087-3), recorded 7/6/27 (Delos Owen, piano).
Victor 20908: Somebody and Me/No Wonder I'm Happy (mxs 39086-3/39085-3), recorded 7/6/27 (Delos Owen, piano).

Sam 'n' Henry, Humorous Dialogues, Recorded and Released by the Victor Talking Machine Company

Victor 20032: Sam Phoning His Sweetheart 'Liza/Sam and Henry at the Dentist (mxs 35328-3/35329-2), recorded 4/20/26.
Victor 20093: Sam's Speech at the Colored Lodge/Sam and Henry at the Fortune Teller's (mx 35066-2/35073-3), recorded 5/27/26 and 5/28/26.
Victor 20375: Sam & Henry Rollin' The Bones/Sam & Henry Buying Insurance (mxs. 35067-2/35068-3), recorded 5/27/26.
Victor 20788: Sam's Big Night/The Morning After (mxs. 39092-2/39093-2), recorded 7/7/27.

Amos 'n' Andy "Chainless Chain" Radio Episodes, Recorded by the Brunswick-Balke-Collender Company for Broadcast Syndication

Episode 360 for broadcast 5/19/29 (mxs XC3255/3256)
Episode 361 for broadcast 5/20/29 (mxs XC3257/3258)
Episode 362 for broadcast 5/21/29 (mxs XC3259/3260)
Episode 363 for broadcast 5/23/29 (mxs XC3261/3262)
Episode 377 for broadcast 6/8/29 (mxs XC3383/3384)
Episode 378 for broadcast 6/9/29 (mxs XC3385/3386)
Episode 379 for broadcast 6/10/29 (mxs XC3387/3388)
Episode 380 for broadcast 6/11/29 (mxs XC3389/3390)
Episode 381 for broadcast 6/13/29 (mxs XC3391/3392)
Episode 382 for broadcast 6/13/29 (mxs XC3393/3394)
Episode 384 for broadcast 6/16/29 (mxs LTR117/118)
Episode 385 for broadcast 6/17/29 (mx LTR119 only—1/2 episode)
Episode 386 for broadcast 6/18/29 (mxs LTR121/122)
Episode 387 for broadcast 6/20/29 (mxs LTR123/124)
Episode 388 for broadcast 6/21/29 (mxs LTR125/126)
Episode 389 for broadcast 6/22/29 (mxs LTR127/128)
Episode 390 for broadcast 6/23/29 (mxs LTR129/130)
Episode 391 for broadcast 6/24/29 (mxs LTR131/132)
Episode 392 for broadcast 6/25/29 (mxs LTR134/135)
Episode 393 for broadcast 6/27/29 (mxs LTR136/137)
Episode 394 for broadcast 6/28/29 (mxs LTR138/139)
Episode 395 for broadcast 6/29/29 (mxs LTR140/141)
Episode 398 for broadcast 7/2/29 (mxs LTR146/147)
Episode 400 for broadcast 7/5/29 (mxs LTR150/151)
Episode 416 for broadcast 7/23/29 (mxs XC3706/3707)
Episode 417 for broadcast 7/25/29 (mxs XC3720/3721)

Network Broadcasts

Episode 1250—3/24/32 (home recording)
Episode 1525—2/15/33 (home recording—fragment)
Episode 1530—2/22/33 (home recording—fragment)

Commercially Released Broadcast Recording Compilations

The Amos 'n' Andy Chronicles. New Rochelle, NY: Great American Audio, 2000 (contains *Amos 'n' Andy Show* episodes of 11/19/43, 12/29/44, 1/6/48, 11/6/49, 11/16/52, and 2/14/54; *Amos 'n' Andy Music Hall* episodes of 8/23/59 and 11/25/60; *Amos 'n' Andy* chainless chain recordings of 6/22 through 6/29/29; and an excerpt from *Command Performance* program 69, recorded 6/5/43).
Amos 'n' Andy Collectors Edition, Volumes 1 through 3. Metacom 2333025, 2333028, 2333031. Plymouth, MN: Metacom, 1995 (contains nearly complete 1943–44 season of *The Amos 'n' Andy Show,* sourced from tape dubs made from the original discs for Charles Correll).

The Rarest Amos 'n' Andy, Radiola MR-1134. Sandy Hook, CT: The Radiola Company, 1981 (contains episodes of 4/3/39, 8/19/36, 12/4/36, and 12/24/41).

In addition to episodes specifically cited above, the author possesses and has reviewed recordings of more than 200 episodes of *The Amos 'n' Andy Show* aired between 1943 and 1955.

Archival Interviews

Charles J. Correll, interviewed on tape by Richard Correll, *Same Time Same Station.* KRLA, Pasadena, CA, broadcast 1/14/73.

Charles J. Correll, interviewed by Richard Lamparski, *Whatever Became of Amos 'n' Andy,* recorded 6/30/69.

Bill Hay interviewed on *Same Time Same Station.* KRLA, Pasadena, CA, broadcast 1/14/73.

Correspondence/Interviews

Freeman F. Gosden, Jr., correspondence with the author, 1/5/98, 1/6/98, 2/10/98, 12/13/99, 11/24/2000, 11/25/2000, 11/27/2000, 4/29/2003.

Jane Gosden, telephone conversation with the author, 5/18/03.

INDEX

Abbott and Costello Show (radio series) 145
Abbott's Monthly 130
Ace, Goodman 144
acrolect and basilect 93
acting, radio 31, 57–58
The Adventures of Amos 'n' Andy: A Social History of an American Phenomenon (book) 202
African American newspapers 130–136
African American vernacular English 37, 87–93, 195
African Americans 9, 11, 26, 55, 116, 118, 127–137, 142, 145–148, 154, 197–198
All About Amos 'n' Andy and Their Creators, Correll and Gosden (book) 202
Allen, Arthur 56
Allen, Fred 140, 169, 173
Amos 'n' Andy (comic strip) 36–37, 190
Amos 'n' Andy (radio series): common view of 1–2; creation of 35–40; origin of character names 38; premiere of 38–39; early storylines 40–42; appeal of characters 42–43; attracts interest of Pepsodent and NBC 43–45; NBC premiere 46–48; sparks nationwide craze 50–53; imitated by other programs 56–57; realism of 58–59; characters of 69–93; women added to cast 82–83; use of dialect in 89–93; plots of 95–114; educational elements of 97–98, 100; ridicules Fascism 100–101; melodrama in 101–105; situational humor in 105–107; undermines racial stereotyping 118–120, 123–124, 154–158; attacked by Pittsburgh Courier 131–137; portrayal of African American attorneys in Breach of Promise storyline 132–133; endorsed by *Northwest Enterprise* 135–136; series ends 140; as assimilationist parable 155–157; as morality play 158–159; long-term popularity of 163–178; not based on Miller & Lyles 192–193
"Amos 'n' Andy and the Debate over American Racial Integration" (article) 202
Amos 'n' Andy Music Hall (radio series) 149–150, 177, 178
The Amos 'n' Andy Radio Program 1928–1937: Its History, Content, and Social Significance (dissertation) 203
Amos 'n' Andy Show (radio series): series begins 140–141; early tone 142; impact of studio audience 143–145; shift in tone 143–145; sold to CBS 147; not censured in NAACP protest 150; ratings of 175–178
Amos 'n' Andy Show (television series) 147–148, 150, 161, 178, 198, 199
Amsterdam News 135
Anderson, Eddie 116, 197
Armed Forces Radio Service (AFRS) 177
Ash, Paul 21–23
Ashby, A.L. 66
Atlanta, Ga. 38
audience, studio 143–145, 198
Aunt Lillian (character) *see* Taylor, Lillian
Ayelsworth, Merlin H. 53, 100

Baltimore *Afro-American* 130, 161
bank holiday, explained by Amos and Andy 97–98
Barnouw, Erik 157, 199
Barton, Charles 148
Baskett, James 142, 145
Bendo, Prince Ali (character) 73, 84, 189
Benny, Jack 167, 169, 199
Benton, William 43
Berg, Gertrude 56
Bergen, Edgar 167

Berlin, Abby 148
bidialectism 88–89
The Big Broadcast of 1936 (motion picture) 192
Birmingham, Al. 30
black English *see* African American vernacular English
blackface 7, 15, 19, 26, 29, 38, 43, 115–116, 118, 124–125, 147, 189
Blake, Sadie (character) 79, 85
Blatz Brewing Company 148
Blue, Genevieve (character) 83–84
Bob Hope Show (radio program) 175
Boniel, Robert 20
Bowles, Minnie (Gosden) 10, 187
Bradley, Dr. Preston 196
Brasch, Dr. Walter M. 88, 91, 195
Brawley, Benjamin 130
breach of promise storylines 62, 66–68, 132–133, 170, 198
Bren, Joe 13, 19–20
Brice, Fannie 169
Briel, Joseph C. 45
Brown, Andrew H. (character): origin of name 39; early traits of 39–41; early days in Harlem 59–60; relationship with Madam Queen 62–66, 80–81; sued for Breach of Promise by Madam Queen 66–68; victimization by Kingfish 70–71; disliked by Gwindell 77; mental games with Lightning 78–79, 106; financial recklessness of 95–96; faddishness of 105–106; emotional vulnerability of 107–108; offended by being called "boy" 108; differs from racial stereotype 115–116; retires debts and takes war job 140; becomes stooge for Kingfish 143–144
Brown, Camila 187
Brown, Garrett "Snowball" 10–12, 40, 89, 187
Brownlee, Roscoe (character) 84
Brunswick-Balke-Collender Company 33
Butler, Benjamin 15
Butterfly, Senorita (character) 84

Calhoun, Algonquin J. (character) 145
Calvin and the Colonel (television series) 150, 199
Campbell Soup Company 140, 175, 201
Cantor, Eddie 165, 169
Carter, Gaylord 150
cartoons, animated 192
Cecil and Sally (radio series) *see* *The Funniest Things*
Century of Progress Exhibition 99
chainless chain 33–35, 42, 187, 190
Chase and Sanborn Hour (radio series) 167, 169
Check and Double Check (motion picture) 53–54, 192

Chesterfield Time (radio series) 165
Chevalier, Maurice 169
Chicago 26, 31, 33–34, 40, 43–44, 55, 118, 135, 150
Chicago *Daily News* 35–36, 127, 191
The Chicago *Defender* 130, 135
Chicago *Tribune* 34, 127
Chicago Urban League 127
Chicago World's Fair, 1933 *see* Century of Progress Exhibition
Childress, Alvin 147
Christian Science Monitor 128
Clarke, A.W. 128–130
Cohen, Octavus Roy 116, 196–197
Collins, Lawyer (character) 67, 84, 118, 133–134
Columbia Broadcasting System Inc. (CBS) 34, 44, 177, 178
comedy 19, 29, 30, 43, 105–107, 115, 143–144, 158
comic strips, serialized 27–28, 189
Connolly, Joe 143
Cook, Johnny (character) 133–134
Coon, Zip (stereotypical figure) 7
Cooper, Jack L. 55
Cooperative Analysis of Broadcasting (CAB) 165, 169
Correll, Alyce (McLaughlin) 150, 189
Correll, Anna (Fiss) 13–14
Correll, Charles J.: birth and childhood 13–15; early employment 15–16; early interest in music 14; joins Metropolitan Quartet 15–16; joins Joe Bren Producing Company 16; meets FFG 13, 16–17; friendship with FFG 19; duties with Joe Bren Producing Company 19; early dabbling in radio 20; at WEBH 20–21; in *Red Hot* 21; move to WGN 23; and *The Gumps* 26; influenced by comic strips 27–28; and *Sam 'n' Henry* 29–38; development of writing technique 31; development of chainless-chain idea 33–35; first network broadcasts 34–35; move to WMAQ 35–36; on poor quality of transcription broadcasts 44; on negotiations with Pepsodent and NBC 44–45; opposes Pepsodent interference 45; visits Harlem 45, 191; bewildered by craze 51; dislikes blackface representations of Amos and Andy 54; as radio actor 57–58; describes scriptwriting technique 57; first photo during broadcast 85; on FFG's speech 90; thanked by FDR 98; understands motivations of characters 106; deliberately avoids blackface clichés 115; portrayal of race relations by 120–124; ceases use of blackface makeup 124; repudiates minstrelsy 126; appears at Chicago

Defender picnic 135; temporary retirement 140; hires writers for sitcom format 141; pressured to go for big laughs 144; attempts to offset postwar stereotypes 145; and television 146–148; sale to CBS 147, 176–177; retirement of 150; death of 150
Correll, Joseph B. 13–14, 15
Correll, Marie (Janes) 189
Correll, Thomas 38
Crawford, John "Brother" (character) 65–66, 74–76, 93, 102, 103, 116, 145
craze, for *Amos 'n' Andy* 50–53, 170
Cripps, Thomas 202
Crosby, John 144
Crossley, Archibald 165
Crow, Jim (stereotypical figure) 7

Damarel, Donna 171
Dandridge, Dorothy 145
Dandridge, Ruby 142
Dandridge, Vivian 145
Davis, Edith 194
The Debunker (magazine) 59, 194
Depression *see* The Great Depression
dialect *see* African American vernacular English
Diamond, Most Precious (character) 31, 69
Dickinson, Dr. W.L. (character) 84
Dillard, J.L. 87, 88, 194
disc jockey format 149–150
Dixie Melody Masters (singing group) 194
Dixon, Earl (character) 195
Dixon, Jack (character) 101–104, 171, 195
Duffy's Tavern (radio series) 145
Dunlap, Orrin E. Jr. 62

Early, Stephen 97
Easy Aces (radio series) 165
Eisenhower, Pres. Dwight D. 150
Eisenhower Medical Center 150
Ellington, Duke 54, 135, 192
Ely, Melvin Patrick 124, 200, 202–203
Ephus and Mr. Bodilly (radio series) 54
The Eveready Hour (radio series) 116–118

fan mail 39, 151
Fascism, ridiculed by A&A 100–101
Fennelly, Parker 56
Fibber McGee & Molly (radio program) 175, 177
Fields, Benny 173
Fields, George 54, 116
Fiss, Joseph 14
Fleischmann's Yeast Hour (radio series) 167
Fonda, James 148
Ford (Rush) and Glenn (Rowell) (harmony team) 20

The Fred Allen Show (radio series) 145, 177
Fresh Air Taxicab Co. of America, Inc. 40–41, 59
The Funniest Things (radio series) 56, 194

Galliccio, Joseph 45, 58, 62
Gardella, Tess 116, 197
Gibson, Gabby (character) 145
Gilles, Hal 37, 56
Gilmore, Art 141
Glenn, Roy 145, 147
Goff, Norris 56–57, 189
Gold Dust Twins (radio team) 43
Gosden, Emma L. (Smith) 8, 10–11, 187
Gosden, Freeman F.: birth and childhood 8–12; family background of 8–9; personality traits 9–10, 17, 19; military service 12–13; early interest in show business 10–13; joins Joe Bren Producing Company 13, 17; meets CJC 13, 17; friendship with CJC 19; duties with Joe Bren Producing Company 19; early dabbling in radio 20; at WEBH 20–21; in Red Hot 21; move to WGN 25; and *The Gumps* 26; influenced by comic strips 27–28; and *Sam 'n' Henry* 29–38; development of writing technique 31; development of chainless-chain idea 33–35; first network broadcasts 34–35; move to WMAQ 35–38; dismisses wisecracking 43; opposes Pepsodent interference 45; visits Harlem 45, 191; upset by poor review 49; bewildered by craze 51; dislikes *Check and Double Check* 54; as radio actor 57–58; portrays Madam Queen 82, 194; first photo during broadcast 85; versatility of 86; as bidialectal 89; stresses fiscal responsibility in scripts 95–96; thanked by FDR 98; understands motivations of characters 106; and "Lord's Prayer" sequence 113, 196; deliberately avoids blackface clichés 115; portrayal of race relations by 120–124; ceases use of blackface makeup 124; describes Chicago Urban League endorsement 127; appears at Chicago *Defender* picnic 135; temporary retirement 140; hires writers for sitcom format 141; supervises writers 142; pressured to go for big laughs 144; attempts to offset postwar stereotypes 145; and television 146–148; sale to CBS 147, 176–177, 199; dislikes television series 148; retirement of 150; friendship with Eisenhower 150; helps found Eisenhower Medical Center 150–151; bothered by controversy 151; honored by Richmond City Council 151; death of 151
Gosden, Freeman F., Jr. 19, 54, 113, 148, 188, 199

Gosden, Harry 10, 38
Gosden, Jane E. (Stoneham) 150, 189
Gosden, John T. 8
Gosden, Leta M. (Schreiber) 25, 189
Gosden, Sarah Ann 8
Gosden, Walter W. 8, 10, 187
Gosden, Walter W., Jr. 9, 10
Gosden, William B. 10, 187
The Great Depression 95–100
The Great Home Bank (storyline) 96, 170
The Great Migration 26, 30
Green, Eddie 116, 145, 197
Gruenwald, Edgar 169, 200
The Gumps (comic strip) 25, 189
Gwindell, Frederick Montgomery (character) 77, 145, 171

Hairston, Jester 142, 147, 150
Hal Roach Studios 148,
Hall, Mourdant 53
Hall Johnson Choir 116
Harlem 45, 59, 117–118, 128, 134, 171, 191
Harriot, Elinor 83, 142, 150, 172, 194
Harris, Flukey (character) 84
Hartford, Ct. 128
Hay, Bill 23, 35, 38, 45–46, 75, 86, 125, 140
Henry, O. 142, 144
Hernandez, Juano 197
Higby, Mary Jane 58
Hilmes, Michelle 153–154, 157, 199
Hinkson, Dr. F.A. 128
Hitler, Adolf 101
Holy Mackerel! The Amos 'n' Andy Story (book) 202
Honest Joe (character) 84
Honeyboy and Sassafrass (radio series) 54–55, 116
Hooper, C.E. Co. 165
Hotchkiss, Mr. (character) 84
Howard, Terry 83, 172
Hutchens, John K. 140
Hypercorrection 90–91

Inner Sanctum Mysteries (radio series) 175, 177

The Jack Benny Program (radio series) 145, 167, 177
Jackson Ward 9, 10, 26, 89
Jefferson, Willie "Lightning" (character) 77–79, 93, 105–106, 116, 124, 172
The Jewels of the Crown 31
Jim and Charley (abandoned title) 38
Jimmy Durante–Garry Moore Program (radio series) 175
Joe Bren Producing Company 13, 19–21
John Henry, Black River Giant (radio series) 116, 197

Johnson, Henry (character) 27
Johnson, Pop (character) 84, 103, 118
Jones, Amos (character): origin of name 39; early traits of 39–41; relationship with Ruby Taylor 59–62, 81–82, 110–111; early days in Harlem 59–60; resolves Andy's Breach of Promise suit 67–68; and Roland Weber 83; evolution of speech 93; financial conservatism of 95–97; assaulted by Jack Dixon 102; accused of murder 102–104, 121–123; childhood poverty of 108–109; accomplishments of 109, 155–157; inner strength of 109–110, 155–157; depth of friendship with Andy 110; marriage and family life of 110–111; birth of Arbadella 111, 113; explains Lord's Prayer to Arbadella 113–114; as war plant worker 139; persistence of 155–157
Jones, Amos, Jr. (character) 142, 173
Jones, Arbadella (character) 84, 111, 113–114, 139–140, 142
Jones, Elijah (character) 84, 109
Jones, Katharine Tift 116, 197
Jones, Ruby (character) *see* Taylor, Ruby
Jones (Billy) and (Ernie) Hare (harmony team) 20
Juvenile Jury (radio series) 175

KaDell, Carlton 141
Kalmar, Bert 53–54
Kaney, A.W. "Sen" 44, 191
Kansas City *Call* 130
KFRC, San Francisco 42
Kingfish *see* Stevens, George "Kingfish"
"Kinky Kids Parade" (song) 21, 23, 26–27, 31
KOA Minstrels (radio series) 43

Labov, William 87, 88, 194
The Landlord (character) 84
Lasker, Albert 43–44, 104
Lauck, Chester 56, 189
Lee, Johnny 145, 147
Lee, Madaline 83
Lever Brothers Company 141, 175
Lewis, Theophilus 135
The Life of Riley (radio series) 145
Lightning (character) *see* Jefferson, Willie "Lightning"
Little Orphan Annie (comic strip) 27
Liza (character) 31–32, 41
Long, Sen. Huey P. 101
Lord, Phillips 56
Lord and Thomas Inc. (agency) 43–44, 104, 112, 189
Lord's Prayer, interpreted by Amos 113–114, 196
Louie's Hungry Five (radio series) 55, 194

Lubin, Lou 145
Lucas, Henry (character) 84
Luke and Timber (radio series) 55
Lum and Abner (radio series) 56, 175, 189
Lux Radio Theatre (radio program) 177
Lyles, Aubrey 56, 116, 192–193

MacRorie, Janet 197
Major Bowes' Original Amateur Hour (radio series) 165
makeup *see* blackface
malapropisms 90–91
Marsh, Orlando 35
Marsh Laboratories Inc. 35
Marx, Louis F. & Sons (manufacturer) 51
McCanna, Benjamin T. 25–26
McIntyre, O.O. 51, 58
merchandising, licensed 34, 51–52
Miller, Flournoy 56, 116, 192–193
Miller and Lyles (comedy team) 56, 116, 192–193
Mills, Clifton (character) 171
minstrelsy 7, 19, 28, 37, 43, 45, 115–116, 118, 124, 126, 187
Mitchell, John, Jr. 9
Moeller, Henry 37
Molasses 'n' January *see* Pick and Pat
Moore, Clifton Newton 55
Moore, Tim 147
Mooseface, Bullneck (character) 171
Moran and Mack *see* Two Black Crows
Mosby's Rangers (military unit) 8
Mosher, Bob 143
Mueller, Charley 36, 37
murder trial, Amos's (1931) 102–104, 171
Muse, Clarence 116, 197
Mussolini, Benito 100, 101
Myrt and Marge (radio series) 165, 171–172
The Mystic Knights of the Sea 69–71, 118, 132, 173

National Association for the Advancement of Colored People (NAACP) 132, 136, 137, 148, 178, 198, 200
National Association of Chiefs of Police 104, 197
National Association of Colored Waiters and Hotel Employees 132
National Broadcasting Company Inc. (NBC) 34, 43–47, 177, 178, 197
New Deal 97–98
New York *Sun* 49
New York *Times* 2, 62, 140
New York World's Fair (1939) 146
Northwest Enterprise (newspaper)

Okey Hotel 171

O'Neil, Lewis "Slim" 12–13

Paley, William S. 148, 150, 199
Pantages Circuit Tour (1929) 42, 147, 191
Pardidon, Jack 16
Parker, Frank 173
Parker, Lulu (character) 62
Patrick, Johnny 56
Paul Ash in Hollywood (stage show) 23
Pearl, Jack 169
Pending, Pat (character) 95–96, 158
People Are Funny (radio program) 177
Peoria, Ill. 13–15
The Pepsodent Company Inc. 43–45, 47, 52, 103–104
Pepsodent Show (radio series) 167
The Perfect Song 145
Peterson, F.L. 130
The Phil Harris–Alice Faye Show (radio series) 145, 175
Philadelphia *Tribune* 130
Photoplay (magazine) 53
Pick and Pat (comedy team) 116, 197
Pittsburgh *Courier* 131–136
postwar radio comedy, extravagance of 145
premiums 39, 42, 111–112
Preston, Billy 194
Psychology (magazine) 43
Punkin' (character) 83, 172

Queen, Madam (character) 62–68, 79–81, 130, 132–133, 137, 169, 171, 198
Queen, Raymond (character) 198

racial othering 123–124, 157
racial portrayals 30, 113, 115–126, 153–158
racism 9, 121–123
Radio Comedy (book) 203
Radio Digest (magazine) 33, 128–130, 198
radio drama 31, 194
radio homes 165, 176
Radio Industries Banquet 34, 190
Randolph, Amanda 147, 197
Randolph, Lillian 142
ratings 140, 163–178, 198, 200
Rayner, E.C. 33
rebroadcasts, for West Coast 50
recorded promotional announcement, radio's first 38
recordings, phonograph 23, 25, 31, 188–189, 190, 199
Red Hot (stage show) 21
Regensberg, J.T. 188
Richmond, Va. 8–12, 151
The Rise of the Goldbergs (radio series) 56, 194
RKO Radio Pictures Inc. 53–54

Robb, Alexander 36
Roberts, Harlow P. 43–44, 47, 49
Roosevelt, Pres. Franklin D. 97–98
Ross, Dale Howard 203
Ross, Robert J. 142
Royal, John F. 197
Ruby, Harry 53–54

Sam 'n' Henry (radio series) 27–28, 29–38, 43, 120, 127, 150, 190
Sambo (stereotypical figure) 116, 157
Sanders, Elizabeth F. (character) 85
Schmitz, J.P. 188
Schuyler, George S. 131, 134
scriptwriting 57
segregation 9, 120–121, 198
Seldes, Gilbert 59
Selinger, Henry 25–26, 189
serial format 30–31, 54, 140, 173–175
Shell Company of California 42, 191
Shipley, Maynard L. 59
The Short Order Cook (character) 84
Shorty the Barber (character) 145
Shuffle Along (stage play) 193
situation comedy format 140–146, 174–175
Sky Ride 99
slang, use of in scripts 92
Smith, Lawyer M. (character) 67, 134
Smith, Sam (character) 27, 29–32
Snoop, Brother (character) 133
social classes, African American 41, 118–119, 134, 145
sponsors, chainless-chain era 191
stage performances 21, 34, 124–126, 190, 191
The Stebbins Boys (radio series) 56
stereotyping, racial 30, 37, 55, 115–118, 143
Stevens, George "Kingfish" (character) 69–73, 93, 95–96, 102, 103, 116, 142–144, 158, 172
Stevens, Sapphire (character) 83, 84, 142–143, 172
stock market crash 97, 196
Stonewall, LaGuardia (character) 145
Strong, Walter 35
studios 46, 57–58
Summa, Louise 20, 21, 57
Sylvester (character) 40–41
syndication *see* chainless chain

Taylor, Lillian (character) 87, 101–102
Taylor, Ruby (character) 41, 59–62, 81–82, 95, 97, 101, 110–111, 113, 139, 154–155, 169, 171–172, 196
Taylor, William L. (character) 41, 97, 103, 118, 154–155, 171, 196, 199
television 146–148, 150, 178
theatres, motion picture 50

time change, broadcast (1929) 49–50
Tom and Harry (abandoned title) 38
Trammell, Niles 44
transcriptions, broadcast 35, 44, 201
Treasury Star Parade (radio series) 140
Trenholm, Kay 49
Tribune Company Inc. 34–35, 194
Troy, Helen 56
Two Black Crows (comedy team) 43, 190

Uncle Abe and David (radio series) 56

Vail, Myrtle 171
Vallee, Rudy 167
Van Beuren Productions 192
Van DeTweezer, Mr. and Mrs. Charles F. (characters) 84
Van (Gus) and (Joe) Schenck (harmony team) 20
Van Porter, Henry (character) 76–77, 93
Vann, Jessie 136
Vann, Robert L. 131–132, 134, 136
Victor Talking Machine Company Inc. 23, 25, 31, 32
Victory Theatre (radio series) 175
voice characterizations 21, 26, 86, 189
Vox Pop (radio series) 175, 177

Wade, Ernestine 84, 141, 143, 147, 151, 194
Walker, Maggie L. 9
Waller, Judith 35
Walls, Bishop W.J. 130–131, 132
war bonds 139–140
Washburn, Dr. Patrick 131
Washington, Fred (character) 40
Washington, Mr. & Mrs. George T. (characters) 84, 119
Washington, D.C. 50
Wasserman, Lew 199
We the People 175
Weber, Annie (character) *see* Butterfly, Senorita
Weber, Roland (character) 84, 118–119
Weber City, NY (location in script) 100, 172
WEBH, Chicago 20–21, 23
wedding, of Amos and Ruby (1935)
Welsh, Johnnie 54–55, 116
WENR Weener Minstrels (radio series) 43
Wertheim, Arthur F. 203
Wetzel, Maurice 33, 35
WGN-WLIB, Chicago 23, 25, 34–35, 36
White, Flossie (character) 84
Whitman, Ernest 116, 142, 197
Widmer, Hariette 82, 197
Wilcox, Harlow 141
Wilkins, Roy 161, 200
Williams, Bert 26

Williams, Spencer, Jr. 147, 197, 199
Williamson Candy Co. (manufacturer) 51
WLS, Chicago 20
WLW Burnt Corkers (radio series) 43
WMAQ, Chicago 35–36, 38, 46, 127, 128, 189
women, portayal of 79–84
Wong, Barbara Jean 84, 195
World War II 139–140, 173
WQJ, Joliet/Chicago 20, 189
Wynn, Ed 169

www.ingramcontent.com/pod-product-compliance
Ingram Content Group UK Ltd.
Pitfield, Milton Keynes, MK11 3LW, UK
UKHW050528150426
5217IPUK00026B/1848